RSACS

Confederate Underwater Warfare

Confederate Underwater Warfare

AN ILLUSTRATED HISTORY

by LOUIS S. SCHAFER

McFarland & Company, Inc., Publishers
Jefferson, North Carolina, and London

British Library Cataloguing-in-Publication data are available

Library of Congress Cataloguing-in-Publication Data

Schafer, Louis S.
    Confederate underwater warfare : an illustrated history / by Louis
S. Schafer.
        p.   cm.
    Includes bibliographical references and index.
    ISBN 0-7864-0114-1 (library binding : 50# alk. paper) ∞
    1. United States — History — Civil War, 1861–1865 — Naval operations —
Submarine.   2. Submarine warfare — Confederate States of America.
I. Title.
E596.S28   1996
973.7'57 — dc20   95-51081
                                                                   CIP

Manufactured in the United States of America

McFarland & Company, Inc., Publishers
   Box 611, Jefferson, North Carolina 28640

Dedicated to my wife, Brenda,
whose patience has allowed me
to journey down pathways of intrigue

Contents

Preface

As a longtime submarine buff and Confederate historian, I have always been troubled and surprised by the scarcity of historical narratives concerning the advent of early American underwater weaponry. I began to explore the subject more intimately during the early 1980s, in an attempt to bridge the chasm between sporadic accounts of submersible explosives and my growing interest in uncovering little-known facts concerning their development, experimentation, and deployment during the American Civil War years. What I found—or should I say, what I did not find—proved to be even more distressing.

While the specific topic of Confederate underwater warfare seemed to me historically important, I found that researchers had paid it little attention; indeed there was little to verify that underwater weapons had been used in the Civil War. If anything the mystery made the topic even more provocative and compelling. I pushed forward with my research, spending long hours in dusty historical libraries and document sections of archives.

Over the course of many months, though I managed to collect a significant number of firsthand accounts, I confronted an even larger number of puzzling aspects of underwater warfare. Though Civil War writers had left behind hundreds of personal diaries, intimate letters, and other primary source documents, their individual perspectives of what had occurred often lacked depth, expression, and creativity. Yet despite all of that, their personal accounts did manage to offer some compelling evidence of both defensive and offensive use of underwater explosives.

Perhaps the most complete available study of naval operations during the war was J. Thomas Sharf's *History of the Confederate States Navy*, first published by Rogers and Sherwood of New York in 1887. It imparts a very real sense from a tactician's point of view of what Civil War naval conflict represented, characterized by patriotism, embargo, privateering, sectionalist fervor, a shortage of adequate supplies, and a vision of uninvited and unwanted reform.

Still, from a Southerner's viewpoint, the question of American pride versus cultural protectionism seemed to overshadow all other conflicts. In fact, the majority of Southerners seemed to be torn between remaining loyal to their country and remaining loyal to their state, which added even more fuel to the fires of war. This sentiment is best witnessed, perhaps, in the personal accounts of Matthew Fontaine Maury, scientist and oceanographer, whose emotional uncertainty over the matter of states' rights versus union was vividly expressed in the Maury Family Papers, found in the Manuscript Division of the Library of Congress: "The State of Virginia gave me birth; within her borders, among many kind friends, the nearest of kin, and troops of excellent neighbors, my children are planting their vine and fig tree. In her green bosom are the graves of my fathers...." Ultimately, his decision to defend his home would prevail, and Maury would resign his commission in the U.S. Army.

Though there seemed to be no lack of Confederate pride during the Civil War years, the region's shortage of supplies is fairly well documented. Still, the many inventive ideas and creative smuggling operations that arose to combat the shortages have remained largely unexamined. Perhaps the most imaginative of all were the extensive efforts devised to overcome the shortage of adequate gunpowder manufacturing facilities, detailed by George Washington Rains in his "History of the Confederate Powder Works," put forth in the pages of the *Chronicle and Constitutionalist* in Atlanta, Georgia, in 1882. Rains described the rather peculiar practice of dividing the Confederacy into districts, into which separate crews were dispatched to dig the earth from beneath privies and latrines in an effort to collect precious niter deposits.

While George Washington Rains explored unique methods of securing the vital ingredients needed to make gunpowder, his older brother, Gabriel, was inventing and experimenting with explosives. Explaining his personal war effort in "Torpedoes," which was later published in the pages of the *Southern Historical Society Papers* in 1877, Gabriel Rains offered significant insight into his motive behind the creation of infernal machines. Though the mysterious Rains brothers have been largely overlooked by historians, they were outstanding munitions makers whose innovations did much to enhance the hopes of victory for a brief time within the failing Confederate ranks.

How do we explain the factors that motivated the development, testing, and deployment of underwater weaponry during the Civil War? Perhaps the best explanation lies in the fact that this particular conflict was, for both sides, the first "modern," tactical war, suddenly devoid of romance or chivalry. Indeed, anything and everything seemed to be fair in gaining an edge over the enemy during this particularly brutal conflict.

To understand the development of underwater warfare, we must first understand that to be a Confederate meant that one cherished beliefs and notions that were generations old. In fact, Southern citizens continued to defend the concept that they were descendants of brave knights in shining armor, romantically singing songs of pride as they marched. They were willing to meet the enemy face-to-face on their own land—a land comprised, in their vision, of honest, hardworking men and women who had held onto the idea of freedom of choice as proudly and tightly as they had the idea of freedom of religion.

From the Union's perspective, strangling the Southern cause in Anaconda-like fashion could be best accomplished by cutting off its ocean imports and exports, while simultaneously attacking by sea and inland river. Knowing that the Confederacy had planted its roots in America's southern soil long before the outbreak of civil conflict, the North should have also realized that Southern waterways were its very lifeblood and, therefore, would not be given up easily. In a valiant attempt to avert the Union's blockade and invasion, the deployment of floating and submersible explosives was the most logical defensive and offensive measure available. The North's response to such an innovative strategy was precisely what the South had hoped for—one of apprehension and caution. In fact, as the geographical concentration of naval war continually shifted, so did the Confederacy's infernal explosives.

While the majority of Southerners believed such weapons to be well warranted and well-intentioned, the Northern press of the 1860s continually responded with condemnations of "evil Rebel barbarity." Mines hidden along busy roadways, submerged within wells, buried around homes, tucked into ordinary bags of flour, and entombed at the bases of telegraph poles had already killed many dozens of Union soldiers and were considered to be nothing less than "immoral booby traps."

Yet, despite the fact that the use of land mines was frowned upon, the majority of Confederate tacticians would eventually become convinced that underwater explosives were an extremely effective means of defending their thousands of miles of ocean shoreline and rivers. Commonly referred to as "torpedoes" during this period, such devices were the invention of a covert unit known as the Confederate Torpedo Division. Different versions could be triggered electrically from shore, or by mechanical means and percussion fuses whenever they came in contact with the hull of an enemy vessel. Intricate details of a variety of these detonating designs, intended to avert an invasion by sea, were offered by J. Thomas Scharf as well as by Hunter Davidson, the latter's in "The Electrical Submarine Mine, 1861–1865," printed in the *Confederate Veteran* of 1908.

Eventually, after managing to keep the Union's navy at bay for several months with the threat of underwater explosives, it became necessary for the South to break up the Union blockade by taking more of an offensive stance. Finding typical floating "drift" mines both unreliable and unpredictable, the Confederate navy attached spar percussion torpedoes to low-slung ships and dispatched submarines to attack specific enemy targets. Perhaps the most telling evidence of the risk and sacrifice was provided not by trained fighters, but by a group of ordinary Southern civilians who volunteered for the dangerous mission of testing one of America's first submersible vessels. On October 15, 1863, the crew disappeared beneath the waters of Charleston Harbor, South Carolina, never to return alive. Days later, when the tiny craft was raised and examined, General P. G. T. Beauregard had this to say about their adventure:

> The unfortunate men were contorted into all kinds of horrible attitudes; some clutching candles, evidently endeavoring to force open the manholes; others lying in the bottom tightly grappled together, and the blackened faces of all presented the expression of their dispair and agony...

Similarly vivid accounts of other offensives were described in numerous testimonials, including William A. Alexander's "Thrilling Chapter in the History of the Confederate States Navy: Work of Submarine Boats," printed in the *Southern Historical Society Papers* in 1902; H. D. Brown's account entitled "The First Successful Torpedo and What It Did," in a rare 1910 edition of the *Confederate Veteran*; and Gordon Levey's "Torpedo Boats at a Louisiana Soldier's Home," first published in a 1909 volume of the *Confederate Veteran*.

Still, with very few exceptions, the stories in their original forms were somewhat stale and, therefore, quite difficult to digest. With that firmly in mind, I began the tedious process of assembling, interpreting, and synthesizing these many accounts, putting the information in a more readable form while attempting to maintain the authoritativeness and factual integrity of the originals. Yet, as I continued to develop and relate my version of the nineteenth century authors' stories, I would eventually come to believe that I was not doing them justice. In fact, my first rough draft had barely managed to scratch the surface by recollecting hundreds of disconnected shreds of historical evidence.

It was then that I first began to explore the more difficult questions of what contributions to history had been made by the people, events and devices I had grown acquainted with through my research—to evaluate, as it were, the much broader picture. Exactly what did it mean to be a Confederate patriot during the 1860s? Precisely what was the emotional and mental impact of daily warfare in the Southern states during the American Civil War? And what had prompted underwater weaponry to be developed and deployed in the South?

Perhaps all of these inquiries were answered by Thomas Jefferson's grandson and the Confederate secretary of war, George Randolph, who disclosed the South's policy and moral disposition when he stated, "It is admissible to plant shells in a parapet to repel assault, or in the road to check pursuit.... It is not admissible to plant shells merely to destroy life and without other design than that of depriving the enemy of a few men."

During the American Civil War, therefore, the common Confederate soldier brimmed with an immense amount of personal pride, but no particular prejudicial hostility or hatred toward his Union counterparts; he was forced to be constantly on guard against those who would change this very way of life; and the weapons of underwater warfare were developed, for the most part, as the optimal defense against an invasive force that wanted to alter his future.

As I began to reread and pull together the various accounts that I had already collected, a much different portrait depicting the human side of the Confederate war came into focus. Slowly, convincingly, as the words took a new direction, old happenings began to live and breathe in the present. Perhaps, more importantly, they had begun to assume a unique identity, with a very real sense of both depth and emotion.

Still, the complete story concerning what it meant to be a Confederate will forever remain elusive. Written documentation from the times concerning the underwater implements of war was discouraged by those who believed that the tactic was simply wrong. Hence, this portion of American history was affected by the great moral dilemma that confronted those who wanted to call themselves both American and Confederate. Their reflections of conflict contained no motivation to incite war or to celebrate victory over their enemies; instead, they were simply willing to lay down their individual lives to protect a precious way of life for the masses.

I continue to investigate all available information concerning Confederate underwater warfare, and I will likely continue to do so for many years to come. I often find small pieces of evidence in university libraries, historical collections, and local museums. Some of these documents offer brief glimpses of the specific incidence of the use of such explosives, fewer offer concise details of the men who fashioned them, and even fewer probe the intricate workings of the weapons themselves.

Illustrations for the book were especially difficult to find. Though a few photographs have been preserved, much needed to be created from scratch. I want to offer my appreciation to my friend Valecia Bryner, of Alma, Michigan, for her unique way of turning a wide variety of verbal descriptions into vivid images.

A special thanks is extended to my wife, Brenda, whose constant support made my determination to finish the book worthwhile. My most heartfelt thanks of all goes to my late father, Louis Schafer, Sr., for bringing me along the road of life with one human trait always at the forefront—the desire always to make the right choices.

Introduction: Beginnings of Underwater Explosives

The torpedo is defined as a self-propelled guided missile that travels underwater. It carries with it an explosive warhead and is designed to sink all types of sea-going vessels, both above and below the surface. Torpedoes can be fired by surface ships or underwater vessels, or they can be dropped by aircraft. During the Civil War, both the Federal government and the Confederacy were fully aware that the concept of using underwater explosives was nothing new to the art of warfare.

In fact, more than 200 years prior to the 1860s, the Dutch had attempted, unsuccessfully, to incorporate similar innovative weaponry against the mighty Spanish navy. Their explosives delivery vehicles were unmanned, air-tight boats, weighted down with rock and gravel and then set adrift just below the surface. In theory, these semisubmerged vessels, which also housed an ample supply of gunpowder and slow-burning fuses, would drift casually toward their victims and explode when they came in contact with the wooden hulls of enemy ships. In reality, however, the Spanish navy somehow managed to escape their devastation time and time again during the course of the conflict.

In 1652, a Frenchman named Le Son constructed an underwater craft in Holland which was known as the Rotterdam Boat. Though little is known of the experiment, history did record the fact that it was intended to be loaded with explosives for use against the British fleet. However, the innovative craft never went into action.

Later, a manned underwater craft was used against the British navy during the American Revolution, an attack which would later be made famous by a satirical poem entitled "Battle of the Kegs." Credit for this ingenious device, designed and constructed in 1773, can be given to the remarkable inventor David Bushnell. Known as the *American Turtle*, this "water-machine" was destined to play a vital role in aiding American technology in the unique concept of underwater warfare.

While studying at Yale University, Bushnell had become obsessed with the idea of perfecting a method of exploding gunpowder underwater. His experiments paid off, resulting in a clever submersible mine that could be triggered by a simple clockwork mechanism. After extensive testing, he calculated that it would take approximately 150 pounds of powder to destroy any British man-of-war then afloat.

Next on Bushnell's agenda was the construction of a hand-propelled craft which could deliver his underwater explosive beneath an unsuspecting enemy vessel. A partial description of the attack vessel, offered by Bushnell himself, is certainly worth reprinting:

> The external shape of the submarine vessel bore some resemblance to two upper tortoise shells of equal size, joined together, the flue ... of entrance into the vessel being represented by the opening made by the swells of the shells at the head of the animal. The inside was capable of containing the operator and air sufficient to support him thirty minutes without receiving fresh air. At the bottom, opposite the entrance, was fixed a quantity of lead for ballast; at one edge, which was directly before the operator, who sat upright, was an oar, for rowing forward or backward; at the other edge was a rudder for steering.
>
> An aperture at the bottom, with its valve, was designed to admit water for the purpose of descending, and two brass forcing-pumps served to eject the water within when necessary for ascending. At the top there was likewise an oar, for ascending or descending, or continuing at any particular depth. A water-gauge or barometer determined the depth of descent; a compass directed the course, and a ventilator within supplied the vessel with fresh air when on the surface.
>
> The entrance into the vessel was elliptical and so small as barely to admit a person. This entrance was surrounded with a broad elliptical iron band, the lower edge of which was let into the wood, of which the body of the vessel was made, in such a manner as to give its utmost support to the body of the vessel against the pressure of the water. Above the upper edge of this iron band there was a brass crown or cover, resembling a hat with its crown and brim, which shut water tight upon the iron band; the crown was hung to the iron band with hinges, so as to turn over sidewise, when opened. To make it perfectly secure when shut, it might be screwed down upon the band by the operator or by a person without....
>
> In the fore part of the brim of the crown of the vessel was a socket, and an iron tube passing through the socket. The tube stood upright, and could slide up and down in the socket six inches. At the top of the tube was a wood screw, fixed by means of a rod which passed through the tube and screwed the wood screw fast upon the top of the tube. By pushing the wood screw up against the bottom of the ship and turning at the same time, it would enter the planks; driving would also answer the same purpose. When the wood screw was firmly fixed, it would be cast off by unscrewing the rod which fastened it upon the top of the tube.
>
> Behind the submarine vessel was a place, above the rudder, for carrying a large powder magazine.
>
> This was made of two pieces of oak timber, large enough, when hollowed out, to contain 150 pounds of powder with the apparatus used in firing it, and was secured in its place by a screw turned by the operator. A strong piece of rope extended from the magazine to the wood screw above mentioned, and was fastened to both. When the wood screw was fixed and was to be cast off from its tube, the magazine was to be cast off likewise by unscrewing it, leaving it hanging to the wood screw. It was lighter than the water, so that it might rise up against the object to which the wood screw and itself were fastened.

The failed attempt by the *American Turtle* submarine to sink a British vessel, the HMS *Eagle* (courtesy of Valecia Bryner).

> Within the magazine was an apparatus constructed to run any proposed length of time under twelve hours; when it had run out its time, it unpinioned a strong lock, resembling a gun lock, which gave fire to the powder. This apparatus was so pinioned that it could not possibly move, till, by casting off the magazine from the vessel, it was set in motion.
>
> The skillful operator could swim so low on the surface of the water as to approach very near a ship in the night without fear of being discovered, and might, if he chose, approach the stem or stern above water with very little danger. He could sink very quickly, keep at any depth he pleased, and row a great distance in any direction he desired without coming to the surface. When he rose to the surface he could soon obtain a fresh supply of air, and then, if necessary, he might descend again, and pursue his course.[1]

Just after midnight, on September 6, 1776, the *American Turtle* was readied for her initial mission. Her target was the HMS *Eagle*, a 64-gun British flagship lying off Governor's Island in New York Harbor. The operator of the submarine, Ezra Lee, a member of the Connecticut regiment of the Continental Army, failed in his attempt to secure the screw to the hull of the ship, however, and he was forced to set the oak cask of gunpowder adrift in the ocean currents. To the disappointment of Bushnell, it harmlessly exploded well away from its target.

Although the *Turtle* made two more attempts to destroy a British ship, neither was successful. A short time later, the *American Turtle* vanished. No one knows for certain whether she was accidentally sunk, dismantled by her builder, or destroyed by the Americans in order to keep her from falling into enemy hands.

After the war was over, David Bushnell changed his identity, choosing to live the remainder of his life in total obscurity. And the concept of using underwater warfare was put to rest for the time being. Later, however, Robert Fulton experimented with his own version of underwater explosives. On October 15, 1805, his submersible craft, known as the *Nautilus*, set out to sink an aging Danish brig called the *Dorothea* as a demonstration for the British government. The event took place at Walmar Roads, near Deal, England, with several British dignitaries looking on. The two-man submarine passed beneath and beyond the target hulk while the mines it was towing struck and exploded against the brig's side, destroying it.

Though the demonstration proved successful, Fulton's timing was off, for just six days later the British defeated the enemy French fleet at the Battle of Trafalgar. After such a resounding victory, the British government no longer saw a need to improve its sea power, and Fulton's vision of creating an innovative underwater weapons system ended abruptly.

One legacy that Fulton did manage to leave behind, however, was the term "torpedo." He was the first to apply it to an underwater explosive device, borrowing it from the name of the *Torpedo electricus*, a type of crampfish which stuns its prey with a powerful electric shock. However, it was not until fifty years after Fulton's death that the term took on its present meaning of "self-propelled" underwater missile.

Next came the work of Samuel Colt, who also experimented with submerged mines. Like Bushnell and Fulton before him, however, his ideas were frowned upon by the United States government. In fact, few government officials, or civilians for that matter, believed that these early torpedoes were of enough worth to devote valuable time to developing them as a primary means of attack. This attitude would change, however, at the onset of the Civil War.

Chapter 1

Maury, at Your Service

Just after 10:00 P.M. on Sunday, July 7, 1861, five small rowboats prepared to depart from the Norfolk, Virginia, dockyards. Earlier that night, before the sun had set, the boats had been loaded down heavily with underwater explosives, along with other necessary equipment to be used in an attack on Union vessels. As their target the man in charge of the operation had chosen a small contingent of warships which were anchored in the bay at nearby Hampton Roads.

On the Friday and Saturday nights immediately preceding the historic mission, a single man, traveling in a smaller rowboat, had been dispatched to spy on the Union vessels. The well-planned espionage measures had, however, been hampered by a tiny steamer, which had maintained a constant vigil circling the larger fleet. Keeping a safe distance, the spy was quite certain that he had not been detected by the smaller scouting craft. He realized that, should the enemy suspect any covert actions, the entire operation would be in jeopardy. Returning to Norfolk, he reported to his superior that the Union fleet seemed to be totally unaware of the impending assault. It was decided that the mission would be carried out, as previously planned, on the following night.

To get within close enough range of the Northern vessels, the men had decided to enter the water approximately three miles upriver, as a further precaution to ensure that their actions would go undetected. Arriving within sight of their target area well after midnight, they spotted their prey bobbing gracefully in the calm waters of the bay. Quickly and quietly, they continued to conduct their business.

One of the major supporters of such an innovative weapon during the conflict between the North and the South, and leader of the assault was an American scientist/oceanographer named Matthew Fontaine Maury. Maury, who had distinguished himself through his extensive research involving the charting of ocean currents and winds, chose to offer his support and ingenuity to the Confederacy following the outbreak of war. Undoubtedly, this could not have been an easy decision for him to reach. He had chosen to resign his commission in the United States Navy on April 20, 1861, after having served 36 dedicated years. Yet, what had been the 54-year-old Virginian's reason for casting his lot with the rebellious Southern states?

Maury had been raised from childhood within "the school of states' rights."[1] Later, he elaborated on his explanation for siding with his home state: "The State of Virginia gave me birth; within her borders, among many kind friends, the nearest of kin, and troops of excellent neighbors, my children are planting their vine and fig tree. In her green bosom are the graves of my fathers...."[2]

Immediately following his official resignation, Maury opted to relocate his entire family from his former job site in Washington, D.C., to the home of a close relative named John Minor, who resided in Fredericksburg, Virginia. Just a single day after his arrival, on Sunday, April 21, 1861, along with Judge John L. Allen and General Francis H. Smith, he became a member of Governor John Letcher's three-man advisory council for the protection of Virginia's waterways.

Maury's unique ability to assimilate a vast amount of facts and figures at a rapid pace offered him a rather bleak mental image of the state's inadequate defense. Of the 60,000 small arms on hand, which were being warehoused in Lexington and Richmond, only about 10 percent were percussion muskets. The remainder fell under the category of flint-locks, which were most definitely not what the Confederate land forces needed for rapid-fire assault. To make matters worse, the state possessed only about 3,200 barrels of gunpowder at the time. It was, therefore, crystal clear to the middle-aged scientist that Virginia, if not the entire Confederacy, would have to incorporate drastic measures in order to overcome the immense firepower of the Union forces.

To this end, Maury suggested the adoption of an innovative underwater weapon, known as the torpedo, for the defense of Virginia's vast waterways. In the days of the Civil War, the term "torpedo" was used to describe any stationary or free-floating mine that could be detonated either mechanically or electrically. And, although they had never really proven themselves in the heat of battle, Maury believed that such a weapon could be effectively used in harbors, bays, and rivers throughout the region.

Maury was correct in his calculations, for, although millions of dollars would eventually be spent by both sides in the conflict to construct a strong navy, fortified ship-to-ship confrontations would, indeed, be rare. In fact, the torpedo would eventually be responsible for the destruction of more Union vessels than would all direct attacks by Confederate warships combined.

However, as Maury would soon find out, it was an extremely difficult task to convince the Southern authorities that underwater explosives were the answer to the defense problem of Confederate waterways. Though he reasoned that, even with the assistance of commissioned vessels, the South would be unable to protect its three thousand miles of coastline, government officials did not yet agree that torpedoes would do an adequate job. However, with the stubbornness of a mule, Maury decided to explore the torpedo's possibilities without their approval.

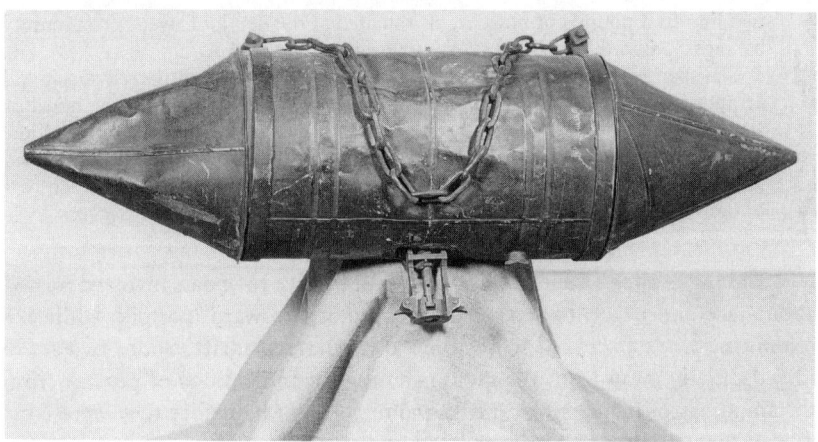

A floating torpedo made of tin which was intended to detonate on contact with an enemy ship. A later version of Maury's wooden torpedo, these were often strung together in pairs with a lengthy rope attached to the detonating chain (courtesy of the West Point Museum Collection).

Initially, Maury experimented with miniature explosives within the secluded home of his banker-stockbroker cousin, Robert H. Maury, who resided in the city of Richmond. Borrowing a large metal washtub used for bathing by the children of the house, he proceeded to detonate small canister-type mines filled with gunpowder. Determined to prove once and for all that his ideas were sound, he then designed several larger oak casks, which were put into tangible form by the Richmond-based Talbott Brothers Company. Filling them with gunpowder, he next affixed homemade fuses to the cylinders. Finally, the underwater explosives were connected together in pairs by lengths of strong hemp rope. In this way, the rope would act as a snare, hooking itself around the front section of an enemy vessel and swinging the torpedoes around to discharge against both bows.

As his first target, Maury chose three of five Northern ships anchored at nearby Hampton Roads. They included a pair of flagships, the USS *Roanoke* and the USS *Minnesota*, as well as a sailing sloop-of-war named the USS *Cumberland*. Along with a select group of friends, the hopeful scientist boarded a train bound for Norfolk, where he arrived on Friday, July 5, 1861. The group departed from the railcar only a few miles upriver from Sewall's Point, overlooking the Roads, where the Union fleet diligently blockaded the mouth of the Elizabeth River and Fortress Monroe. Hidden in wooden crates were Maury's deadly devices:

They (the torpedoes) were in pairs connected together by a span 500 feet long. The span was floated on the surface by corks, and the torpedo barrels, containing

two hundred pounds of powder, also floated at the depth of twenty feet, empty barrages, painted lead color, so as not readily to be seen....
    The span was connected with a trigger in the head of each barrel, so set and arranged that when the torpedo, being let go in a tide way under the bows ... would be drifted alongside, and in so drifting tauten the span, and so set off the fuse, which was driven precisely at a ten second shot fuse, only it was calculated to burn fifty-four seconds, because it could not be known exactly in which part of the sweep alongside the strain would be sufficient to set off the trigger.[3]

Having dropped their explosives, two of the five rowboats involved turned about-face and began to retrace their route back toward Norfolk, while the remaining three prepared to set their own charges adrift. Soon, two more rowed quietly away from the area, listening for indications of pursuit from the small patrolling steamer. Tense moments went by before they were convinced that they had not been spotted by the enemy.

While the rest of his men continued their return journey, Matthew Maury's boat waited patiently for the explosion, but it never came. Disappointed, the entire crew regrouped and returned to the Confederate capital of Richmond, perplexed by what had gone wrong. Later, they were to determine that the failure was, in all likelihood, due to a simple miscalculation: it seems that the type of fuse Maury had designed would, indeed, readily burn at a depth of 15 feet; however, it was stifled by the 20-foot depths at which it had been dropped.

A few weeks after the failed attempt, the Union Navy discovered a single unexploded torpedo drifting harmlessly near Hampton Roads, which was, more than likely, one of the explosives Maury had implemented in his attack. In examining the potentially dangerous weapon more closely, Union officials surmised that it had failed to detonate because of a slight leakage in the wooden encasement, which had resulted in wet gunpowder.

After a brief visit to Fredericksburg to spend time with his family, Maury returned to Richmond in order to continue his experiments. After resolving the problem with the fuse used on his initial attack, he confidently approached Stephen Russell Mallory, the Secretary of the Confederate Navy, asking for financial support for his torpedo project. In late July, he exhibited a pair of explosives which he had recently constructed, hoping that he could convince the Secretary of their worth. Yet Mallory remained unimpressed. Like so many other "experts" on the subject offensive warfare, the Secretary of the Navy failed to see the vast potential of such a weapon.

Discouraged, yet not to the point of despair, Maury set out to convince others of the importance of using his creation. And, despite Mallory's negative attitude, he was able to find support from Governor Letcher, his longtime friend.

Subsequently, two large barrels of gunpowder were given over to be used at Maury's own discretion, and the scientist prepared for a full-scale test to be

Matthew Fontaine Maury (courtesy of the Library of Congress).

conducted at Rockett's Wharf, located just south of Richmond. With such a convincing demonstration, he hoped that Mallory might alter his view concerning underwater warfare, and swing his support in the torpedo's direction.

On a humid day in the middle of August, a host of dignitaries, including Governor Letcher, Secretary Mallory, and the Congressional Committee on Naval Affairs, gathered along the banks of the James River. With the assistance of his son, Richard, Matthew Maury departed from the CSS *Patrick Henry* and rowed out into the middle of the river. There, he placed his torpedo carefully in the water, and articulately prepared the trigger. Next, he allowed it to drift delicately into the current. Moments later, after the father and son had moved a safe distance from the submerged explosive, young Richard yanked hard on the connecting rope, and "the explosion was instantaneous: up went a column of water fifteen or twenty feet…. Many stunned or dead fish floated around…."[4]

The doubters, including the stubborn Secretary of the Navy, must have been thoroughly convinced of the torpedo's value, for Maury was soon promoted to the position of "Chief of the Sea-Coast, Harbor, and River Defenses of the South." Furthermore, $50,000 was appropriated by the Confederate Congress to be used to develop underwater explosives. The elated inventor quickly set about organizing the construction of a complete arsenal of torpedoes.

Corresponding with his first few weeks as Chief of the Sea-Coast, Harbor, and River Defenses, Maury contacted officials responsible for the defense of the Mississippi River. At that time, he advised them that torpedoes might be incorporated to mine the western frontier of the Confederacy.

Major General Leonidas Polk, then in charge of the western waterway, must have liked what he heard, for he soon requested that Maury be assigned to the Mississippi region. Prior to an answer on the Major General's requisition, however, Maury took it upon himself to order a number of torpedoes to be manufactured and transported to the western front. All of Maury's dealings with Polk, though they were conducted over a relatively brief period of time, were regarded as being highly secret. In fact, all contact between the two was executed by the well-trained Secret Service of the Confederate States. Later, Maury was forced to dispatch detailed instructions to the Mississippi region on the care and use of torpedoes, since Major General Polk's plea was eventually denied. Evidently, Maury had suddenly become a valuable asset to the Virginia officials, who had decided that he could not be spared.

Matthew Maury planned a second attempt at sinking Union warships to be carried out in the same vicinity as the first, near Hampton Roads at Fortress Monroe. On this occasion, the assault on the USS *Minnesota* and the USS *Savannah* would take place on the overcast night of Wednesday, October 9, when there would be no light from the moon hampering their expedition.

However, just a few short days before the planned attack, Maury's hopes were dashed by the Secretary of the Navy, who opted to place him on another assignment. The scientist was extremely upset by the entire affair when he learned of the specifics surrounding this so-called "special duty," and he spoke of his bitterness in a letter to a friend and kinsman, Franklin Minor:

> The governor has made a contract with certain individuals in New Orleans to purchase arms, etc., in Cuba and is furnishing the money. So you see I am sent simply to hold the purse strings and see that the arms are good, a duty for which any officer of the Army or Navy is as well qualified as I.
> I am ordered by Mallory to report to New Orleans for this duty, the Secretary of War, not having an Army officer to send, asks for a Navy officer. I am sent, thus showing that in Mallory's judgment I can be better spared than any officer of the Army or Navy....[5]

On October 5, 1861, Captain Franklin Buchanan, who was in command of the Confederate States Navy Office of Orders and Detail, dispatched a memo

A semi-submerged torpedo, attached by lengths of rope to chunks of driftwood which would, in theory, snag an enemy vessel, thus forcing the torpedo upward to explode against the enemy's hull (courtesy of Valecia Bryner).

which ordered that a replacement be found for Maury on the Hampton Roads project. To fill the vacancy, Lieutenant Robert D. Minor was selected, and he was told to receive from Maury "such instructions as will enable you to carry out his views relating to it" (i.e., torpedo experiments).[6]

Aside from the planned attack near Hampton Roads, Maury was further upset at having to interrupt another pet project, which he had more recently been promoting.

Earlier, he had proposed that the Confederacy design and construct a fleet of highly mobile, small steam launches, armed with powerful guns. In Maury's opinion, these "mosquitoes" would be able to cruise through smooth waterways in groups, firing upon the enemy from a safe distance. Hopefully, they would be more than able to defend the South's bays and rivers, perhaps even clearing them entirely of blockading Federal vessels. Instead of investing a great amount of time and effort constructing larger ironclads, Maury's smaller crafts could be built in approximately 120 days.

A few weeks prior to his scheduled departure to New Orleans, on October 8, Maury had outlined his entire mosquito proposal in detail to Governor Letcher. Each miniature attack vessel would be 112 feet in length, 21 feet in beam, draw six feet of water, and boast a pair of rifled pivot guns of the largest available caliber. Propelled by steam, the greatest portion of each craft would be hidden from view below the surface, and their gun carriages would rise a mere two feet above waterline. In this way, Maury had further explained, they would present the smallest of targets to the enemy fleet. Finally, the scientist had estimated that each would have a total cost of $10,000.

Early in the morning on October 9, Robert D. Minor, Maury's replacement on the torpedo assault project, stepped aboard the CSS *Patrick Henry*, which was anchored near Mulberry Point on the James River. After meeting with Commander John R. Tucker, he secured two able-bodied volunteers to assist him in the torpedo venture. After receiving instructions from Minor, Midshipman Alexander M. Mason and Master Thomas L. Dornin spent the rest of the day preparing for the upcoming attack. Under the cover of darkness that same night, the three enterprising navy men carried out the preplanned siege on the USS *Savannah*:

> The boats were ... lowered, the magazines carefully slung, buoys bent on intervals of seven feet.... Acting Master Dornin, with ... Mason, took the left side of the channel, while I took the right. Pulling down the river some 600 or 700 yards, the boats were then allowed to drift with the rapid ebb tide, while the end of the cork line was passed over to Mr. Dornin and the line tautened by the boats pulling in opposite directions. The buoys were then thrown overboard, the guard lines on the triggers cut, the levers fitted and pinned, the trip line made fast to the bight at the end of the lever, and the safety screws removed, the magazines carefully lowered in the water ... and all set fairly adrift within 800 yards of the ship and 400 yards of the battery on the bluff above the point. So near were we that voices were heard on the shore.... Pulling back a short distance and hearing no explosion we returned to the ship [*Patrick Henry*].[7]

Lieutenant Minor had dropped the floating torpedoes at a distance of 800 yards from the Union warship, which Maury later determined to be too far away to assure accurate drift angle. Hence, distance, not depth or faulty encasements, had been the cause of this, their second consecutive failure.

The only hope that Maury retained in achieving success with underwater explosives was the thought that Jack Maury, a cousin, would contact him with good news. Secretly, without the Navy department's consent, the scientist had instructed Jack to conduct an attack on the USS *Minnesota*. Sadly, however, it was not meant to be: on October 16, Maury received a letter reporting that the mission had not even gotten off the ground. It seems that Jack had opted to engage a boat pilot to transport him and his weapon out to a place near the Union vessel. However, the pair had failed to locate the huge warship, losing her beneath the cover of darkness. Despite the misdirection, however, cousin Jack had managed to retain his explosives equipment, and vowed that he would try again.

In the meantime, Secretary of the Navy Stephen R. Mallory seems to have received a good deal of criticism concerning his decision to reassign Matthew Maury on "special duty." Of the chief complainers was the Naval Affairs Chairman, Charles Magill Conrad, who believed that Mallory's orders would have a harmful effect on the progress of torpedo development. Evidently such opposition helped to prompt the Secretary to rethink his position on the Maury affair, for the scientist received word on October 24, 1861, stating that the reassignment orders had been canceled.

Two months later, on December 23, both houses of the Confederate Congress passed "An Act to authorize the President to be constructed a certain number of gunboats." The following day, President Jefferson Davis signed into law the bill, which gave Matthew Fontaine Maury the right to design and build not more than 100 of his small mosquito patrol boats. With a hefty appropriation of $2,000,000, the rejuvenated inventor went to work on the construction of his fleet.

By the middle of January 1862 Maury found himself in Richmond, Virginia, pushing hard to secure materials and able-bodied workmen for his gunboat project. However, once again he was delayed in his endeavors, pleading continually with Mallory for well-versed carpenters and artisans. Hopefully, he thought, when completed, the 100 mosquitoes could be divided into divisions of between five and ten vessels, each under the command of an individual officer. He estimated that each division would require a crew of about 40 men.

Although the construction phase had already begun, at such sites as Rappahannock (lying along the Pamunkey River), at York, and at the Norfolk Navy Yard, all work was stopped abruptly by the House Committee on Naval Affairs. On March 17, 1862, the Confederate House of Representatives had passed a bill authorizing President Davis to suspend the building and testing of the mosquito squadron. Instead, the remainder of the funding would be put toward the design and construction of ironclad vessels equipped with rams. Maury was forced to accept the disheartening fact that his dream fleet would never see action.

With the work on his gunboats ended, Matthew Maury settled down to the business of torpedo experimentation once again, intensifying his efforts toward their perfected development. Even though he would later plan and carry out two separate attacks on Union vessels, incorporating his initial mechanical version, he began to become more interested in electrically-charged torpedoes, which could be detonated from the safety of dry land.

With this concept in mind, insulated wire became an extremely valuable commodity for Maury's experiments. Yet the scientist soon came to realize that there was a severe shortage of such wire throughout the Confederate States. In order to help alleviate the problem, Maury dispatched a purchasing agent to New York City, to attempt to buy telegraph wire from the enemy. However, the mission failed miserably, for the agent never returned. To this day, there is no record of what became of him. It is interesting to note that during this same period of time the Union Secret Service managed to detain a reported Confederate spy in Philadelphia. Evidently, the captured agent had recently spent some time in the New York area, in order "to get some telegraphic material"[8]

Since the science of electricity was still in its infant stage during the Civil War, Maury called upon the services of Dr. William Norris, the Chief Signal Officer of the Confederacy and perhaps the South's foremost expert on the subject. Though he initially declined to give his valuable assistance, Norris would eventually provide a great deal of technical data, along with an adequate supply of used Federal underwater cable, to the Confederate cause. Though the cable, which had earlier been confiscated from the beaches of Willoughby Spit following a storm, was in poor condition, Maury referred to it as a "God-send."[9]

New funds were appropriated by the Confederate Congress, enabling Maury to continue his experiments. Aging cast-iron steamboat and locomotive boilers were used as waterproof tanks, into which the gunpowder was loaded. These were referred to by the scientist as "magazines."

For the electrical charge Maury incorporated Wollaston batteries, which were the only type available. Each individual battery consisted of a bank of cells which housed 18 pairs of 10-by-12 inch zinc plates, submerged in 36 gallons of sulfuric acid. Such a charge had the ability to detonate a single torpedo positioned up to 250 feet away. Due to the fact that the underwater explosives would need to reach much further out into specific waterways, Maury determined this to be too short a distance. To overcome this distance problem, he opted to set up his torpedoes in clusters, which he referred to as "ranges." Thus, the first charge would be used to detonate a string of explosives in a domino fashion.

When the invading Union forces began to make their move up the James River later that same year, Maury sent a message to the Confederate Secretary of War, George W. Randolph:

I beg to call your attention to our river defenses, and to say that the most effectual way of keeping off the enemy with his shot-proof vessels is to mine the channelways, and blow up by means of electricity when he attempts the passage.[10]

Randolph took heed of Maury's plea and granted the scientist permission to put his knowledge and weaponry to good use. Assigned a tug vessel known as the CSS *Teaser*, Maury set about coordinating the strategic placement of his deadly explosives. Each torpedo in the single range of four contained 1,500 pounds of gunpowder, and they were carefully positioned above Chaffin's Bluff, just south of Richmond. A second range, consisting of fifteen smaller charges, were placed below the bluff, and Maury described them in detail:

They (torpedoes) were arranged in rows, those of each row being 30 feet apart. Each tank is contained in a water-tight wooden cask, capable of floating it, but anchored and held below the surface from 3 to 8 feet, according to the state of the tide. The anchors to each are an 18-inch shell and a piece of kentledge... The wire for the return current from the battery is passed from shell to shell along the connecting rope, which lies at the bottom. The wire that passes from cask to cask is stopped slack at the buoy rope from the shell up to the cask.... The return wire is stopped in like manner down along the span to the next shell....[11]

Even though Maury had established no less than twenty-one Wollaston batteries along the shoreline, to act as backups in case of electrical failure, he never had the opportunity to detonate his explosives. Before any enemy vessels ventured into his James River network, a sudden spring freshet managed to wash away his hidden tanks. They were never recovered.

Matthew Maury's waning hopes of destroying a Union warship were completely dashed when he was, without warning, dispatched on a lengthy and important mission to Europe in mid-1862. His torpedo research and development was turned over to Lieutenant Hunter Davidson, whom Maury had been training since April. Davidson, who assumed control of the entire operation in late June, had the immediate misfortune of running the *Teaser* aground on July 4, 1862. Shortly thereafter, the helpless vessel fell into the hands of the enemy, along with Maury's descriptions, instructions, and diagrams. Also among the contraband was a detailed account of the precise location of his mines, all anchored below the surface of the James River. Though the Union fleet did not conduct a search of the region, they received the information seriously and avoided traveling along the river for several months to come.

Much later, after the Maury torpedoes had long since held the enemy at bay, and had utterly destroyed one of their vessels, Maury had this to say:

All the electrical torpedoes in that river were prepared and laid either by myself or by Lieutenant Davidson, who relieved me after having been instructed by me as to the details of the system. These were the first electrical torpedoes that were successfully used against an enemy at war.[12]

There can be no doubt, therefore, that Matthew Fontaine Maury, though he has not been given the credit, is responsible for establishing the foundation for underwater warfare used during the Civil War.

Chapter 2

The Anaconda and the Rabbit

During the greatest portion of 1862 the primary objective concerning underwater explosives was restricted to the invention and testing of new devices. One Confederate officer, who had the unique opportunity to observe much of this development in torpedo warfare, had this to say:

> There were torpedo twin boats, propelled by rockets; diving apparatus by ... which torpedoes might be attached to the bottom of the enemy's ship; balloons that were to ascend, and, when arrived just above the vessel ... drop some kind of torpedo on the deck; rotation torpedo rockets to be fired under water; submarine boats with torpedoes attached to a spar; in fine, any variety of plans, and yet but a very few practical ones....[1]

Though it seems quite clear that Matthew Fontaine Maury had initiated the rejuvenation of the torpedo concept during the early weeks of the Civil War, he was by no means the lone Confederate to pursue such matters during the course of the four-year conflict. Quite literally, a large troop of dedicated Southern citizens and military personnel followed closely on the boot heels of Maury, with each contributing a new piece of knowledge to the puzzle of torpedo technology. Yet, what prompted this newfound intense interest in the study and development of underwater warfare? To fully understand the magnetic forces which attracted inventors by the dozens toward such worldly, and often dangerous, endeavors, we must first take a closer look at Northern strategists rather than those in the South.

Within one week of the day when shooting first broke out at Fort Sumter, South Carolina, the entire world was shocked by the Proclamation of Blockade outlined by the Northern government. It was intended to be carried out between the "Capes of Virginia to the mouth of the Rio Grande."[2] A full description was provided by William H. Seward, Secretary of State under Abraham Lincoln:

> Washington, April 19 — The President has issued a proclamation as follows:
> An insurrection against the Government of the United States has broken out in the states of South Carolina, Georgia, Alabama, Florida, Mississippi, Louisiana and Texas, and the laws of the United States for the collection of the revenue

cannot be effectually executed therein comfortably by that provision of the Constitution which requires the duties to be uniform throughout the United States.

And, further, a combination of persons engaged in such insurrection have threatened to grant pretenders letters of marque to authorize the bearers thereof to commit assaults on the lives, vessels and property of good citizens of the country, engaged in commerce on the high seas and in the waters of the United States.

And whereas an Executive proclamation has been already issued, requiring the persons engaged in these disorderly proceedings to desist therefrom, calling out a militia force for the purpose of repressing the same ... the President with a view to the same purposes before mentioned, and to the protection of public peace and the lives and property of quiet and orderly citizens pursuing their lawful occupations ... has further deemed it advisable to set on foot a blockade of the ports within the States aforesaid....

For this purpose a competent force will be posted so as to prevent the entrance and exit of vessels from the ports aforesaid.

If, therefore, with a view to violate such blockade, any vessel shall attempt to leave any of said ports, the vessel will be duly warned by the commander of one of said blockading vessels, who will endorse on her register the fact and date of such naming, and if the same vessel shall again attempt to enter or leave the blockaded port, she will be captured and sent to the nearest commercial port, for such proceedings against her and her cargo as may be deemed advisable.[3]

During the mid–1800s, the threat and implementation of a blockade was interpreted as being a clear act of war between independent nations. No country in the world had even considered the possibility that the United States government would suggest placing a blockade upon her own ports in the South. The *New York Herald* voiced the majority opinion by proclaiming that "no government can blockade its own ports. It may lay an embargo on goods leaving its ports, but it cannot legally and constitutionally prevent the ships of other nations from entering its ports while it is at peace with those nations."[4]

Thus, Secretary of State Seward's use of the term "blockade" not only established the Confederates as independent belligerents, but it created an atmosphere for retaliation by the Confederate States. In fact, it would long be remembered as one of the major political blunders in all of American history. Cutting off the South's avenues of supply, both outgoing and incoming, was, indeed, an act of aggression. It angered longtime foreign trading countries, as well as the Southern states themselves, and established a solid foundation of friendship between them. When all was said and done, nations such as England would opt to side with the South during the war — not because the English government condoned slavery, but because of the heavy cotton trade flowing into her ports from the Confederacy.

Winfield Scott, a longtime United States general, who had built a solid reputation as a strategist in both the War of 1812 and the Mexican-American conflict, was given the difficult task of implementing the North's blockading tactics. His complicated undertaking would become known as the "Anaconda Plan."

In a pair of letters dispatched to General George B. McClellan in May of 1861, Scott outlined his proposal:

> A powerful movement down the Mississippi ... [in order] to clear out and keep open the great line of communication in connection with the strict blockade of the sea-board ... (will) envelop the insurgent States and bring them to terms with less bloodshed than by any other plan.[5]

The inventor of the term "Anaconda" is unknown, though it has been attributed to both a Cincinnati newswriter and General McClellan himself. Robert H. Newell, author of the *Orpheus C. Kerr Papers*, attempted to offer a more visual portrait of the plan when he wrote: "The great anaconda has gathered itself in a circle around the doomed rabbit of rebellion, and if the rabbit swells he's a goner."[6] Newell might have done better to take his ideas one step further, however, for he did not put forth a complete description of the situation. Winfield Scott's plan did not limit itself to a mere strangulation of the Confederate supply routes: it would also be a unique means of clearing a pathway for the transportation of Union troops, munitions, and supplies to those areas where they would be most in demand or least expected. Thus, the anaconda (Union forces) would be able to attack at will, as well as put a chokehold upon the South.

Furthermore, Newell said nothing of the South's reaction toward such harsh and aggressive behavior. Most people can certainly understand that a "doomed rabbit," when cornered and afraid, will retaliate to the best of its ability. Thus the Anaconda Plan provided a breeding ground for the implementation of a radical new defense against the relentless northern naval forces — namely, underwater warfare.

Whatever the specific details of the plan may have been, in reality, the possibility of the northern militia taking complete and utter control of the southern seacoast is quite difficult to comprehend for modern historians. The fact of the matter is, if Americans of today truly wish to understand the situation of civil war between the Confederacy and the United States in 1861, including the unique struggle for control of the South's coastline, we must look beyond the memorabilia now gathering dust within museums throughout the country. To engage in a ferry cruise up the James River, or to visit such battle scenes as Charleston Harbor and New Orleans, is not enough. We must, instead, attempt to visualize precisely what thoughts cascaded through the minds of those who developed and implemented the intricate blockading tactics. Indeed, we must bring ourselves to think as they had once thought; to feel as they had once felt; and to see what they had, most assuredly, seen. Only then can we claim a true insight into America's Civil War past.

Yet, when we do make the concerted effort to explore this mysterious world known as "history," we immediately unearth one major flaw in Winfield Scott's Anaconda Plan: the obvious lack of ready manpower and equipment to carry out such an enormous task.

Examples of large, iron-jacketed mines, intended to be detonated from shore with an electrical charge originating at a battery station.

In the United States, which has grown by leaps and bounds since the days of the Civil War, we may find it quite difficult to comprehend a nation which once possessed a very minute military force. In 1861, when fighting first began, the total population of the country was only about 31.5 million. Furthermore, there were only 16,257 soldiers enlisted in the U.S. Army, and a mere 7,500 then serving in the U.S. Navy. Taking our observations one step further, the vast majority of these enlisted men were permanently stationed along the western front, in order to control any sudden Indian uprisings. As of March 1861, the Union government had only 42 ships in its commission, and just over 200 men stationed on the Atlantic coastline. Of these available vessels, just 26 were steamers. Without question, then, the active military forces of the North could not even hope to muster enough manpower in the foreseeable future to fill the huge order demanded by Scott's plan of blockade.

However, the Northern government immediately went to work on strengthening its forces, quickly altering its seemingly hopeless situation. Five distinct and specific goals, if the North hoped to carry out its complicated blockading plan with any effectiveness, were laid down. First and foremost, orders were dispatched overseas to speed up the return of all warships. Government-owned shipyards all along the northeastern coast began to build around the clock; and the Navy Department initiated contacts with privately-owned shipping merchants in New York as well as other large cities, hoping to enlarge their fleet by way of both charters and purchases. No offers were turned away. Barks, ferries, schooners, sloops, tugs, and anything else that floated and could transport supplies or men were accepted.

Actual bargaining was conducted by the Department of the Navy, or, often, by operatives acting under its directive. As of July 1, 1861, a dozen steamers had been located and secured, with nine of these being employed under charter. Later, the business of purchasing suitable vessels would be placed in the hands of private agents. After each transaction was approved by a special board of naval officers, the vessel would be made ready for warfare. The ships were of varied descriptions, including everything from small tugboats to 2,000-ton screw-steamers. By the end of that first year of fighting, 418 vessels would be purchased, including 313 steamers and 105 sailing ships.

The second important objective was the immediate construction of sloops-of-war; sailing vessels which could transport between eighteen and thirty-two guns each. In February 1861 Congress authorized the construction of eight of these sailing ships, half of which would be near-identical copies of three sloops built in 1858.

With no lengthy delays in design procedures, due to the fact that the North already was in possession of working models, the construction of the sloops went smoothly. During the latter half of 1861, six additional sloops were commissioned, each of which was of the same general design, only larger.

Third on the list of goals was to hire private citizens to construct much more compact, heavily-armed screw-gunboats. Twenty-three of these were built quite rapidly, being afloat, armed, and manned within a three-month period. Because of their quick construction, they were given the nickname "ninety-day gunboats,"[7] and they were actively employed in both blockading measures and a variety of offensive maneuvers.

A fourth class of vessels which were desperately needed was those with the ability to patrol rivers and narrow sounds. In order to meet this need, twelve paddle wheel steamers were designed and constructed. Though they outweighed the screw-gunboats by three to four hundred tons, they were shallow enough to do the job adequately. To avoid the necessity of turning around in cramped quarters, they were each outfitted with a double bow and a rudder at each end. These "double-enders,"[8] as they were called, were built of both wood and iron.

The final measure which would increase the North's naval power was the design and construction of iron-clad, ocean-going war machines. In August 1861 Congress appropriated $1,500,000 for these armored vessels. From this fund such ships as the *New Ironsides*, the *Gelena*, and the *Monitor* would be built.

It seems clear that Winfield Scott, whose Anaconda Plan was thoroughly outlined in his letters to General George B. McClellan, considered the

Mississippi River as part of the South's available seacoast — as it well should have been. Yet Scott was to encounter obstacles in his attempt to implement his blockading formula, for not everyone agreed with his methods.

Perhaps one of the most outspoken critics of Scott's anaconda strategy was Gideon Welles, the Secretary of the Navy under President Abraham Lincoln. In his candid diary of the war, Welles wrote:

> I had, in the early stages of the War, disapproved of the policy of General Scott — non-intercourse with the insurgents, shut them out from the world by blockade and military frontier lines, but not to invade their territory. The anaconda policy was, I then thought and still think, unwise for the country.[9]

When General Scott had first outlined his plan to shut off Southern port cities, it was believed that the measures could adequately be carried out by simply dispatching a small squadron of vessels to the major commercial harbors throughout the Confederacy. It was later decided, however, that between two and six ships, positioned well away from each harbor, would be needed at each designated site. In addition, in order to supplement this action, large numbers of slow-moving cruising vessels would be needed to continually travel freelance up and down the coast. Acting upon this belief, the Northern government pinpointed ten to twelve "problem" areas, situated from the Atlantic to the Gulf of Mexico, and proceeded with the operation.

The USS *Niagara*, which had recently returned from overseas duty in Japan, was dispatched to cruise the waters off Charleston; the USS *Powhatan* and USS *Brooklyn* moved southward, then westward, around the southern tip of Florida into the Gulf; and the USS *Keystone State* was directed to keep a close watch over the Hampton Roads area of Virginia. Later, the screw-steamer *South Carolina*, weighing 1,165 tons, would arrive off Pensacola, with the USS *Massachusetts* equally as prompt in reaching Key West.

The city of Savannah was, for all intents and purposes, effectively blockaded by May 28, with Mobile and New Orleans receiving notice of such action just two days earlier. And a single month later the *South Carolina* was secure in the harbor near Galveston, Texas.

However, despite the North's concerted efforts to implement the Anaconda Plan at full strength, the chain of blockade was far from being complete. In fact, it could hardly be referred to as a chain at all, for there were so many weak and missing links.

Blockade-running quickly became widespread at most Confederate ports, due to the fact that it was rather easy to move large vessels in and out of a harbor without being detected. The majority of Confederate business, with the South trading cotton for gunpowder and weapons, was being conducted secretly with Great Britain. On their return routes, all ships sailing out of British ports toward the Southern states began to incorporate a system of stopping-off points along the way. To this end, all available neutral ports in the vicinity of the Confederacy were employed, including Bermuda, Nassau, Havana, and Matamoros. Since this practice continued as the war dragged on, the North was forced to alter its original blockading procedure. Measures were initiated to increase its naval forces even more, for the North believed that a much closer scrutiny would result in the end of contraband trade. Therefore, the old traditional idea of a blockade being maintained by a few well-armed vessels moving up and down the coastline gave way to an entirely novel practice. Instead, a large number of small and mobile steamers would be used to clog up the South's harbors and to move up and down inland rivers.

By the time that this decision had been reached, Secretary of the Navy Gideon Welles seems to have taken a complete and utter turnaround in his earlier opinion of the blockading of southern ports. In fact, he went as far as to devise his very own unique method of stopping vessels from entering and exiting the Confederacy — that of intentionally sinking ships, loaded down heavily with stone and gravel, in both Charleston Harbor and the mouth of the Savannah River. In this way, he hoped to plug up the shallow main channels of travel into both cities. Of Welles' innovative strategy, the *New York Herald* had this to say:

> There are twenty-five vessels, averaging 335 tons each, and they will be so heavily loaded with stone that, when once sunk, it will be no easy matter to raise them. They will thus become the real blockading fleet, that no storm or fog can interfere with or no small craft pass by.[10]

It quickly became quite apparent, therefore, that any and all strategies that the North might improvise were believed to be fair during wartime maneuvers. However, the task of blockading its own southern ports would become increasingly more difficult as the months went by, due to the fact that the Confederacy continued to incorporate underwater explosives.

Perhaps Antoine Jomini inadvertently assisted the Southern strategists toward making the decision to incorporate torpedo warfare when he recognized the importance of open supply routes by stating: "The vicinity of the sea is invaluable for the transportation of supplies. Whoever is master on this element can supply himself at will...."[11] As the Anaconda Plan went into full swing, the South began to implement its newfound defensive measures. The Confederate Torpedo Division, under the direction of the newly-appointed Hunter Davidson, continued the work with electrical torpedoes initiated by Matthew Fontaine Maury. Davidson's crew operated primarily on the James and Cape Fear rivers of Virginia. Though the force was quite compact, it was elastic enough to spread out to other points throughout the region. At the outset, other than Davidson himself, there was an electrician and his assistant, two men at each battery station on shore, three telegraph operators, two scouts, and the well-trained crew of a tugboat. In all they numbered approximately 50 men.

As we have already said, a problem within his covert organization arose soon after Davidson took the helm. On Independence Day of 1862, the United States gunboat *Maratanza* surprised and captured the marooned CSS *Teaser*, which had been designated as Davidson's main headquarters. On board, the Union navy men discovered a good deal of detailed written material outlining Maury's earlier experiments, as well as mine-laying equipment of the highest quality. Their haul included copper wire, batteries, gunpowder, and an odd multicolored inflatable balloon "made up of old frocks."[12] This crudely designed aircraft was to be used at a later date to spy on the Union forces at Harrison's Landing.

Davidson's headquarters were replaced almost immediately, with a second small steam-tug, fittingly dubbed the CSS *Torpedo*. The new vessel carried a pair of Parrott rifles for emergencies, should there be any further problems with patroling enemy ships. In a tiny cabin aboard this craft, Davidson would plan, design, and implement a variety of underwater weapons.

The initial objective which had to be met, prior to any testing of torpedoes, was the development of an extremely sensitive fuse. Made up of a fulminate of mercury, it was to be used in conjunction with an electrical charge passing through an ultra-fine length of platinum wire. Each individual fuse was constructed by taking a piece of one-half-inch hollow quill and filling it with the liquid mercury. A short length of platinum was then inserted through the center, with both ends of the quill being sealed with a small amount of beeswax. Each end of the platinum wire was then connected to a heavier length of insulated copper wiring, which led away from the submerged torpedo to dry land. Finally, the entire fuse apparatus was secured within a cartridge bag made of durable red flannel stuffed with gunpowder. Only then was it ready to be inserted into a torpedo tank.

Each explosive, designed by Davidson himself, possessed an encasement fashioned out of one-half-inch boiler iron, with a single opening to load the gunpowder and to insert the fuse. The opening would then be filled with a screwplug, which had been specifically designed with a pair of miniature holes through which the copper wiring would pass. Greased cotton was used to ensure that there would be no leakage of moisture through these holes into the inside of the tank. Eventually, most of these torpedo tanks would be constructed by the Tredegar Iron Works of Richmond, and each would be thoroughly tested with heavy hydraulic pressure in order to locate any possible flaws in workmanship.

Before deciding on the ideal shape of his explosive, Davidson and his crew spent countless days testing a variety of ideas and suggestions. One of the first, a soda tank constructed of copper, was capable of holding between 100 and 150 pounds of gunpowder, an amount believed to be perfect for their needs. A heavy iron ring was positioned around the belly of the prototype tank in a belt-like fashion. This, in turn, was attached to a 20-foot length of chain, whose opposite end was connected to a mushroom anchor. The torpedo, minus its fuse, was then positioned beneath the moving waters of the James River for a period of time to see how well it might endure.

Later, when the fuseless tank was hoisted to the surface, Davidson discovered that the continuous oscillating rotary motion of the current had caused the copper wiring to twist and, eventually, break. Furthermore, from daily observation, the crew noticed that the tank tended to hover approximately halfway between the river's bottom and the surface. Thus, whenever such a setup was detonated, it would spend 50 percent of its force downward and the other half upward, losing a good portion of its effectiveness. It was determined that further experimentation would be needed before any suitable explosive could be crafted.

As had been the case with Matthew Maury's earlier experiments, shortages of necessary materials continued to hamper the progress of the Confederate Torpedo Division. At the beginning of July 1862, there were only about 2,000 feet of insulated copper wiring available throughout the entire South. Furthermore, Davidson's crew was only able to secure four or five feet of the precious platinum wire which they so desperately needed. Finally, to top it off, ready-made batteries were extremely scarce, and battery acid could only be obtained from the limited amounts then in the possession of druggists scattered throughout the region.

Not one to give up easily, Davidson opted to attempt the construction of homemade batteries to detonate his underwater charges. Yet, to set up such an innovative system without the necessary glass tumblers to hold acid or platinum strips to submerge in the nitric acid was going to be extremely difficult, to say the least. There were virtually no glass factories located within the Confederacy, and the only platinum suitable for his purpose was already being used in the guts of batteries owned by the few telegraph offices sprinkled throughout the region.

Finally, however, a homemade model was designed by Davidson's electrician, R. O. Crowley, from available materials:

> ...with the zinc plates formerly used in the Wollaston battery in our early experiments, I had a number of zinc cells cast in the shape of an ordinary glass tumbler, having a projecting arm for a handle as well as to connect it with the next adjoining cell in the series. The inside of these zinc tumblers was amalgamated with mercury, and a solution of sulphuric acid, composed of one part of acid and thirteen parts of water, was poured into each tumbler or cell. In this solution was placed a cylindrical porous cup, open at the top, and filled with nitric acid. In the nitric acid was immersed a piece of cast-iron having four projecting leaves and a projecting handle connected with a corresponding handle of the adjoining zinc cell by an ordinary brass clamp.[13]

The cast-iron strips, it was discovered, were not instantaneously consumed by the abrasive nitric acid, as the group of experimenters had initially believed they would be. In fact, they found that the strips could remain submerged for several hours at a time without noticeable alterations in their composition. If left too long, however, the nitric acid would change into nitrous oxide, a useless chemical compound that would eventually effervesce without warning.

At that point, Crowley realized that it was only necessary to refill the porous cups with fresh nitric acid. Though the electrician's homemade battery was relatively sufficient for the Torpedo Division's needs, it could not produce an electrical current beyond a distance of two miles of circuitry.

By the autumn of 1862, Davidson's crew had developed what they believed was the ideal underwater explosive. The oscillation motion, as well as the depth problem, had been solved. Three of these copper torpedoes, each containing approximately 150 pounds of gunpowder, were planted in the waters of the Rappahannock River, just inland from Port Royal, Virginia. Their hopes of destroying any Union blockading vessels moving upriver were squelched, however, when their secret operations were disclosed to the enemy by a Federal spy.[14]

Hunter Davidson dispatched electrician Crowley to the nearby township of Port Royal when it became apparent that the North's General Ambrose Burnside was on the verge of moving his troops into nearby Fredericksburg, thus endangering the Torpedo Division's continuing experiments. Crowley's mission was to save all explosives material and completed torpedoes from falling into enemy hands. This included the scarce copper and platinum wiring as well as the limited number of handcrafted batteries. Before abandoning their strategic position along the Rappahannock River, however, the crew took the time to detonate the previously planted underwater charges, which could not be salvaged. This destruction operation managed to frighten numerous residents throughout the area, prompting them to take steps toward evacuation.

The entire 50-man troop, which had, by this time, become an irreplaceable part of the Torpedo Division, began their retreat aboard a local Fredericksburg train, taking with them their valuable cargo. While passing through Ashland, Virginia, just a few days later, the engineers discovered that the village was already occupied by invading Union Cavalry under the direction of Colonel Judson Kilpatrick. After stopping the train in mid-flight, the Union leader ordered everyone off before demolishing its railcars and running the engine from the tracks.

Long before this potentially devastating incident took place, Davidson and the others had been ordered to carry documents on their persons whenever they traveled, in the likely event that they might be captured by the enemy. These important papers were supplied to them by the Confederate States Navy Department, and read as follows:

> The bearer ... is in the service of the Confederate States Navy ... and in case of his capture by the United States forces, he will be exchanged for any general officer of their army who may be in our hands.
>
> [signed] S. R. Mallory
> Secty. of the Navy.[15]

Opting to keep the papers hidden among his personal effects for the time being, electrician R. O. Crowley opted to approach Colonel Kilpatrick and blatantly inquired: "Colonel, what shall you do with citizens?"[16]

The Union leader thought for a moment, and then responded that all Southern citizens would be allowed to go free. Without hesitation, the members of the Davidson's crew vanished into the crowd. Had the colonel understood what a valuable group of prisoners he had within his grasp, the Torpedo Division might well have ceased to exist right then and there. As it was, however, they managed to escape and make their way southward, deciding to reestablish their operation along the muddy banks of the busy James River.

Chapter 3

With Patience Comes Success

With the Confederate Torpedo Division's system very close to being perfected, Hunter Davidson's explosives engineers established themselves along the banks of the James River, approximately six miles south of Richmond. Here, they planted a pair of strong iron tanks 12 feet deep, filled with 1,000 pounds of gunpowder each. Copper wires led from the torpedoes to a galvanic battery located on shore, situated within a small wooden hut camouflaged within the confines of a deep ravine. From this battery house, the wires continued up to an elevated lookout station nearby, where a scout could continually monitor the movement of enemy ships.

The exact location of the sunken torpedoes was marked by a pair of ordinary sticks, spaced about ten feet apart and positioned on the bluff, in line with one another and the depth charges. The watchman's job was simple enough: whenever an enemy vessel came in line with the two sticks, the torpedoes were to be detonated by merely touching the two bared copper wire ends together, thus completing the circuit.

Just a few weeks after everything was in place, while the rest of the crew was in Richmond securing supplies, an inexperienced lookout spotted a Union vessel steaming up the river. This was the Torpedo Division's first opportunity to test the system under actual battle conditions.

However, the lone lookout must have grown impatient in waiting for the exact alignment, for he touched the copper wires together prematurely. Up went a huge geyser of water, missing the unsuspecting gunboat by some 20 or 30 yards. The fast-moving Federal vessel was unable to stop her engines quickly enough, however, and she plunged into the large trough of water. The ensuing wave washed over her deck, and six or seven sailors were swept overboard. The steamer then prepared to reverse its direction, after pausing long enough to snatch up her lost crewmen. Though there was still ample opportunity to destroy the vessel on her turnaround maneuver by simply firing the remaining torpedo, the ship made it safely back to Richmond without incident. Evidently, the lookout had panicked and had vacated his post immediately following the initial explosion.

The success of detonating the first torpedo by a man in Davidson's crew, though no damage was done, helped to establish a fear of underwater explosives throughout the Union ranks. From that day forward, it would demand a great deal of courage on the part of the Northern navy to travel the treacherous waters of the South. This, however, was detrimental to the Torpedo Division's goal of sinking enemy vessels.

The work of installing other torpedoes beneath the waters of the James River took Davidson and his men the entire summer of 1862. By the end of October they had completed their mission, and Davidson informed a friend:

> I am getting on slowly here with the submarines [torpedoes]. I shall soon have about 12,000 pounds of powder down at different stations on the river.
>
> My later experiments prove that powerful galvanic batteries can be relied on to act with unerring certainty at the distance of a half mile under water. This is the way we should obstruct all our rivers if sufficient powder can be got. I don't believe you can find a Yankee to risk a blowing up.[1]

A description of the Confederate Torpedo Division's defenses of the James would not be complete without details surrounding the huge barricade established at Drewry's Bluff, Virginia. It was strategically positioned within an area where the river became extremely narrow and deep. On one side, the bank rose abruptly to a high, precipitous bluff. On the other side was a low flatland. The spot was ideal for any lookout stationed at the top of the hill to see for several miles up and down the winding waterway.

The barricade itself had been fashioned by driving long piles into the soft, sandy river bottom in such a way that they formed cribs. Into these cribs were dropped tons of granite, which had been transported from Richmond specifically for that purpose. Arranged in a zig-zag row, the cribs stretched from one side of the narrows to the other, and could only be seen by an extremely watchful eye at low tide. The only direct passage that was left open was a compact route along the bank that stretched out onto the flatland and was protected by a few well-placed torpedoes. Several Union steamboats and schooners would eventually be scuttled along this dangerous portion of the James River.

When it came time for Confederate ironclads to bypass Drewry's Bluff, the Torpedo Division was instructed to blow up some of the cribs. After the large ships had passed safely, new cribs were reconstructed where the old ones had been removed. The major reason for building this protective barricade in the first place was to keep enemy vessels at bay during highly secretive nighttime maneuvers. The widespread belief, however, was that during a full-scale invasion by the enemy, the Torpedo Division would be able to defend the passageway for only a few short hours at most.

Hence, steps were taken to build similar defensive underwater cribs farther up the James, in order to guard against any Union vessels which might chance to get by the first series of obstacles. Construction was undertaken at numerous strategic points, incorporating larger, 2,000-pound explosives

A friction torpedo, which was activated by an operator stationed on shore who pulled a lanyard when an enemy ship was in the right position. Often used when batteries for electrically detonated torpedoes were in short supply (courtesy of West Point Museum Collection).

submerged beneath the narrow passageways. At the Confederates' southern-most telegraph station on the James, located at General Pickett's Turkey Island plantation, a 100-foot-high spy tower was erected. From this vantage point, lookouts could see Federal gunboats as far away as City Point, several miles to the northwest.

Depending heavily on this tower for sightings of all advancing forces, the Confederate Torpedo Division constructed a torpedo barricade in an area known as Deep Bottom, approximately five miles from City Point. Whenever the lookout on duty spotted an enemy vessel moving within the vicinity, a signal would be passed on to the Deep Bottom battery station, and the crew would prepare itself for the destruction of the incoming ship.

Since their explosives were positioned so near to the enemy lines, the engineers generally worked at planting the torpedoes under the cover of darkness, in precise spots designated by trained surveyors during the day. The galvanic battery which would detonate the torpedoes at Deep Bottom was well-concealed in a five-foot-deep pit, covered with twigs and brush, along the immediate shoreline. A short distance away, a second pit was dug, possessing a backup battery.

In early August of 1863, a Union fleet pushed upriver past the Deep Bottom torpedo station. The batterymen were in Richmond once again, however, constructing more depth charges to plant along the James. At approximately 4:30 in the afternoon on August 5, the enemy decided to retrace their path by turning the ships around and traveling back downstream.

In the meantime, the battery operators had returned to their posts, and were waiting when the vessels passed. One Union ship known as the *Commodore Barney*, a converted New York ferry, floated almost directly over one of the hidden underwater explosives. Excitedly, the Confederate crew set about to destroy the 513-ton gunboat. Suddenly, a force of water streamed up beneath its bow, followed by the aftersounds of a deafening explosion. The ship rocked violently, as heavy white foam and chunks of riverbed from a 50-foot geyser crashed across her deck:

> It was terrible.... The vessel was lifted ... upward of ten feet out of the water, and an immense jet of water was hurled from her bow into the air, falling over and completely deluging her....[2]

Although 20 crewmen of the *Commodore Barney* went overboard into the swirling waters, only two were killed, and the vessel miraculously managed to remain afloat. The major damage inflicted upon her was a broken steam pipe, which temporarily disabled her engine-works. Another Union ship, the *Cohasset*, came to the disabled vessel's rescue, towing her approximately five miles to dock in Dutch Gap. There, technicians repaired her engine.

Though the Torpedo Division did not manage to destroy the *Commodore Barney*, they disclosed, with certainty, the fact that the James River was well-laid with torpedoes. It would literally be months before a second advance by the Union Navy would take place on these waters.

Finally, in the spring of 1864, another Federal patrol squadron made its move up the James River from Bermuda Hundred, traveling toward Drewry's Bluff. Rounding the point just below Presque Isle on May 6, the flotilla spotted the Confederate lookout tower, and proceeded to demolish it with explosive shells. Next, a battalion of Northern foot soldiers, who had been transported to the area aboard the gunboat *Mackinaw*, landed on both shores. They were ordered to search for the hidden location of the galvanic batteries. Almost simultaneously, a squadron of search vessels, heavily armed with munitions, traveled in advance of the approaching fleet, dragging grapnel hooks to uncover hidden wiring and torpedoes. However, they passed over the wires and underwater explosives several times without locating them.

Determining that there were no torpedoes in the vicinity, the *Commodore Jones*, a double-ender gunboat manned by 200 men and eight guns, was ordered to continue the advance. The vessel chanced to pass directly over the Deep Bottom underwater explosives, yet no detonation took place.

The explanation for the inactivity was simple to understand: convinced that the Union ironclad *Atlanta*, which had recently been captured by Federal forces from the Confederate Navy station at Savannah, would soon be dispatched to follow, lookout Peter W. Smith opted to be patient before he gave the signal to the battery man below to explode the mine . He understood that this prestigious vessel would be a much more valuable target.

When the *Commodore Jones* landed on the wharf at Deep Bottom and discovered the Confederate hideaway vacant, the order was given for her to retreat. Fearing that the entire squadron was on the verge of falling back out of range, the Torpedo Division's lookout changed his thinking, deciding to attempt the destruction of the *Commodore Jones* after all. As she floated back up the river, at approximately two o'clock in the afternoon, she happened to pass directly over one of the larger 2,000-pound mines which had been submerged beneath the surface for nearly 22 months.

Peter Smith was unsure as to whether or not the explosive could be detonated, as he ordered the battery operator to touch the bare wires against the cable. Without warning, the *Commodore Jones* was shattered into thousands of pieces by a terrific explosion:

> Suddenly she appeared to be lifted bodily, her wheels revolving in mid-air; persons declared they could see the green ... of the banks beneath her keel. Then, through her shot to a great height, a fountain of foaming water, followed by a dense column thick with mud. She absolutely crumbled to pieces — dissolved as it were in mid-air, enveloped by the falling spray, mud, water, and smoke....[3]

An estimated 40 Federal navy men perished in the surprise attack, and a portion of the flotilla retreated back toward Bermuda Hundred in utter terror.

Undaunted by the danger, the Union marine squadron continued their avid search along the shoreline, managing to capture and kill the frightened battery man. Once again, the smaller Union vessels resumed their intricate search for underwater wiring and hidden explosives. Finally, after several minutes of retracing their course back and forth, their grapnel hooks latched onto something. Slowly, a length of copper wiring was yanked to the surface.

The Federal searchers followed the line to the bank, where they discovered and made prisoners of the Confederate lookout and his assistant. The pair, later identified as Peter W. Smith and Jeffries Johnson, were then dragged aboard the double-ender gunboat *Eutaw*, where they were savagely tied in a conspicuous place along the wheelhouse. This was done not so much to flaunt their capture, but as a protective measure against any further unexpected attacks. Eventually, the two prisoners would be transferred to the Union prison at Fort Warren, only to become part of a prisoner exchange 12 months later. Hunter Davidson and the remainder of his crew managed to escape detection by the Union search party.

During the upcoming weeks, while the Torpedo Division continued to plant their electrically-powered submersible mines along the James River, numerous mechanical torpedoes which detonated on contact, were also being employed by the Confederate States Army in rivers throughout the South. Since the army and navy were seldom in close collaboration with one another, they could not have known at the time that they were simultaneously mining the same areas, quite often the same stretches of waterway. And even though Secretary of War Mallory ordered the contact type of torpedo to be removed, accidents did occur from time to time.

One such mishap involved the Confederate steamship *A. H. Schultz*, which had originally been constructed as a passenger vessel and had traveled between Richmond and Norfolk. During the war she was taken control of by the Confederate States government for the purpose of shipping prisoners of war from Varina, situated on the James River, to various points. At these points, the captured Northern soldiers would be exchanged for Confederate prisoners.

On one particular outing, while the *A. H. Schultz* was transporting 450 Federal soldiers down the river, she passed the barricades of Drewry's Bluff safely and landed at her secret destination. It was believed at the time that she would trade these prisoners for a like number of Southern soldiers being held by the North. However, due to a miscommunication, she was forced to sail to Richmond empty. When the vacant vessel reached a position just beyond the Deep Bottom Bluff, she ran into an errant contact mine. A massive explosion followed, killing the two firemen and two Confederate soldiers on board. The steamer sank below the surface of the James River within five minutes, and she was a total loss.

It was extremely fortunate that the ill-fated *A. H. Schultz* did not chance to come in contact with the mechanical mine on her downward journey, for it is more than likely that many Federal prisoners would have been killed. This, in turn, would have resulted in a good deal of abrasive criticism at the inept handling of prisoners of war being transported under a flag of truce.

With the eventual advance of Northern troops toward Richmond during the upcoming months, the Torpedo Division was once again forced to move its base of operations. This time, they packed up their equipment and traveled to Wilmington, North Carolina. Here, their major objective was to make certain that no Federal vessels passed Fort Caswell and Fort Fisher, located at the mouth of the Cape Fear River.

Hunter Davidson and his men were faced with a new challenge in their newest location; how to plant underwater explosives in the ocean, whose ebb and flow pushed through a rather wide channel. They discovered, however, that, despite the fact that the channel off Fort Fisher was about one-half mile in width, there was barely enough room at the bar for more than one or two vessels to pass at a time. Hence, they selected this narrowing passageway as their primary area of concentration, and they proceeded to submerge a total of seven 2,000-pound torpedo tanks spaced evenly. The copper wires leading from the hidden explosives to the battery pit on shore were buried beneath the soft sand. Each mine was assigned an individual identification number, from one through seven. Next, markers in the form of ordinary sticks were positioned above the numbered explosives. In this way, a lookout would easily be able to decide when an enemy ship was close enough for detonation procedures to begin.

Upriver from Fort Fisher, toward Wilmington, the Torpedo Division planted a pair of mines weighing 1,000 pounds apiece. The wiring ran up the shore to an aging earthwork situated along the bank. There they were connected to a Wheatstone battery, which was one of an extremely limited supply that had recently been smuggled in from Europe through the strong Federal blockade. During a heavy thunderstorm, however, while the Division's crewmen waited for the Union fleet to make its move, the copper wiring was struck by lightning. This sudden surge of power worked to detonate both explosives simultaneously, warning the Union naval forces of the mining operations. Thus, they decided to curtail their immediate plans to advance toward the forts.

Though to many experts Davidson's torpedoes may have seemed rather large for the job they were designed to do, they did not even come close to the size of one constructed by the North, which housed more than 215 tons of fused powder. The purpose of this monstrous explosive was not only to destroy the Confederate gunboat *Louisiana*, which had been built in New Orleans in 1861, but to demolish Fort Fisher as well. Yet, an expected confrontation between the two opposing sides, with each employing underwater explosives, failed to materialize. Furthermore, the "H-bomb" of the Civil War, as it would later be called, failed because of poorly conceived fuses. When Fort Fisher was eventually invaded by advancing Federal land forces late in the war, a Confederate prisoner was asked about the effects of the giant explosive. Evidently, the inquisitive Northerner had not been informed that the bomb had never exploded. Amused, however, by the lack of information, the Confederate soldier exaggerated by answering: "It was horrible! Woke up every man in the fort!"[4]

Several other types of underwater explosives, most of which were successful, were developed by the South during the first two years of the conflict. One, known as the "drift" torpedo, gave the Union Navy a good deal of worry. It consisted of an outer shell made of tin, and housed approximately 70 pounds of gunpowder. Numerous wires led from a friction fuse to small chunks of driftwood floating on the surface. In theory, these "trigger" lines would inevitably become entangled within the enemy's propellers. As early as January 1863, one of these devices was discovered by the USS *Essex* as she made her way up the Mississippi River.

Another widely-used explosive which had been devised by the Confederate navy was known as the "stationary" torpedo, and it was detailed as being

...comprised [of] a spar fastened by a universal joint to a fixed block at the bottom of the river and bearing the torpedo at its summit. Swinging with the current and tide, this torpedo was always kept at a uniform depth below the surface, and was out of sight. The torpedo was studded with sensitive caps, and no matter where a ship touched it it would explode. They could not be grappled for, and it was only by good luck, care and ingenuity that the Federals got them out....[5]

As time went by, Union vessels were becoming more and more leery of most well-traveled waterways, and the South began to realize that defensive weapons might not be the answer. Perhaps, they reasoned, if the enemy would not come to them, then they would be forced to go to the enemy. Because of this realization, Hunter Davidson and crew began to tinker with the concept of offensive underwater explosives. Yet it would be many months before such a system would be implemented.

Near the end of the war, just a few days after the fall of Richmond, Chief Electrician R. O. Crowley was captured by three members of the Union cavalry. They were instructed by their superior to transport him directly to General Alfred H. Terry's headquarters in Washington, D.C.

There had been frequent rumors throughout the four-year campaign which indicated that any man captured who was believed to be engaged in the business of planting torpedoes would be shot or hanged. And now, Crowley feared that he would be the first to be executed for such treachery by the Northern justice system, as an example to the rest of the Confederacy. After a few brief words with the general, Crowley was taken aboard the flagship *Malvern*, where he expected to be interrogated by Admiral David D. Porter. Yet, to his surprise, he was met by not only Porter, but President Abraham Lincoln. The two prominent Union officials informed Crowley of their desire to be informed as to where any unexploded torpedoes were located.

"The war is ended," Porter proclaimed, "and we must clear the river for navigation."[6]

Crowley explained that there was absolutely no danger from these underwater explosives, which had been planted by the Confederate Torpedo Division, since they could only be detonated by an electrical charge. The two dignitaries insisted that he cooperate, however, and Crowley finally agreed to lead them to the secret locations.

The following morning, aboard the steamship *Unadilla*, Crowley traveled up the James River and disclosed the various positions of the underwater mines. In a few short weeks, they would be removed, once again making the waterway safe for peacetime navigation.

Chapter 4

Supply and Demand

As Lieutenant Hunter Davidson and other military personnel and Confederate citizens continued to establish their inventions of destruction throughout the South, it soon became apparent that there would be immense problems in securing an ample supply of critical raw materials. Of these resources, the most essential to the development of torpedo warfare was undoubtedly potassium nitrate, the foundation of modern-day gunpowder. Without it, the strategy of designing and constructing submerged explosives, let alone the ability to use land guns and cannons, would be hopeless.

Prior to the outbreak of the war, gunpowder had not been warehoused in any of the Southern states, except for extremely minute amounts. As for enough powder to fill the wants and needs of a large-scale military operation, however, only a small fraction had been confiscated from the Navy Yard at Norfolk and other such installations. All total, this amounted to only about 30 tons.

This, coupled with the problem of possessing no large-scale powder mills, made the entire situation seem rather bleak for the Confederacy. One of the South's high-ranking officers, Brigadier General Josiah Gorgas, later remembered it this way:

> We began in April 1861, without an arsenal, laboratory or powder mill of any capacity, and with no foundry or rolling-mill except at Richmond…. During the harassments of war, while holding our own in the field defiantly and successfully against a powerful enemy; crippled by a depreciated currency; throttled with a blockade that deprived us of nearly all the means of getting material or workmen; obliged to send almost every able-bodied man to the field; unable to use slave-labor, with which we were abundantly supplied, except in the most unskilled departments of production; hampered by want of transportation even of the commonest supplies of food; with no stock on hand even of articles such as steel, copper, leather, iron, which we must have to build up our establishments….[1]

Letters began to pour into the War Department, located in Richmond, urgently requesting immediate shipments of gunpowder. One such plea, written by Governor Francis Wilkinson Pickens of South Carolina, offers us a prime example of the situation at hand:

I earnestly beg, if possible, that you will order me, if you have it at Norfolk, 40,000 pounds of cannon powder. I loaned the Governor of North Carolina 25,000 pounds, and also the Governor of Florida, for Fernandina and Saint Augustine, 5,000 pounds, besides what I sent to Memphis, Tennessee. If I could be sure of getting 40,000 pounds as a reserve for Charleston, I would immediately order a full supply of cannon powder for about 100 guns I have now on our coast below Charleston. As it is, I fear to drain Charleston entirely. I bought for the state, last December and January, about 300,000 pounds from Hazard's Mills in Connecticut, but I have distributed all of it but about 40,000 pounds....[2]

In the past, the major supplier of potassium nitrate, which was also known as saltpeter and nitre, into Southern port cities had been British India. Yet, when the Confederate government realized that what they were able to smuggle past the Union blockade was not nearly enough to keep up with the rising demand, they immediately began making plans to institute a large-scale nitre mining operation.

The initial attempts to supplement what little nitre they could secure from British India and other foreign sources began in the late autumn and early winter of 1861. In order to meet the stringent demands, a laboratory was established in the city of New Orleans. There the Confederacy attempted to manufacture fuses, primers, and gunpowder. The operation was headed by Lieutenant Beverly Kennon, with the job later being delegated to Lieutenant John R. Eggleston and Acting Master W. A. Robins. Furthermore, two mills at the New Orleans site, which had been placed under the direction of General Mansfield Lovell, were putting out an excellent grade of gunpowder. Yet, this was still not nearly enough to supply the needs and desires of the entire Southern militia.

By the first week of December 1861 the New Orleans mills were producing just over two tons per day. Yet, they had outstanding orders for an additional 200 tons. Then, on December 28, one of these powder mills met with tragedy when it accidentally exploded, putting the entire operation at a standstill. Orders for gunpowder, at 83 cents per pound, continued to come in nonstop.

By January 13, 1862, the total stockpile in New Orleans had dwindled to just over 116,000 pounds. As with any shortage of supply that would soon confront the struggling nation, the price quickly skyrocketed, reaching an astounding $1.14 per pound by the end of the month, and it was destined to go even higher.

Southern laborers began to work low-grade nitre deposits which had been discovered in the lengthy limestone caverns of Tennessee and Kentucky. However, the majority of these underground passageways would soon fall victim to invading Union forces during the spring of 1862, and the Confederacy's nitre supply would fall still further. By April of that same year, total output of domestic nitre mining was somewhere in the neighborhood of 500 pounds

Mechanical torpedo, designed to be detonated when its "plunger," attached to a lengthy wire, was pulled down when snagged by a passing ship (courtesy of West Point Museum Collection).

per day. In a desperate attempt to reinforce the diminishing stockpile, the Confederate Congress implemented an act establishing the Nitre Bureau as a separate department under the jurisdiction of the Secretary of War.

Major I. M. St. John, who was given the post of Nitre Bureau Chief, detailed a four-part plan of operations, which included:

1. A systematic exploration of all Confederate territory in search of nitre deposits;
2. stimulation of private mining operations throughout the South;
3. large-scale production output by the government-controlled Nitre Corps; and
4. importation of nitre from neighboring Mexico.[3]

On April 27, 1862, what was to become the largest powder mill operation in the entire Confederacy was established in Augusta, Georgia. It, as well as all other similar operations sprinkled throughout the South, was placed under the direction of the newly established Nitre Bureau, and Colonel George Washington Rains was appointed to oversee the entire operation. Within a few short months the mills were in full swing, turning out almost 10,000 pounds of powder in each 15-hour period. And by the end of the war the Augusta plant would be responsible for having shipped well over 1.5 million pounds of powder to the city of Richmond alone.

Colonel Rains, who would be responsible for having provided most of the gunpowder for underwater torpedoes and floating mines, as well as the greatest portion used by the Confederacy east of the Mississippi River, had acquired an excellent education at West Point. Graduating at the top of his class in 1842, and majoring in scientific studies, he had gone on to serve as a member of the university staff as a professor of chemistry, geology, and mineralogy. Yet, at the time of his appointment as the man in charge of gunpowder manufacturing in the South, he had not even laid eyes on a powder mill. Even so, Chief of Ordnance Josiah Gorgas offered him complete power to locate, mine, refine, and purchase all needed supplies for the large-scale venture.

The gunpowder of the day, as Colonel Rains quickly came to realize, was made up of three-fourths potassium nitrate and smaller amounts of charcoal and sulphur. It seemed extremely doubtful that he would be able to secure enough of these important ingredients, however, to fill the growing number of back orders. Simply put, Rains was quite convinced that the best he might hope for would be an insufficient supply of second-rate gunpowder.

Acting as if he were prospecting for gold, the Colonel went underground, into the limestone caverns of Arkansas, Alabama, Tennessee, and, eventually, Georgia. To his amazement, he uncovered earth that was highly concentrated with the valuable nitrate of lime, and he immediately ordered that work crews be brought in to begin digging. By incorporating a rather simple chemical process — the saturation of this freshly mined earth with lye made out of wood ashes — he transformed this seemingly ordinary commodity into saltpeter. An abandoned mill located near Nashville was soon producing an excellent grade of powder, with a nearby stamping mill furnishing its ingredients. By July 10, 1862, the Nashville mill was able to produce nearly 3,000 pounds per day after just four short months of operation.

Colonel Rains wrote a booklet on the subject of collecting saltpeter, later to be used by others involved in the expanding Nitre Bureau operation, and then he proceeded to begin the arduous task of recruiting and training an ample work force. This, it was later reported, would be nearly as difficult as establishing the powder mills themselves:

> The chief (problem) is the diminution of skilled workmen. Without statistics, I can only assure you that the number and quality of workmen have greatly fallen off … it was difficult to get machinery, (and) we have now a surplus and cannot get workmen to run it…. While we are importing workmen by two they are leaving us by the hundreds.[4]

While the miners continued to search for nitre, Colonel Rains returned to the capital city of Richmond, where he began to establish a smuggling operation for potassium nitrate from Europe. Profits for those involved were immense, with captains of the blockade-running vessels earning up to $5,000 per trip. The chief officer aboard received $1,250, the chief engineer $2,500, the pilot $3,500, the second and third mates $750 each, and the crew and fireman a respectable $250 apiece.

It was often a long and dangerous journey between the two continents, and crews were known to break the tension in a variety of ways. One method was to participate in the consumption of expensive alcohol, and those involved made the following toast well-known during the war:

> Here's to the Confederates that grow the cotton,
> the Yanks that keep up the price by blockade,
> the Limeys that pay the high prices for it —
> to all three and a long war.[5]

A total of 66 vessels are known to have departed from English ports bound for the Confederacy during the four year stretch between 1861 and 1865, and about 40 of these were eventually captured or destroyed. The anaconda net caught only 10 percent of the blockade-runners during the first year of the war, one in eight in the second, one in four during the third year, and nearly half in 1865.

In all, the total number of vessels coming and going from Southern ports is estimated to have been 1,650, with each averaging five or six successful trips, transporting goods worth approximately $2 billion. When it came to gunpowder, Colonel Rains was able to smuggle in about 2,700,000 pounds through the Federal blockading forces.

As the blockading system and smuggling operations settled down into a well-calculated chess game between the North and the South, the Confederacy was able to set up a near-perfect routine. Large British steamers, loaded down heavily with gunpowder, arms, and other luxuries from Europe, would dock at Bermuda, Nassau, or any other open stop-over port. The final few miles, just before slipping into Confederate ports, were then covered by swifter, light-draft vessels designed for shallow waters, all painted either foggy gray or coal black. Furthermore, all blockade-runners traversed familiar sea lanes into the South: Bermuda to Wilmington, for example, was the longest, covering a distance of 674 miles. It was 515 miles between Nassau and Charleston, and a mere 500 to Savannah.

Individual quantities were often impressive, leaving some Confederate troops better armed than their Northern adversaries. The blockade-running *Fingal*, for instance, transported 7,500 Enfield rifles and 17,000 pounds of gunpowder into the Confederacy during early November of 1861. Another, known as the *Banshee*, almost met her demise a few months later when a purebred Arabian horse being imported from Egypt for President Jefferson Davis neighed while the ship was attempting to sneak past a Union fleet. Though enemy vessels opened fire, the *Banshee's* skipper, Captain Thomas Taylor, managed to escape into the darkness with both his Arabian horse and gunpowder intact.

Back in the South, Colonel Rains was still hard at work organizing production of gunpowder. Perhaps the most intriguing activity instituted during his lengthy career was the division of the Confederacy into districts, each of which was assigned a well-trained crew to dig the earth from beneath privies and latrines. Here, they would find saltpeter, which had been artificially produced by mingling human waste, containing nitrogenous matter, with quicklime deposits. This substance was then transported to a nitre bed for processing and purification. Some of the war's most humorous jingles, merrily sung by both sides in the conflict, came out of this unusual practice of patriotism.

By November 1861 Colonel Rains had managed to produce a daily output of 1,500 pounds from his Richmond plant. He then made the most important discovery of his young career: he found a little-known pamphlet, originally published in London, which detailed the most up-to-date gunpowder plant in existence, the Waltham Abbey Works. Even though the booklet failed to provide illustrations, it was certainly well-outlined. With the assistance of C. Shaler Smith, an aspiring architect and engineer, Rains took his first steps toward establishing the finest powder-works of the day.

As a suitable construction site, Colonel Rains chose a two-mile stretch along a man-made canal near Augusta, Georgia. The complex itself would be built from excess materials shipped in from all over the South.

From the huge Tredegar Iron Works at Richmond, Colonel Rains received a dozen circular iron plates and 24 rollers weighing five tons each. All in all, it amounted to more than 250 tons of machinery. An additional four rollers came from the city of Chattanooga, Tennessee, and from an area just south of Macon, Georgia. A gear wheel, 16 feet in diameter, was cast in Atlanta and shipped east. Finally, Colonel Rains imported a 300-foot iron shaft, measuring 12 inches thick at its center.

Further materials were still needed before the Augusta gunpowder mill could be put into total operation. An aging 130-horsepower steam engine was located, decaying within the confines of an abandoned cotton mill, and it was disassembled and transported by rail. Made up of five huge boilers and a 14-ton flywheel, the entire machine had been manufactured in the North prior to the war.

Colonel Rains ordered one dozen evaporating pans from an iron works located along the Cumberland River in Tennessee; copper boilers were constructed from converted turpentine and whiskey stills confiscated in the backwoods of Kentucky; and giant retorts and iron slip cylinders came out of Augusta.

Raw coal and iron ore came from North Carolina, raw copper was sent from Ducktown, Tennessee, and zinc for the warehouse roofs was dispatched from far-away Mobile, Alabama.

By April 1862 Colonel Rains was finally prepared to begin full-scale operations. His stretch of newly-constructed buildings concealed a variety of secrets developed by himself and his skilled crew members. One obstacle which they had been forced to deal with was the impurities often found in potassium nitrate. Such impurities made the finished product virtually worthless, due to the fact that it would easily absorb unwanted moisture. Clearly, then, the vital artery of the entire compound was the sulphur refining area.

Colonel Rains knew that the cleaning process demanded the removal of all traces of acid and other moistures, and that his incoming supply was far from being "pure." Much of the sulphur was purchased from Louisiana sugar growers, who had imported it prior to the war in order to refine their harvest. The powder, after treatment, would have to hold up to the strict test of standing on glass without leaving a residual stain behind. Building a sound distillery was the key to obtaining a satisfactory product.

The method incorporated by Colonel Rains to refine and crystallize the powder was a rather complicated procedure. He had ingeniously arranged a series of evaporation pans within the refining area. Water from the nearby canal flowed beneath some of these pans, in order that they might be more easily cooled, while others were heated by a row of furnaces. This setup made certain that the entire area would be free from the contamination of smoke and ashes. When the Colonel discovered that his crew could not keep up with the demand manually, he devised an automated system by which the pans could be filled, dumping the boiling water into individual draining and crystallizing vats. He would later contend that he could run the entire process three times per day, on a set schedule, with only two or three workmen on duty at a time.[6]

The distilling process began with the melting of the sulphur, which was then poured into wooden boxes five feet high and ten inches square at the bottom, with the sides gradually tapering toward the top. As the chemical slowly cooled, impurities settled toward the bottom, leaving the upper portion of the material relatively pure. After transferring the near-perfect sulphur into large vats, it was then vaporized and condensed inside of water-cooled coils. Next, the material was recollected, to be pulverized like flour by five-foot iron rollers. Finally, the powdery substance was sifted through a large sheet of silk.

Later, when the Confederacy's silk supply was all but gone, Colonel Rains was forced to come up with another idea for the final stage of purification. The new step which he devised was, in fact, far more efficient than using silk as a sifter. By simply attaching hollowed-out axles, filled with tiny pinholes, through the middle of revolving barrels, he was able to blow the fine sulphur dust into an adjoining room by using periodic blasts of hot air. Even though this seemed to take care of the biggest of his puzzles, however, his problems were not yet completely solved.

Charcoal, which was another essential ingredient in the production of gunpowder, was also scarce during this early portion of the war. In the past, willow trees had been used in its manufacture, and they were believed to be the best source available. Yet, since the supply of willow had quickly become exhausted in the South, Colonel Rains was forced to test other types of wood. He soon discovered, to his delight, that cottonwood was just as good; perhaps even better, since it seldom contained knots.

The cottonwood logs were first split into two-inch square boards and packed into six-foot-long iron cylinders. Retorts were then attached over the skins of the cylinders and sealed with red Georgia clay. Next, with the bottoms perforated to allow gases to escape, the wood was set on fire. It took approximately two hours for the cottonwood to burn down to charcoal.

The heated cylinders were then lowered into the canal for cooling, after which the charred cottonwood was transferred into pulverizing barrels, where it would be powdered by the continual rolling of heavy bronze balls. After it underwent a sifting process, it was transported to the weighing room, to be carefully mixed with the other important ingredients.

Later, Colonel Rains would manufacture his own version of underwater explosive by combining nine pounds of charcoal with 45 pounds of nitre and six pounds of sulphur. These "charges" were then individually saturated with water and steamed until the mixture became slushy. Hence, Rains was the first to incorporate the method of reducing gunpowder to slush, thus allowing the nitre to partially crystallize within the charred carbon. Such ingenuity cut the final rolling time from four hours down to less than one.

Eventually, after each batch was cooled into solid cakes, he placed samples from each under his microscope for further observations. After scrutinizing his unique mixture for several days, Colonel Rains decided that the carbon particles were still far too pitted with minute holes. Yet, since nitre was the active ingredient in gunpowder, he opted to use that very same nitre to fill these tiny pores, which was another entirely new concept in the art of making gunpowder.

Colonel Rains went on to establish at least a dozen rolling-mills within the Augusta complex, each of which stretched nearly 300 feet along the banks of the canal. These mills were separated, for safety's sake, with wooden sidewalks nearly ten feet thick. The front of each mill was outfitted with a thick glass shield in case of an accidental explosion. Trained workers operated long levers by a friction gear built beneath each building's floors, in order that the dangerous rollers could be adequately controlled from a distance. As a further safety precaution, Colonel Rains constructed a 30-gallon water tank above each roller. Rigged so that these tanks could spill their contents at a moment's notice, he wanted to make absolutely certain that there would be no chain-reaction incidents within his network of buildings.

Colonel Rains also took the time to implement similar precautions at his gunpowder mining sites. The powder magazines, themselves, were situated beneath the ground, and were divided at the surface by thick brick traverses. Each buried mound was individually covered by lightweight zinc roofs, in order to protect the finished product from the elements, and were designed in such a fashion that any individual explosion would not cause damage to the magazine's nearest neighbor. These storehouses, as well as the mines and mills, were guarded around the clock by a contingency of young soldiers between the ages of 16 and 18, whose numbers reached well into the hundreds.

Throughout its three-year operation period, following the implementation of the Colonel's safety measures, the Augusta Powder Works suffered only three accidents, with only one of these causing serious injury.

Yet, before the extensive safety precautions had initially been installed, a catastrophic explosion outside the main plant had taught all present a sound lesson concerning the dangerous risks involved. On that occasion, seven good men had been killed instantly, and nearly three tons of powder had been destroyed. The force of the charge had sent up a huge column of smoke, gravel, and flame into the air, to a height of more than 500 feet. Later, it was discovered that the casualties had been the result of a careless workman disobeying strictly enforced rules: seconds before the mishap, he had been observed by his co-workers smoking a cigarette within the restricted area.

Colonel Rains managed to produce 2.75 million pounds of high-quality gunpowder at his Augusta mills over the course of just 36 months. Though his plant never truly reached capacity output, he was more than able to fill every demand that came in. By the end of 1861, the cost of smuggled powder had risen to new record highs — nearly $3 per pound. Colonel Rains calculated that his mills had manufactured more than one million pounds that same year, which had saved the Confederacy nearly $2 million. And his huge Augusta complex had cost the South less than one-fifth that amount.

The comprehensive mining exploration paid off rather quickly, also, for a large new nitre deposit was discovered in Texas, and production output rose dramatically. By August of 1862, the South had increased its mining operation to 1,200 pounds per day; and by the end of October it would swell to well over 2,000 pounds. In a five-month period, between May and October 1862, the Confederacy's stockpile of raw nitre reached an astounding 2,000 tons.

Despite the fact that the South would lose much of this supply to invading Union forces, and despite being cut off from their mining operations in Texas, the Nitre Bureau was able to maintain an output of 2,000 pounds of gunpowder per day until the war reached its ending. Late in the conflict, 50 percent of all Confederate gunpowder would come from private businesses, with the majority of the remainder coming from mills designed and organized by Colonel Rains.

Chapter 5

Torpedoes on the Yazoo

On February 13, 1862, a flotilla of Union vessels from recently-captured Port Royal, South Carolina, ran across a few rudely constructed objects. Led by Lieutenant J. P. Bankhead, their mission was to search along the mouth of the Wright River where it emptied into the Savannah. At the time they were not looking for underwater mining devices, but rather for a small channel that would allow them passage into the city of Savannah without being detected.

The crews aboard the Federal ships, USS *Seneca* and USS *Pembina*, spotted debris bobbing up and down in the shallow waters. Perhaps, they surmised, it was nothing more than flotsam — the remaining wreckage of a sunken ship or its cargo. Yet, something seemed strange about the alignment of the five floating chunks; it was as if they were positioned in a straight line across the channel. Furthermore, all seemed to be tied down in some mysterious way, for they were only visible at low tide. With these two odd facts in mind, Lieutenant J. G. Sproston decided that the ordinary-looking objects might not be so ordinary after all. In fact, he concluded that they might, indeed, be buoys attached to some of the Confederacy's newly-developed underwater mines. Lieutenant Bankhead ordered his men to investigate further, but to do so with utmost caution.

The following day, three search vessels from the flotilla traveled carefully up and down the channel, hoping to spot the flotsam once again. Or, if they could no longer see the debris, then perhaps they might snag something with their grapnel hooks. A strange-looking device was subsequently caught and brought aboard the *Pembina*. Later, it was transferred to the *Unadilla* for closer scrutinization.

What the Union fleet had, indeed, discovered was one of a series of "tin-can" torpedoes anchored to the muddy bottom of the river by grapnel hooks. The one that they had managed to latch onto consisted of a tapered cylindrical body, which was designed to lay on its side. Inside was an air chamber and an ample supply of gunpowder. Inserted neatly into the top, situated next to a riveted lifting handle, was a well-designed cannon-friction primer attached to a length of wire. A single tug on the wire would force the primer to be ignited, thus starting a chain reaction which would detonate the explosive.

Top left: An illustration of the torpedo rake, extended upward while not in use; this was the ingenious invention of Colonel Charles R. Ellet. *Bottom left:* An illustration of the Ellet torpedo rake in use. *Top right:* Example of a typical, low-slung ironclad vessel constructed by the North. *Bottom right:* A second example of an ironclad vessel, more oval-shaped than earlier models (courtesy of Valecia Bryner).

Union officer John Rodgers regarded this and all underwater mines as "Confederate murder weapons." Angrily, he ordered that it be taken ashore where it could safely be destroyed with musket fire.

Later that same day, at a few minutes before midnight, the entire contingent of navy men was jarred awake by a loud, booming explosion. One of their vessels, the USS *Susquehanna*, had been in the process of towing an ammunition barge downriver when the barge had apparently tripped one of the hidden torpedo wires as it passed. However, since the actual explosion had occurred some 200 yards from the surprised *Susquehanna*, no damage had been inflicted.

Still upset about the apparent Confederate "treachery," commanding officer Rodgers assumed that some of the mines in the river had been wired to a battery house located within nearby Fort Pulaski. Though he was incorrect in his assumption, he decided not to risk the lives of his men, refusing to take his flotilla any further upriver.

The following morning, Lieutenant Bankhead escorted a group of Union navy men out on an expedition to destroy any remaining torpedoes. This was accomplished by employing a variety of methods, including shooting rifle balls

An illustration of a drift or floating torpedo, similar to those deployed on the Yazoo River in a successful attack on the USS *Cairo* on October 9, 1861 (courtesy of Valecia Bryner).

into their encasements, detonating them from a distance by using hand-held grapnels, or simply cutting their wires. Little did they realize at the time how dangerous these seemingly "harmless" methods were.

Another type of torpedo, discovered later by General Ambrose Burnside as he and his men traveled up the Neuse River toward New Bern, North Carolina, in March 1862, consisted of:

> ...a stout sheet-iron cylinder, pointed at both ends, about five-and-one-half feet long and one foot in diameter. The iron lever was three-and-one-half feet long, and armed with prongs to catch in the bottom of a boat. This lever was constructed to move the iron rod on [the] inside of [the] cylinder, thus acting upon the trigger of the lock to explode the cap and fire the powder. The machine was anchored, presenting the prongs in such a way that boats going down-river should slide over them, but those coming up should catch.[1]

One of the earliest investigators of underwater explosives was Lieutenant Beverly Kennon, who experimented with such devices on Lake Ponchartrain, near New Orleans, in August 1861. A few weeks earlier, in July, the ambitious lieutenant had attempted to sink the USS *Pawnee* as it patrolled the choppy waters of the Potomac River. Instead, the well-armed vessel, which had been searching for small boats smuggling supplies across the waterway near Acquia Creek, discovered a pair of barrels connected together by a long rope. Suspended beneath these barrels were the would-be mines: two heavy iron containers filled with gunpowder. Kennon's homemade explosives were the first to be seen by the Union forces during the Civil War.

Though Lieutenant Kennon was unsuccessful in this early attempt to sink a Union warship, he did not give up hope. In fact, it is known that he offered his expertise to Acting Master Zedekiah McDaniel, who was then stationed at Vicksburg. McDaniel, with the assistance of Acting Master Francis M. Ewing, earned the dubious distinction of becoming the first Confederates to destroy a Union vessel with an underwater torpedo.

This initial success occurred within the slow-moving waters of the Yazoo River, a branch of the Mississippi River, which few people even thought valuable during the early months of the war. In late July 1862 Captain Isaac N. Brown of the Confederate States Navy was placed in charge of defending the Yazoo from invading Union forces. Brown, the son of a Presbyterian minister, was born and raised in Kentucky, and he had spent 28 years of his life in the United States Navy prior to the outbreak of war. Opting to side with the South, he quickly moved up in rank, from commander of the ironclad CSS *Arkansas*, to the man in charge of protecting other vessels, under construction at Yazoo City, against Union attack.

During the autumn of 1862, McDaniel and Ewing offered Captain Brown the knowledge they had previously acquired from Lieutenant Kennon. As a further help, they even volunteered to assist him with the mining of the water route leading to Yazoo City. Brown later recalled their initial experiments in graphic detail:

> So poor in resources were we, that in order to make a beginning I borrowed a five-gallon glass demijohn, and procuring from the army the powder to fill it and an artillery friction tube to explode it, I set these two enterprising men (McDaniel and Ewing) to work with a coil of small iron wire which they stretched from bank to bank, the demijohn filled with inflammable material being suspended from the middle, some feet below the surface of the water, and so connected with the friction tube inside as to ignite when a (Union) vessel should come in contact with the wire....[2]

By the final week of November 1862 two new Confederate ironclads had been completed at the Yazoo City naval yard, and a third was under construction. Though it had been a busy cotton exporting port before the war, with more than 1,000 inhabitants, Yazoo had since lost a good deal of its appeal. It was rather inaccessible after the annual spring floods, wagons no longer brought cotton to the docks to be loaded on steamers, and more and more of its eligible citizens were going off to fight the war.

Yet, in the weeks leading up to the end of 1862, Yazoo had gained a small bit of its usefulness. Not only did it now possess the largest sawmill on the river, but shipyards, machine shops, and blacksmith businesses had recently been incorporated. And the Union Navy was out to destroy these various facilities at all costs.

At eight o'clock in the morning on December 13, 1862, a flotilla of Federal

The USS *Cairo*, sunk in the Yazoo River in December 1862 (courtesy of the U.S. Navy).

gunboats departed from Vicksburg, Mississippi, and began to make their way up the winding, murky, flood-risen Yazoo. Under the command of Captain Henry Walke, the fleet included the USS *Marmora*, USS *Pittsburgh*, USS *Signal*, and USS *Cairo*, along with an ironclad ram known as the USS *Queen of the West*.

The USS *Cairo* had been designed by S. M. Pook, and had been completed under the direction of James B. Eades in St. Louis, Missouri, in July 1861. She was turtle-shaped, weighed 512 tons, carried 12 guns and one howitzer, and drew six feet of water. She was extremely long and sleek compared to other gunboats of the times, and was plated with 2½-inch iron. Her maximum speed was just over nine miles per hour.

Captain Walke's mission was to bombard any Confederate batteries located along the thickly-wooded shores of the Yazoo River, and to attempt a breakthrough to the city of Yazoo. Furthermore, the captain had instructed his men to destroy any floating debris which might seem out of the ordinary. After all, torpedoes came in all shapes and sizes.

The flotilla encountered few problems during the early stages of their mission as they traveled slowly up the narrow waterway. As she rounded a tight bend near Yazoo City, the USS *Marmora*, transporting eight howitzers and leading the convoy, came under heavy musket fire. Her commanding officer, Lieutenant Robert Getty, ordered his crew to reverse course and allow the ship to take on water, hoping that she might be able to negotiate an about-face.

At about this time, the USS *Cairo* joined the USS *Marmora* at the forefront.

Her crew aimed their eight-inch rifles and 32-pound howitzer toward the wooded banks, attempting to disperse any enemy sharpshooters. The *Cairo's* commander, Lieutenant Thomas O. Selfridge, was intrigued when he saw the crew of the lead vessel shooting at what seemed to be an ordinary piece of drift-wood floating on the river's surface. He did notice, however, something strange about the bobbing object — it did not seem to be "drifting," but was rather stable in the water. He ordered the *Marmora's* men to cease firing and instead concentrate their efforts toward the banks. Furthermore, he instructed them to lower a search vessel to investigate the floating object. However, the men aboard the *Marmora* failed to obey these orders, and the *Cairo's* crew was forced to put down their own boats to inspect the floating chunk of wood.

Ensign Walter E. H. Fentress, who had finally been dispatched from the *Marmora* moments later, was the first to discover a taut wire line positioned near the river's surface. Believing it to be a torpedo lanyard, he immediately severed it with his cutlass. Shortly thereafter, a second lanyard line was found by Fentress. He tugged slightly on the wire to check for slack and, deciding that it was harmless, prepared to tow it ashore.

Luckily, the underwater explosive attached to the opposite end failed to detonate, and the inexperienced ensign managed to bring it safely on dry land. Suddenly, as he began to dismantle and destroy the mine, he heard a violent explosion at close range behind him. Whirling around, he spotted a ship's anchor flying through the air. What occurred next was later described by Lieutenant Selfridge:

> Two sudden explosions in quick succession occurred, one close to my port quarter, the other apparently under my port bow ... the latter so severe as to raise the guns under it some distance from the deck.
> She commenced to fill so rapidly that in two or three minutes the water was over her forecastle. I shoved her immediately for the bank, but a few yards distant; got out a hawser to a tree, hoping to keep her from sliding off into deep water. The pumps, steam and hand, were ... manned, and everything (was) done that could be.
> Her whole frame was so completely shattered that I found ... that nothing more could be effected than to move the sick and the arms. The Cairo sunk ... minutes after the explosion.... Though some half a dozen men were injured, no lives were lost....[3]

Early reports which circulated throughout the Federal Navy speculated that the USS *Cairo* had been destroyed by a galvanic battery. Later, however, researchers would learn the truth: that she had been the happenstance victim of two five-gallon demijohns hidden within wooden boxes.

In studying the circumstances surrounding the sinking it became clear that the *Cairo* had, in fact, nearly missed this chance contact with the underwater explosives. One had detonated beneath her bow, with the second one exploding near the port quarter. Evidently, she managed to snag the first

Torpedo rake in action, as used by Admiral Porter aboard the USS *Lioness* in an attempt to snag the torpedoes blocking the harbor (courtesy of Valecia Bryner).

torpedo lanyard very near to the right bank of the channel, eased it snugly against her bow with forward motion, and then pulled the second mine hard against her port side. When this explosive detonated on contact, the ship's crew made a sudden maneuver to escape the apparent onslaught, thus triggering another explosion. It was this second mine that inflicted the damage that caused the *Cairo* to sink.

Unknown to the Northern flotilla, Captain Isaac N. Brown had watched the entire affair from the hidden confines of a nearby rifle pit, along with Acting Masters Zedekiah McDaniel and Francis M. Ewing. The Captain would later admit his mixed emotions concerning the sinking of the great enemy ironclad. Reportedly, he felt "much like a schoolboy ... whose practical joke has taken a more serious shape than he expected...."[4]

After the crew of the *Cairo* had been rescued, the heaviest vessel in the flotilla, *Queen of the West*, steamed up and proceeded to drag away the sunken ship's smokestacks. Apparently this was done to keep the wreck from being discovered by Confederate forces. During this upcoming days, other Union vessels would continue to shell the shoreline of the Yazoo River in an effort to protect smaller "tag-along" boats searching the waterway's muddy bottom for additional underwater explosives. Approximately one dozen of these crude mines were subsequently discovered and destroyed, along with Captain Brown's secret cache of gunpowder and torpedo encasements.

Five days before Christmas, 1862, a second Federal fleet, including the USS *Baron de Kalb*, USS *Signal*, USS *Queen of the West*, USS *Benton*, USS *Tyler*, and USS *Lexington*, made their way toward the lazy Yazoo River. They reached its mouth on December 23. Led by Rear Admiral David D. Porter, the flotilla hoped to make its way to the enemy's heaviest batteries, located near Haynes Bluff, by the first of the year.

On board one of these advancing vessels was General William T. Sherman, who planned to seize the high ground along the left bank. Next, he would proceed onward to Vicksburg for a joint attack, with Ulysses S. Grant invading the city from the opposite side. Before departing on this essential tactical mission, Admiral Porter had warned his men about possible underwater mines, offering instructions that "the brightest lookout must be kept.... Have plenty of rowboats to go ahead ... with drags and searches of all kinds."[5]

Heeding the admiral's warning, small cutters were dispatched to scrape the edges of the banks with large grapnel hooks, while the larger vessels would drag the center channel for torpedoes and wires. Whenever a floating object was sighted, a team of trained navy men would approach it with extreme caution. If it were, indeed, found to be an explosive, they would then haul it to shore with a lengthy rope, so it could be safely destroyed. These sailors were given "a diagram of the river and the manner in which torpedoes are laid, for the rebels have a regular ... system which we can avoid...."[6]

On the twenty-fourth of December, near the spot where the USS *Cairo* had gone down, the *Queen of the West* ran over a torpedo wire which had been spotted by a lookout at the last moment. Unable to reverse direction in time to avoid it, the officers and crew of the mighty ram braced themselves for the inevitable explosion, yet nothing happened.

Quickly, small search boats were lowered into the water, as the mother ship waited for them to investigate. However, before they were able to bring up the failed mine, Confederate snipers hiding along the shoreline thicket began harassing them with pepper-shot. With no place to take cover on the open waters, the search mission was immediately aborted. After four days of sporadic sniper fire, the Union fleet decided to pull back downriver.

On the final day of 1862, Admiral Porter attempted once again to make a push up the Yazoo River. However, on this occasion he had come better prepared: one of his accompanying ships, the USS *Lioness*, had been equipped with a huge sixty-five-foot "torpedo rake," an ingenious invention designed by Colonel Charles R. Ellet. In theory, the somewhat awkward tool would latch onto hidden mines and pull them to the surface. Constructed of logs, with dozens of grappling hooks dangling from them, the rake was bootjack-shaped.

Soon, because of its effectiveness, the invention would become standard equipment aboard all Union search vessels. It seems quite likely, however, that

Fretwell-Singer torpedo, exhibiting a plunger activated when a saucer-shaped iron weight was knocked from the deck of the air chamber, thus pulling out a safety pin (courtesy of West Point Museum Collection).

the contrivance might have been a bit too dangerous to use, causing underwater explosives to detonate too near a searching vessel. In fact, the crew of the USS *Lioness* must have felt quite relieved when a dense fog rolled in on this, their initial exploratory mission. In short order, the thick mist was followed by heavy rains, and Admiral Porter decided to postpone the use of the torpedo rake for the time being.

Just a few days later, during the first week of the new year, Porter had this to say concerning the 1862 operations on the Yazoo River:

> We have had lively times up the Yazoo. Imagine the Yazoo becoming the theater of war! We waded through 16 miles of torpedoes to get at the forts (seven in number), but when we got that far the [gun] fire on the boats from the riflemen in pits dug for miles along the river and from the batteries became very annoying, and that gallant fellow [Lieutenant Commander William] Gwin thought he would check them, which he did until he was knocked over with the most fearful wound I ever saw. We could not advance, the torpedoes popping up ahead as thick as mushrooms, and we have had pretty good evidence of their power to do mischief. I never saw more daring displayed than by the brave fellows who did the work. The forts are powerful works, out of the reach of ships, and on high hills, plunging their shot through the upper deck, and the river so narrow that only one vessel could engage them until the torpedoes could all be removed.[7]

During the early months of 1863, Captain Isaac N. Brown traveled to Yazoo City, Mississippi, on a number of occasions. He realized that the city was quite vulnerable to enemy invasion at any time, and that a strong Federal fleet could force its way past Haynes Bluff, located just downriver. Brown made an appeal to General John Pemberton, who was in command of the entire Yazoo Valley, to strengthen the Confederate defenses. When his plea was all but ignored, he decided to turn to other sources to accomplish this goal.

In the spring of 1863, as the heavy seasonal rains inundated the river, the situation grew tense for the workmen laboring to finish the ironclads being constructed at Yazoo City's local shipyards. The waters swirled around the stocks where the huge iron ships lay dormant, causing the ground to cave in occasionally and the heavy vessels to lean precariously.

Downriver, Captain Brown was quite certain that several of his torpedoes had been washed away by the flooding torrent. This prompted him to contract for 50 or more newly developed underwater explosives, which had been designed by two Texans, Dr. J. R. Fretwell and E. C. Singer (a gunsmith and a relative of the sewing machine entrepreneur). These explosives were described as possessing "automatic action on being brought in contact with a vessel or boat."[8]

The Fretwell-Singer torpedo consisted of a floating cone, which was constructed of tin and was filled two-thirds of the way with gunpowder. An iron rod with a spring-triggered plunger extended through the heart of the encasement, with an equal length protruding from the opposite end. The torpedo would be activated when a saucer-shaped iron plate fell from the deck of the cone, pulling out the safety pin. Thus, the spring-driven plunger would be released, smashing a percussion cap hidden within the water-tight compartment.

It wasn't until the first week of July, however, that the Confederate Examining Board finally reached a decision concerning the largescale production of the Fretwell-Singer underwater torpedo:

The lock is simple, strong and not liable at any time to be out of order; and … the caps … are not likely to be affected by moisture. By the peculiar and excellent arrangement of the lock … the certainty of explosion is almost absolute. One great advantage this possesses over many others is, that its explosion does not depend upon the judgement of any individual; that it … cannot readily be ascertained by an enemy's vessels.

We are so well satisfied … that we recommend the engineer's department … have some … placed at an early date in some of the river approaches to Richmond.[9]

The ruling by this committee came weeks too late, however, for the citizens of Yazoo City. During the first few days of May 1863, Federal warships once again moved up the Yazoo River. The scattering of troops and batteries that had recently been defending the valley had been withdrawn to assist in the defense of Vicksburg, thus enabling the enemy to move at will toward the unprotected city. The citizens were warned to evacuate, and one local newsman reported:

Thursday, the 21, our town presented a scene of bustle and confusion…. Squads of gold laced gentlemen with their staffs and dependents might be seen hurrying to and fro making ready to leave our "dear, damned, deserted town." The rumbling of ambulances and wagons and rattling of hoofs told our people that they would soon be left to the mercy of a dreaded foe….[10]

Under the direction of Captain Isaac Brown, the dismantling of Yazoo City's navy yard and vessels was set in motion, as salvageable equipment was hoisted onto flatbed wagons for shipment to nearby Selma, Alabama. By the time Admiral Porter's earliest invading gunboats had arrived, very little of value remained. Subsequently, the Federal navy men finished the job of destroying the city.

Captain Brown refused to depart from the region, however, for he was determined to gain some semblance of revenge upon the Federal Navy. Unable to secure his contracted number of Fretwell-Singer torpedoes by the time the enemy had broken through his blockade at Haynes Bluff, due to the difficulty of obtaining the needed materials for their manufacture, he went into hiding. Eventually, he was issued a limited cache of underwater explosives, which he planted in the waters of the Yazoo River on July 13, 1863.

It seems that Lady Luck was, indeed, in Captain Brown's favor during this venture, for just two days earlier, Admiral David D. Porter had received a note from General Ulysses S. Grant, inquiring as to whether or not it would be wise to "stand up a fleet of gunboats and some troops and nip in the bud any attempt to concentrate a force there [Yazoo City]?"[11]

Adhering to the request almost immediately, several of Porter's vessels were dispatched once again up the Yazoo River. On this occasion, the flotilla included the armored gunboats USS *Baron de Kalb* (formerly the *St. Louis*),

USS *Kenwood*, USS *New National*, and USS *Signal*. All were placed under the joint command of Lieutenant John G. Walker.

Backed up by Major General Francis J. Herron's 5,000 foot soldiers, ready to roust any Confederates who might be hiding in the thick woods along the banks, the fleet cautiously moved upriver on July 13 just hours after Captain Brown had managed to sink his explosives. The *Baron de Kalb*, weighing 512 tons and mounting 18 guns of various sizes, was ambushed by a battery of Confederate soldiers as she floated just south of Yazoo City. The powerful vessel was forced to fall back, waiting until Major General Herron had the opportunity to land his troops. Later, through the combined efforts of the flotilla and the soldiers, the Southern snipers would be forced to surrender; yet, not before they managed to exact a tremendous loss of lives to the attaching Federal forces.

While supporting the advance, the *Baron de Kalb* was rocked by an immense explosion beneath her bow. As water gushed through a huge gash in her belly, the mighty vessel began to lag. A few moments later, a second explosion occurred just beneath her stern section, inflicting further devastation to the fragile victim's underside. Within a 15-minute period, the mighty ironclad ram would be lying helplessly on the river bottom. Captain Isaac Brown had, indeed, gotten his revenge, though, miraculously, none of her crew were killed. Later, Brown recorded what took place on that fateful afternoon in July:

> On the morning of the Union advance upon Yazoo City, I had myself placed two of these "Fretwells" half a mile below our land battery of one rifle 6-inch gun — handled by the same men — the same gun, in fact, that had aided in the defense of Fort Pemberton. The *De Kalb* had there felt this gun, and it came twice within its range on this day — retiring both times without unreasonable delay — but when our sailor crew found themselves uncovered by our land force, and a whole division of Union men within rifle-range, they withdrew under orders, and the *De Kalb*, seeing our gun silent, advanced for the third time, getting as far as the torpedoes, and there suddenly disappeared beneath the waters of the Yazoo.[12]

The Union flotilla confiscated more than 3,000 bales of cotton from the captured Yazoo area, though the trade was most certainly not balanced. In exchange for Captain Brown's daring, the Confederacy learned one very important lesson; that persistence in the game of underwater warfare led to sporadic, immense success.

Chapter 6

Birth of the Spar Torpedo

As early as the spring of 1862, inventors living in the Confederate states began contemplating the concept and feasibility of outfitting attack vessels with a weapon that would become known as the "spar torpedo." Some of these offensive devices were constructed of cylindrically-shaped copper jackets with vortex ends; others were much larger, and fashioned to resemble giant eggs. Whatever their design, all were made to be attached to the extreme end of a long pole, or spar, projecting from the front section of a vessel:

> The spar was attached to the vessel by a goose-neck fitted to a socket bolted to the bow, near the water-line. Guys from the spar to the side of the vessel kept the spar in its position when the torpedo was submerged for an attack, and it was lowered and raised by tricing lines and tackles. Usually seven fuses made to explode by contact were fixed to each torpedo....[1]

The spar torpedo was initially the idea of Robert Fulton, who constructed and designed the first in 1801, but it was never used successfully in battle until the days of the Civil War. During the early weeks of October 1862, while stationed in Savannah, Georgia, General George A. Mercer gained recognition for reviving the concept when he wrote:

> I have proposed to the General to endeavor to initiate an experiment ... to attach a concussion shell to an arm running out from the ram of a gunboat, and then destroy the enemy's vessels by striking them below the iron plates.... I never heard anyone suggest the above idea, but I have mentioned it to several, and all agree with me that it is perfectly practicable.[2]

The CSS *Atlanta* was, for all intents and purposes, the first Confederate vessel to be outfitted with such an innovative contrivance as the spar torpedo, though she had not initially been designed to incorporate this formidable weapon.

In November 1861, the *Fingal*, a large merchant steamer constructed with a reinforced iron hull, slipped its way through the Federal blockade then strangling Savannah Harbor. She had been constructed in Great Britain, and she was later purchased by the Confederacy to be used for the transport of gunpowder,

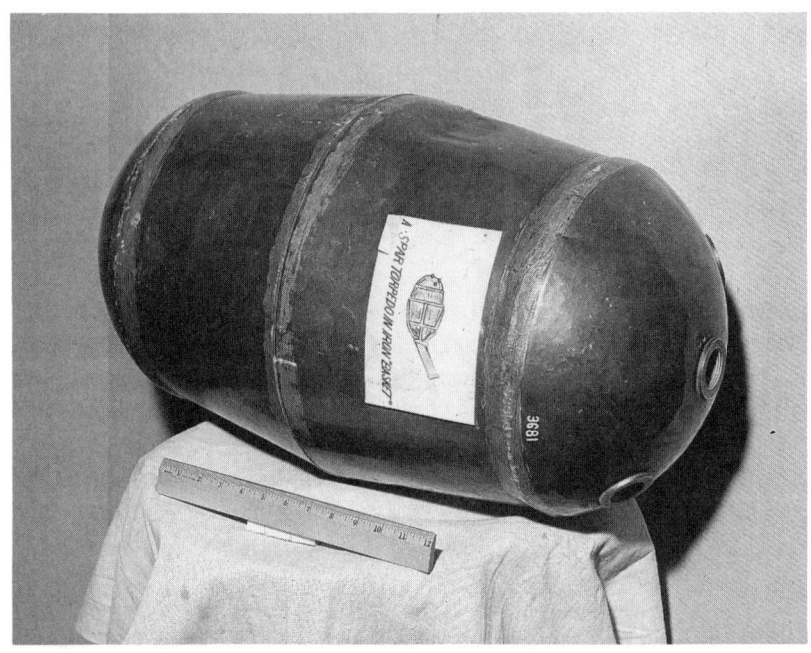

A rather large, egg-shaped spar torpedo, made of iron. Attached to a spar, which extended from a goose-necked fitting positioned at the bow near the water-line. This example housed six fuses constructed to detonate on contact (courtesy of West Point Museum Collection).

weapons, and ammunition. During this, her maiden voyage across the Anaconda lines, her cargo

> …consisted of 10,000 Enfield rifles, 1,000,000 ball cartridges, 2,000,000 percussion caps, 3,000 cavalry sabres, 1,000 short rifles and cutlass bayonets, 1,000 rounds of ammunition per rifle, 500 revolvers and ammunition, a couple of large rifled cannon and their gear, two smaller rifled guns, 400 barrels of cannon powder, and a lot of medical stores and material for clothing.[3]

Nearly four weeks went by before the CSS *Fingal* was reloaded with a large supply of valuable raw cotton and made ready to begin her return voyage across the Atlantic to England. She was unable to break through the strengthening Union blockade, however, and was forced to remain idle on the Southern coastline for several months. Finally, in the spring of 1862, after suffering delay upon delay, it was decided that she would be converted from a simple merchant ship into an imposing offensive vehicle. Subsequently, she was handed over to Asa and Nelson Tift, two brothers who were old friends of Secretary of the Confederate Navy Stephen R. Mallory.

The Tift brothers possessed only limited experience when it came to the job of shipbuilding and conversion. On August 25, 1861, they had come to Richmond, Virginia, to confer with Mallory on the subject of designing and constructing ironclad vessels. At that time the Tifts were novices in such endeavors; Nelson had spent the better part of his life as a Georgia plantation owner, while Asa had been the editor of a newspaper, president of a railroad company, a merchant, a state legislator, and an owner/operator of a small boat repair yard in Key West, Florida.

Despite their lack of expertise, however, Nelson Tift was able to convince Mallory of their knowledge by exhibiting a model of an ironclad ship which he himself had recently designed. The miniature version possessed no curves, nor did it have rounded ends. Therefore, Nelson reasoned, the building of such an innovative craft would not require skilled construction workers; in fact, he informed Mallory, it could even be constructed by ordinary house carpenters.

The Secretary of the Confederate Navy must have been somewhat impressed with Nelson's presentation, for he accepted the proposal almost immediately. As a further temptation to Mallory, the Tift brothers had offered their services in exchange for no financial compensation, except for traveling expenses. On September 1, 1861, Mallory wrote, "I have concluded to build a large ship at New Orleans upon Nelson Tift's plan and will push it...."[4]

Despite the fact that the Tift's initial project—the construction of the ironclad CSS *Mississippi*—turned out to be an utter disaster, with the vessel never seeing action, Mallory remained confident in his old friends. They were given total and unlimited authority in the reconstruction of the CSS *Fingal*. Nelson later commented on the project:

> The *Fingal* was converted into the ironclad *Atlanta* ... on the same plan, so far as practicable, as the ironclad *Mississippi*. The conversion ... was far more difficult, though not so extensive nor as formidable a work.... She was strongly and quickly built.[5]

To the ordinary Southern citizen, the CSS *Atlanta* might have looked very similar to most other Confederate ironclad vessels operating in the open waters of the Atlantic Ocean and Gulf of Mexico:

> Her extreme length was 204 feet, breadth of beam 41 feet ... draft of water 15 feet 9 inches. She was cut down to the main deck, which was widened amidships and overlaid with a foot of wood and iron plating, and upon this foundation was built the casemate, the sides and end inclining at an angle of thirty degrees. The top of the casemate was flat, and the pilothouse rose above the roof about three feet. The sloping sides and ends of the casemate were covered with four inches of iron plates in two layers, secured to a backing of three inches of oak and fifteen inches of pine. A ram was attached to the bow, which was also fitted with a spar to carry a percussion torpedo. Her armament was two 7-inch Brooke guns on bow and stern pivots, and two 6-inch Brooke rifles in broadside. The larger guns

were so arranged that they could be worked in broadside as well as for fore-and-aft fire, and the ship could therefore fight two 7-inch and one 6-inch piece on either side....[6]

Within her belly, the CSS *Atlanta* was outfitted with relatively new, English-built machinery. She housed high-pressure, reciprocating, single-expansion vertical engines which were quite unique aboard fighting vessels. Her boiler, on the other hand, were of a more typical variety, being a horizontal-fire-tube design with double-return flues. Perhaps, however, the Tifts should have had the foresight to install draft fans in order to assist in the rapid generation of steam power. As it was, her crew was forced to rely upon the more conventional concept of natural draft.

Although the *Atlanta* seemed adequately armored and armed to do battle against the imposing Union blockaders, she was still not without her faults. The *Savannah Morning News* reported that when she was loaded down with coal prior to her initial test run, sea water came in at such a rapid pace that her berth deck and wardroom were submerged in more than a foot of water after only a brief period of time. Evidently, the Tifts failed to correct the problem, for she would continue to be plagued with leakage problems throughout her entire career. One man, who would later be assigned to the vessel, put it bluntly when he claimed:

> I would defy anyone in the world to tell when it is day or night if he is confined below without any way of marking time.... I would venture to say that if a person were blindfolded and carried below and then turned loose he would imagine himself in a swamp, for the water is trickling in all of the time and everything is so damp.[7]

Damp or not, Commodore Josiah Tattnall, who had been placed in charge of the Savannah shoreline defense forces, was most anxious to move his newly-converted offensive vessel out in the open waters to face the enemy.

By the final week of July 1862, work had progressed at a rapid enough pace that the CSS *Atlanta* was ready for a trial run down the Savannah River. Present for the occasion were Nelson and Asa Tift, Commodore Tattnall, and numerous other high-ranking Confederate navy officials. After viewing her smoothness of operation, they all agreed that she had proven herself more than seaworthy. Despite their apparent satisfaction, however, it would be another four months before the *Atlanta* would be officially commissioned into the service of the Confederate navy.

Three weeks after receiving her official charter, on January 5, 1863, the CSS *Atlanta* was ordered to get up steam in preparation for her initial assault. Commodore Tattnall had visions of clearing nearby Wassaw and Ossabaw sounds of wooden Federal blockaders before they could be reinforced with recently-constructed monitors. After traveling several miles downstream

A copper-jacketed spar torpedo, designed to be attached to the extreme end of a long pole projecting from the front of an attacking David or submarine (courtesy of West Point Museum Collection).

toward Savannah, however, the Confederate ram was once again delayed, this time by huge wooden cribs filled with paving stone. These imposing obstacles had been placed beneath the river's current by the Confederate navy in an attempt to prevent invading Union vessels from traveling upstream. And, although army engineers promised Tattnall that the river passage would be cleared within a few short hours, it would be an additional month before the cribs could be removed by a labor force working around the clock.

Time was running out for the *Atlanta*, whose crew had hoped to take the Federal blockading fleet by surprise. While Commodore Tattnall waited impatiently for the river to be cleared, Rear Admiral Samuel Francis Du Pont, the naval officer in command of the North's South Atlantic Blockading Squadron, became aware of the *Atlanta*'s threat to his fleet. In order to help strengthen his forces, Du Pont decided to order the USS *Montauk* and USS *Passaic* to the Savannah Harbor region. Although the *Passaic* would be delayed in nearby Port Royal, South Carolina, by inclement weather, the *Montauk* arrived and dropped anchor off Ossabaw Bar on the twenty-fourth of January. Just three days later, this mighty Union ironclad, with the use of her pair of forceful

Dahlgren guns and the support of four other vessels, layed siege to Fort McAllister.

A few miles from the battle, on the Georgia mainland, the townspeople of Savannah listened to the bombardment with growing concern. Soon a request for assistance in defending the fort came to Tattnall from the Savannah City Council. Reluctantly, the commodore agreed to send his new ironclad, though he had recently come to realize the *Atlanta*'s shortcomings:

> I considered the *Atlanta* no match for the monitor class of vessel at close quarters, and in shoal waters particularly, as owing to the necessity [of making her lighter in order] ... to cross the flats and operate in the Sounds, at least two feet of her hull below the knuckle were exposed, covered with but two inches of iron.[8]

The offensive maneuvers by the CSS *Atlanta* against the *Montauk* did not occur on this particular occasion, however, for the overdue *Passaic* finally arrived from Port Royal on January 30. It was quite obvious to Tattnall, with his many years of experience, that his ship could not do battle against two Federal monitors, so he opted to wait until he received further orders.

General Hugh W. Mercer suggested that Tattnall move the *Atlanta* to a nearby sand fort located at Causton's Bluff, on Augustine Creek, a small, winding stream which connected the Savannah River with Wassaw Sound. In this way, reasoned Mercer, the Confederate ship could offer support to the Confederate Army, which was in the process of relocating its strategic land batteries. Reluctantly, Commodore Tattnall conceded.

The waterway had finally been cleared through the Savannah River obstructions, and soundings were conducted in order to determine precisely when the water level was high enough for safe passage. The night before the movement was scheduled to commence, on February 2, a freezing wind developed out of the northwest, and by 4:00 A.M. it had reached near-gale proportions. The operation was subsequently cancelled. One disappointed midshipman wrote:

> ...I fear we will be unable to get out on this spring tide ... of course we will be branded as cowards.... These people never stop to enquire into the cause [of] these delays; but stigmatize the navy generally, because we did not go down and *sink* the enemy's fleet even *before* the obstruction had been removed from the river....[9]

With one delay after another, Commodore Tattnall was relieved of his command in March 1863. He was replaced by Commander Richard L. Page. Ironically, just two weeks after Tattnall had been reassigned, Rear Admiral Du Pont ordered the USS *Montauk* and the USS *Passaic* away from the Savannah Harbor region. They were to take part in an offensive against Fort Sumter, South Carolina. Thus, rather unknowingly, Du Pont had cleared the way for an attack by the *Atlanta*.

Commander Page was unable to take advantage of the situation, however,

Illustration of an early Cushing spar torpedo, which was extended from the front end of an attacking row boat and used to ram an enemy vessel (courtesy of Valecia Bryner).

due to the fact that the *Atlanta*'s steering gear had been damaged while she was enroute to Savannah for her change in command. Perhaps because of this, along with a growing agitation at the inactivity of the Confederate forces in and around Savannah, Page was unceremoniously removed from his new post within the next few weeks.

During the early portion of May, the Confederacy's Savannah squadron was blessed with its third commander in less than 12 months. Commander William A. Webb, a headstrong Virginian who had participated in the battle of Hampton Roads as captain aboard the converted tugboat *Teaser*, took the helm.

Webb's aggressive nature soon became evident, for within one week of taking command he informed Secretary Mallory of his plan to attack the enemy at the next high tide. His luck, however, seemed to be no better than that of the officers who had preceded him. On May 30, after having taken on a full load of coal and being armed, the *Atlanta* made her way past the now unobstructed waterway. But while steaming down the southern channel of the Savannah River, the vessel's forward engine broke down, and the proud ship ran aground. It took more than 24 hours to pull her free, and Webb was then forced to wait for the next spring tide.

In the meantime, while the *Atlanta*'s engine was under repair, Secretary of the Navy Mallory suggested that Webb delay his offensive until the ironclad *Savannah* could come to his assistance. Webb agreed, but informed Mallory that he would then "raise the blockade between here and Charleston, attack Port Royal, and then blockade Fort Pulaski." Though his immediate hopes had been dashed, Webb's confidence showed no signs of diminishing.

Rear Admiral Du Pont's intelligence sources throughout the region were adequate and up-to-date. As early as March of 1863, while the Savannah squadron was still under the watchful eye of Commodore Tattnall, Du Pont had begun to gather valuable information concerning the *Atlanta*'s planned movements. During that time, a pair of disgruntled Irish seamen belonging to the Confederate navy had deserted to Fort Pulaski, which was under the control of Union forces. When they were questioned, one of them had claimed that he had overheard Tattnall's plans to mount an offensive against the blockading Federal fleet. Then, during the first week of June, as Webb was awaiting the arrival of the *Savannah*, Du Pont received further insight into the *Atlanta*'s upcoming maneuvers. He ordered the USS *Weehawken*, USS *Nahant*, and USS *Montauk* into Savannah Harbor.

The night of June 16, 1863, was hot and humid, and the men aboard the CSS *Atlanta* perspired heavily as they worked to fill the ship's bunkers with coal. Just before dawn, at approximately 4:00 A.M., the ship weighed anchor and floated down the dark river, hoping to confront the enemy just before sunrise. She had come prepared, for she was armed with more than enough chilled, armor-piercing shot and shell in her magazine to sink any of the North's ironclads then stationed in the region. Furthermore, a single powerful torpedo was in place at the end of her spar, and an additional five underwater explosives were being kept in reserve. Commander Webb had intentions of ramming the closest monitor with the submerged mine and then aggressively attacking a second with gunfire.

At exactly 4:10 in the morning of June 17, a watchman aboard the *Weehawken* spotted an ominous vessel approaching from the narrows of the Wilmington River. He sounded the alarm almost immediately. The commanding officer of the Federal ironclad, Captain John Rodgers, had a veteran crew on board. They quickly came to quarters, prepared to do battle, and took the USS *Weehawken* downriver, picking up steam as they went. Behind them was the USS *Nahant*, a monitor commanded by John Downes, which was ready to offer its assistance. Ten minutes later the *Weehawken* turned itself in the direction of the *Atlanta*, and commenced to close the gap between the opposing vessels.

When the distance separating the ships had decreased to about 1.5 miles, the invading Confederate ironclad opened fire, its initial shot sailing over the *Weehawken* and striking the water at close range to the *Nahant*. It was more than apparent that Webb meant business, as he continued to close the gap.

Yet, Captain Rodgers became perplexed a few moments later when the *Atlanta* ceased her advance. Strangely, the Confederate vessel had stopped dead in its wake, and was vulnerably positioned crosswise in the channel. This sort of maneuver was like nothing he had ever seen, and was certainly not expected from a ship attempting to make its way out into the open waters of the Atlantic Ocean.

The *Atlanta*'s unusual position in the Savannah Harbor was not, in fact, any sort of surprise tactic; the ship had simply run aground. Upon entering the mouth of the Wilmington River, Webb's men had spotted the blockading monitors, and he had ordered them to proceed full speed ahead. Webb's enthusiasm had apparently caused the ship to leave the main channel accidentally and run into a large sandbar. She had reversed engines and gotten free, but because of the shallow waters she ran aground a second time, leaning slightly to one side.

The situation was hopeless for the Confederate ram. With her spar torpedo lowered beneath the surface, she was now susceptible to a full-force attack. The USS *Weehawken* continued to advance on the helpless ship at full speed, and at a distance of 300 yards opened fire. Although the Federal monitor fired only five times, four shots found their mark.

The initial strike, which had been fired from the 15-inch Dahlgren, hit the *Atlanta* on her starboard side casement. Although it did not penetrate the hull, iron and wood fragments sprayed in all directions, severely wounding a number of Confederate sailors. With somewhere in the neighborhood of 50 men lying hurt on the deck, a second blow slightly damaged the knuckle of the ship. Then, just as the crew had finished loading their guns and were in the process of raising the porthole shutter, a third shot came down upon them. More than half of the gun crew were taken out by this strike. The fourth and final strike from the *Weehawken* managed to blow away the upper portion of the pilot house, wounding two pilots in the process.

The *Atlanta* was only able to get off seven shots of her own, none of which found their mark due to the improper angle of trajectory. After a mere 15 minutes into the confrontation, Webb was forced to raise the white flag of surrender. At this point he addressed his crew:

> I have surrendered our vessel because circumstances over which I had no control have compelled me to do so. I know that you started upon this expedition with high hopes, and you have been disappointed. I most earnestly wish that it had happened otherwise, but Providence, for some good reason, has interfered with our plans, and we have failed of success. You all know that, if we had not run aground, the result would have been different, and now that a regard for your lives has influenced me in this surrender, I would advise you to submit quietly to the fate which has overtaken us. I hope that we all may soon be returned to our homes, and meet again in a common brotherhood.[10]

Lieutenant Commander David B. Harmony of the USS *Nahant* stepped aboard the fallen ship, immediately changing flags. Webb stood by, along with the rest of his hapless crew, allowing the young officer his moment in the spotlight. However, when Harmony proceeded to begin dropping the *Atlanta's* anchor, Webb stopped him, explaining that there was a percussion torpedo beneath the bow.

"I don't care anything about your torpedoes," snapped Harmony. "I can stand them if you can, and if you don't wish to be blown up with me, you had better tell me how to raise the torpedo!"[11]

Soon enough the spar was up out of the water, and a group of Union sailors was instructed to remove the explosive caps and douse them with water. Later, a Northern newsman had this to write concerning the *Atlanta's* underwater weaponry:

> It is evident that the rebels have taught us a good lesson on the torpedo subject ... how a torpedo could be safely carried in front of a vessel without interfering with its steering and other movements, and be at the same time secure from any explosion until the proper time. The *Atlanta's* torpedo gearing solves the question. The forward part of the ram ... is [of] solid iron, twenty feet in length, and so overlaid by steel bars, with their ends protruding below ... that a huge steel saw is formed....
>
> From the deck ... arises a strong iron bar with a pivot at its top, to which is attached a massive iron boom which runs just over the ram's prow, and then forming an elbow, it descends three feet below the water line, where it forms another elbow, and ... some two feet ... [a] socket.... In this ... another iron boom ... and at its end ... a torpedo, all capped and ready. You can hardly conceive of a more perfect or effective engine of destruction....[12]

More than 160 seamen were taken prisoner from the CSS *Atlanta*, including officers and crew. With the exception of the wounded, they were all transported to a prison in Fort Lafayette, near New York City. The *Atlanta* herself would later see active duty once again, for in February 1864 she was dispatched to Fortress Monroe, where she became one of the North's fighting monitors.

Despite the fact that the *Atlanta's* spar torpedo was never used by the Confederates upon a Union vessel, it remained a strong belief throughout the Southern ranks that such a weapon could still be incorporated to inflict devastation upon Union blockaders. In fact, this idea was so prevalent that the Confederacy continued to experiment with what some historians have called, a "technologically advanced invention for the times."

Chapter 7

The Rains Torpedo

When the Civil War had reached its inevitable conclusion, Captain James H. Tomb, who had been involved in numerous torpedo exploits along the coast of South Carolina, wrote:

> There were three lines of torpedoes between Fort Sumter and Fort Moultrie on Sullivan's Island, and also three ropes attached to floats which had torpedoes attached to them.... The first line of torpedoes was directly between Fort Sumter and Fort Moultrie, leaving an open space between the torpedoes and the fort in the channel for ships to pass through.[1]

An expert from the Confederate Torpedo Division who had been responsible for these "lines of torpedoes," was even more specific, claiming that he had planted exactly 123 underwater explosives in Charleston Harbor and the nearby Stono River. Furthermore, during the four years of fighting, it had been an accepted fact that the Federal fleet was completely afraid even to go near anything that resembled a floating beer barrel.

The man responsible for instilling this fear throughout the South Carolina region was General Gabriel J. Rains, brother of George Washington Rains (of gunpowder fame). He was the eldest of a New Bern, North Carolina, cabinetmaker, and a proud West Point graduate. Initially, General Rains began his experimentation with explosives during his days in the Seminole Indian War. Later, he would become one of the world's foremost underwater munitions manufacturers, and he would contribute a great deal of expertise toward the improvement of submerged explosives.

Gabriel Rains was 58 years old when the Civil War began, and he was promoted to brigadier general in early 1862. Soon thereafter, as the invading Northern troops made their way between the York and James rivers toward Richmond, Virginia, Rains gained a reputation as a "ruthless" leader when he planted highly explosive mines beneath the soft, sandy roadways leading into the capital city. Casualties were considerable, and the Northern press poured out headline after headline concerning Confederate barbarity. According to their "sources," underground mines had been discharged in water wells, front yards, bags of flour, and around telegraph poles. All, they claimed, had taken the lives of dozens of "innocent" citizens. Fearful of the possible repercussions from the bad publicity, both General Joseph E. Johnston and General James Longstreet ordered General Rains to discontinue the use of these "harsh implements of war."

Gabriel Rains vehemently denied all charges and accusations that he had "intentionally" planted booby-trap mines in order to harm innocent bystanders, although he did openly admit to having placed the land mines in roadways often traversed by Union troops. From his personal point of view, such activities were not "murderous and barbarous," as described by Union General George B. McClellan. Rather, they were simply a sound defensive measure.

The entire affair was destined to become a thorn in the side of Southern soldiers who felt that gentlemen should face their enemies in combat. Furthermore, a Confederate policy squabble developed, prompting General Rains to appeal to the Secretary of War, George W. Randolph, for a final decision on the matter. Randolph announced official policy by stating:

> It is admissible to plant shells in a parapet to repel assaults, or in a road to check pursuit.... It is not admissible to plant shells merely to destroy life and without other design than that of depriving the enemy of a few men.
> It is admissible to plant torpedoes in a river or harbor, because they can drive off blockading or attacking fleets.[2]

Though his statement actually vindicated General Rains' actions, Randolph was quite aware of the fact that friction had increased between Rains and his superiors. In order to "smooth over" any possible future resentment between the two disagreeing sides, the Secretary of War suggested that the explosives expert be reassigned to the James River defenses. All involved, including Rains himself, agreed to the transfer.

General Rains' initial assignment in the field of constructing underwater explosives came from General Robert E. Lee, who was in the process of formulating a defense against the Union Navy's plans to bring their warships up the James River:

> Soon after the battle of Seven Pines ... General R. E. Lee ... sent for General Rains and said to him, "The enemy have upwards of one hundred vessels in the James River, and we think that they are about making an advance that way upon Richmond, and if there is a man in the whole Southern Confederacy that can stop them, you are the man. Will you undertake it?"[3]

Although Matthew Fontaine Maury had already been designated as the man in charge of electrically-detonated torpedoes, it had quickly become clear that something more was needed — preferably an explosive that could be made in greater numbers, and at a much quicker pace. According to Rains, "ironclads

Example of a Rains keg torpedo believed to be the most widely deployed mine on land or sea. Found near Charleston in August of 1863 (courtesy of West Point Museum Collection).

were invulnerable to cannon of all calibre used and were really masters of rivers and harbors; it required submarine inventions to checkmate and conquer them."[4] Hence, on June 18, 1862, General Gabriel Rains accepted a position which placed him in command of the "submarine defenses of the James and Appomattox Rivers."

A few months after taking this responsibility, Rains was able to fill General Lee's order for hundreds of underwater explosives, which were subsequently dropped into the James River. They were to be the first of two successful types of mines invented by Rains, and were dubbed the "keg torpedoes":

> Lager-beer barrels were confiscated everywhere in the Confederacy for making these instruments, and when caulked and pitched, [were] loaded with from 35 to 120 pounds of powder, capped with friction fuses and moored in a channel ... they proved excellent for defense, causing the loss of more vessels than any other kind used by the Confederacy....[5]

The key to Rains' success with underwater explosives would prove to be his highly-sensitive fuse. Eventually, after weeks of trial and error, he was able to design a primer which could be detonated with just seven pounds of applied pressure, and it was equally effective under both land and water. The formula for the "Rains fuse," as it came to be known, was, however, a carefully guarded secret throughout the entire war. Much later, the confidential ingredients would become a matter of public record. Each torpedo contained fuses made up of 50 parts potassium chlorate, 30 parts sulphuret of antimony, and 20 parts powdered glass. The keg torpedoes were constructed in such a way that gravity forced the fused side upward, so these sensitive primers would be activated whenever a thin, copper protective shield was just slightly dented. This, in turn, would cause Rains' secret formula to detonate, thus setting off the explosive.

When the Naval Submarine Battery Service was initially established, the Confederate States government was not yet willing to hand over enormous amounts of money to finance the operation. Thus, General Rains began with a meager appropriation of just $20,000, which was approved by the Confederate Congress in May 1863. Though this was raised to nearly $250,000 as of June 1864, General Rains was dissatisfied with the insufficient funds made available to him:

> For three years the Confederate Congress legislated on this subject, a bill passing each house alternately for an organized torpedo corps, until the third year, when it passed both houses with acclamation, and $6,000,000 was appropriated, but too late; and the delay was not shortened by the enormous appropriation.[6]

Despite the continual money problems, General Rains would eventually establish torpedo production in Richmond, Mobile, Wilmington, Savannah, and Charleston. In one such "factory," located along the banks of the Mississippi River, he had a handful of men packing demijohns under the cover of a small, insignificant shed. After attaching his sensitive fuses, the explosives would routinely be loaded into a flatbed wagon, covered with a tarp, and transported to the various designated drop sites by an aging Negro known only as "Old Pat." Then it would be up to the river's current to carry them among the unsuspecting Federal fleet.

Even though the floating keg torpedoes developed by Rains would prove to be immensely useful, due to the fact that they could be constructed very quickly, it would be his second design that would score an initial "hit" against a Northern warship. Known as the "frame torpedo," it was comprised of:

> Three heavy pieces of timber, placed in the position, at the bottom of which was ... a box filled with old iron, stones and other heavy materials, was sunk in the river, and then inclined forward at an angle of forty-five degrees by means of ropes and weights. This heavy frame was capped by a cylinder of iron, about ten inches in diameter. Into this was fitted a shell, which was heavily loaded, resting on a set of springs, so arranged that the least pressure on the cylinder would instantly discharge the shell by means of a percussion cap ingeniously placed.[7]

Each of Rains' frame torpedoes possessed a 15-inch artillery shell weighing nearly 400 pounds. The timbers and shells were packed with approximately 27 pounds of deadly gunpowder and positioned in rows across the river's channel. In addition, each explosive could be raised or lowered simply by removing or adding weights.

These ingenious weapons soon found their way beneath most Confederate waterways and became an effective means of repelling the enemy. When Southern General Pierre G. T. Beauregard heard of their apparent effectiveness, he made certain that they were placed around a variety of strategic points under his command. One of these was Fort McAllister, which overlooked the approaches to the Ogeechee River near Savannah.

Nine frame torpedoes constructed by Rains were placed in the channel leading to the installation in early 1863. This action was conducted for two reasons: not only had General Beauregard wired General Mercer in Savannah at the end of January with information warning him that no less than 40 transports, four frigates, and four gunboats were positioned at nearby Hilton Head, but the Confederate chief also wished to protect the newly-converted *Atlanta*, as well as a successful blockade-runner known as the *Nashville*.

According to record, the CSS *Nashville* had been the first vessel commissioned with a letter of marque as a publicly-armed cruiser of the Confederate States. The speedy, side-wheeled steamer had managed to cross through the Federal blockade into Savannah in July 1862, transporting a heavy cargo of valuable arms. From that day forward, however, she had been bottled up in the same vicinity, unable to escape the ever-increasing Federal stranglehold.

Then in January 1863 Union Commander John L. Worden was ordered to take his squadron on a mission into the region, in order that he might do battle against the imposing Confederate land artillery forces. His fleet comprised a half-dozen ships, including the USS *Dawn*, USS *James Adger*, USS *Seneca*, USS *Williams*, USS *Wissahickon*, and a brand-new turreted monitor known as the USS *Montauk*. After arriving late one evening, all dropped anchor well out of reach of Fort McAllister.

The Confederate fortification itself was situated at the mouth of the Ogeechee River, about 16 miles south of the Savannah River and just six miles from Ossabaw Sound. It had been erected on the mainland, overlooking the river bank, and protected the waterway's entrance for more than a mile and a half on either side. The bluff upon which it stood was known in local circles as Genesis Point.

On February 27, 1863, after several "stand-off" battles with the fort, the Federal monitor *Montauk* was dispatched into the Ogeechee waters to renew the assault upon the installation from a different angle. While the *Montauk* was making its move, lookouts on board spotted the CSS *Nashville* waiting patiently for her opportunity to make a dash for the open seas. Commander John L. Worden ordered the crew of his monitor to prepare for an attack on the idled steamer at sunrise the next day.

However, the *Nashville*'s captain decided to attempt the escape then and there, guessing that the enemy had spotted her. Yet, while steaming a bit to the north and west of Fort McAllister, she accidentally ran heavily aground. In this position, she offered the Union flotilla an inviting target. Carefully, the Federals formed columns and moved into the river's mouth, unaware of the explosives that were submerged all around them.

Cannon fire from the fort came to the aid of the ailing Confederate vessel, sending up geysers of water within yards of the Union ships. Miraculously, none of them were hit, though the *Nashville* had now joined the shelling. Even more amazing, perhaps, was the fact that the six Northern ships managed to evade Rains' torpedoes, hidden within mere feet of their bows. Deliberately taking a steady aim at their prey, the Federal attackers opened fire on the defenseless *Nashville*, as Worden describes:

> By moving up close to the obstructions in the river, I was enabled, although under a heavy fire from the battery, to approach the *Nashville*, still aground, within the distance of 1,200 yards. A few well-directed shells determined the range, and I soon succeeded in striking her with 11-inch and 15-inch shells.
> I soon had the satisfaction of observing that the *Nashville* had caught fire from the shells exploding in her in several places, and in less than twenty minutes she was in flames forward, aft, and amidships. At 9:20 A.M. her smoke-chimney went by the board, and at 9:55 her magazine exploded with tremendous violence, shattering her in smoking ruins; nothing remains of her.[8]

With victory apparently in hand, the Federal flotilla began the precarious task of backtracking through the mine-filled waters. At precisely 9:30 A.M., as the crew watched the *Nashville* going up in flames, the USS *Montauk* came in contact with one of the Rains torpedoes. Just a few yards beyond an inlet known as Harvey's Cut, the 844-ton monitor suddenly shifted violently in the water, knocking her crewmen to the deck. At first, the sailors believed that their ship had been struck by a direct hit from Fort McAllister. Yet there did not seem to be any damage to the *Montauk*'s topside. Water gushed through a gash in the monitor's belly, as worried engineers attempted to drain her with their pumps. Only a few moments passed before they became convinced that their efforts were in vain, for any attempt at keeping her afloat would be a lost cause. Hence, Commander Worden ordered his men to intentionally ground her. The once-mighty monitor was steered into a nearby mudbank, where during the next low tide a closer inspection would be made of her ravaged hull.

What the engineers later found absolutely astonished them. There, at the very bottom-most section of the vessel, near the boiler compartment, were thick iron plates that had been twisted upward nearly three and a half inches. Furthermore, a ten-foot slash had been sliced into her reinforced skin. The only weapon that could have inflicted such devastating damage, they knew, was an underwater mine.

Spare pieces of boiler iron were used to make temporary repairs and, with her pumps running full-bore, the water-logged ship managed to limp back to Port Royal, South Carolina, towed by the USS *James Adger*. It would be a full four weeks before she would be placed back into service.

On January 24, 1863, just a month before the *Montauk* was severely damaged by a Rains frame torpedo, the Confederate Torpedo Division had suffered a "casualty" of its own. While Rains was working on one of the sensitive primers in the Richmond plant, it had exploded in his right hand, inflicting irreparable damage to his thumb and forefinger. Though "he was scarcely able to sign his name to official documents,"[9] General Gabriel Rains continued his work on underwater explosives.

During March 1863, Rains completed a manuscript detailing his work on explosive weaponry. It contained a complete description, along with diagrams, explaining precisely how to manufacture torpedoes and land mines. Sadly, however, only a single complete copy was written, which General Rains submitted to President Jefferson Davis for approval. It was the inventor's desire to have the manuscript reprinted and distributed to every general and admiral in the field. The president refused the request, however, claiming that "no printed paper could be kept secret." To this day, Rains' single manuscript has not been located.

If nothing else, General Rains' booklet did manage to convince President Davis that his ideas were sound. According to Special Order No. 124, dated May 25, 1863, Rains was to be dispatched to the Mississippi region:

> The President has confidence in his [Rains'] inventions and is desirous that they should be employed on both land and river....[10]

In charge of the Confederate armies of the west was one of General Rains' aforementioned political opponents, General Joseph E. Johnston, and the underwater explosives expert would be forced to try once again to convince him of his invention's value.

Gabriel Rains departed from Richmond soon thereafter, transporting his needed equipment hidden within a specially-constructed wooden chest. Planning to assemble the torpedoes at his final destination, he stopped off in Augusta, where he requested other materials from his brother. Later, when he arrived in Jackson, Mississippi, he rented a room in which he established a makeshift laboratory for the manufacture of the fuses. However, General Rains' journey would prove to be too late to stop the invading Union forces, and President Davis was bitterly disappointed:

> There could scarcely have been presented a better opportunity for their [torpedoes] use than ... [against] the heavy column marching against Jackson, and the enemy would have been taken at a great disadvantage if our troops had met them midway between Jackson and Clinton....[11]

For the next several months, General Gabriel Rains traveled throughout the South, implementing the use of his torpedoes and land mines in every corner of strategic importance. Finally, on September 2, 1863, he arrived in Charleston, and was immediately ordered to begin burying his underground explosives in and around Fort Wagner. President Davis knew all too well that if the Federal troops ever gained control of this particular fortification it would mean that they would then control the total southern shoreline of Charleston Harbor.

Meanwhile, back in Mississippi, the men who had learned the trade of making explosives from General Rains were having periodic success with torpedo warfare. In one such incident, on March 14, 1863, the 1,928-ton, heavily-armed screw sloop, USS *Richmond*, was nearly destroyed by an underwater explosive believed to be the masterpiece of General Rains.

As the *Richmond* floated past Fort Hudson, under the direction of Admiral David G. Farragut, a mine was detonated almost directly beneath her stern. The blast heaved up a 30-foot column of water and mud, swaying the ship violently and shattering its windows. Parts of a nine-inch turret gun tumbled overboard during the ensuing wash. The ship managed to escape serious damage, however, for the torpedo happened to push a good deal of its force downward.

At the start of 1864, General Rains developed a strategy to lure one of the Federal blockaders at Charleston into his network of torpedoes. On January 10, mines were positioned in the Stono River near Legareville, and an imitation battery station was erected at Grimball to "induce the *Pawnee* or some other boat to pass through the opening in the piling...."[12]

A unit was assigned to General Rains from the Twenty-first Division of the South Carolina Infantry. They were under the command of Engineer Lieutenant J. T. E. Andrews, who described their initial mission:

> I deemed it impracticable to operate, and returned to "Battery Pringle" with the determination of prosecuting the work the next night. Upon making my intention known to the men, I learned that a majority of them would refuse to accompany me, intimating at the same time that it was my intention to surrender them to the enemy.[13]

Disgusted, Rains returned the unit to the Twenty-first Division and requested a second volunteer group. However, a few days later he would be further frustrated when someone from the second unit snuck away from Battery Pringle and informed the enemy of the plan.

In all probability, the "traitorous scoundrel" did not tell the Union forces anything that they didn't already know — officials aboard the USS *Pawnee* had, for all intents and purposes, figured out that the battery was only a "dummy" intended to lure them up the channel. It seems that they had become suspicious for two reasons: workmen building the structure had not seemed to care much when the *Pawnee* made her way past the installation and, though the ship was well within range, Confederate soldiers had failed to fire a single shot. On January 11, the *Pawnee*'s skipper opted to retreat back to the safety of the harbor, making Rains' plan a total failure.

By the middle of the month, a Federal search vessel was dispatched into the area, with the intention of locating the Rains torpedoes. It found several, and one was shipped to the U.S. Military Academy in order that it might be "a lasting testimonial of the contribution of the traitor Pierre G. T. Beauregard to the country...."[14]

A few days later, Beauregard gave Rains the order to place floating mines in the main channel near Morris Island, as well as in the Stono, Ashepoo, and Combahee Rivers. Before he could carry out the general's command, the torpedo expert was reassigned to Mobile, Alabama, which demanded his immediate and complete attention. As we shall later see, although his activities in the defense of Charleston Harbor were complete, his contributions to the development of underwater warfare were far from over.

Chapter 8

Captain Lee's Torpedo Ram

The torpedo ram, according to its original design, was a low-floating, extremely quick, heavily armored steamer. It was different than any other type of offensive vessel used during the Civil War in that it transported few, if any, guns aboard. Instead the ram came equipped with a single deadly spar torpedo, attached to its bow and containing a heavy charge of gunpowder and sensitive fuses ready to explode on contact. The inventor of this ingenious attack vessel was described by a close acquaintance as "an intelligent young Engineer officer"[1] by the name of Francis D. Lee, who served on the staff of General Pierre G. T. Beauregard in Charleston, South Carolina.

Born in 1827, Lee was a member of one of Charleston's most illustrious families, and he grew up to become a well-respected architect. After assisting with the design and construction of Fort Wagner, located along the shoreline of Morris Island, he became extremely interested in the concept of underwater weaponry. The best torpedoes, he surmised, were those that could be detonated by chemically-reacting fuses.

These fuses, which were similar in nature to those later developed by Hunter Davidson, were not the typical variety known as "powder-train" fuses: in fact, they were far more advanced. Made up of tiny leaden tubes, they were topped off with hemispherical caps constructed of extremely thin metal. Within their curved forms, Lee inserted similarly-shaped glass test tubes, which were hermetically sealed after being filled with a sulfuric acid concoction. Between the glass and metal covering was a layered composition of his secret formula: a carefully measured dose of chlorate of potassa, powdered sugar, and very fine rifle powder pellets.

Theoretically, whenever the thin, outer jacket of lead came in contact with a hard surface it would easily be dented. This in turn would shatter the interior glass test tube, forcing the sulfuric acid to mingle with the chlorate of potassa, powdered sugar, and gunpowder. The resulting flame produced by the spontaneous chemical reaction would lead to an instantaneous explosion of the gunpowder charge housed within an ordinary torpedo case.

After he had managed to perfect this ingenious detonating device, Captain Lee continued his work by designing a copper cylinder to hold the gunpowder.

Containing between 50 and 150 pounds of powder, each cylinder came equipped with a dual-purpose socket, allowing it to be either pushed by a long wooden spar or dragged by a length of rope.

On August 29, 1862, special orders were dispatched to General Pierre G. T. Beauregard, assigning him to the command of South Carolina and Georgia sea defense. His headquarters were immediately established in Charleston, where he arrived on September 15, relieving General John C. Pemberton.

The task of defending this coastal region seemed immense to Beauregard, as rumors floated throughout the ranks that the Federal navy was on the brink of initiating a major sea invasion of Charleston. The General, who was quite familiar with such assaults, felt that the city was totally unprepared for a siege of any proportion.

The relationship between the newly-appointed officer and the Confederate navy department was one of enormous strain and friction. Beauregard's major criticism was directed against what he thought was the ineffectiveness of the gunboats then patrolling Charleston Harbor:

> The *Palmetto* and *Chicora* were, unfortunately, of too heavy a draught to be of much practical use in the defense of the harbor. They were also lacking in motive power, consequently in speed; and their guns, on account of the smallness of the port-holes, could not be sufficiently elevated, and were but very short range.[2]

And, to top it off, Beauregard claimed that these gunboats were quite "unseaworthy," unable to stand up to the rigorous motion of unsettled tides. As evidence of their "total failure," they had not fired a single shot in the defense of Fort Sumter during the Federal naval attack of April 7, 1862.

Stephen R. Mallory, Secretary of the Navy, was utterly outraged by Beauregard's criticism of the gunboats, claiming that:

> ...[the] failure to fire on the occasions indicated resulted from the judgement of the commander. His ships were designed to fight the enemy's ironclads, which they could only do with fair chances of success at the close range already indicated.[3]

A few months later, Beauregard would continue the disagreement between himself and Secretary Mallory in a more abrasive assault by saying:

> Of course, I do not suppose that Mr. Mallory can possibly admit they [the gunboats] are worse than useless, since he is still going on with their construction. Moreover, they are to a certain extent the children of his own creation, and if he be a good father he cannot disown them or admit that they are defective, any more than the owl can admit that its young ones are ugly. But I do believe that Congress ought to interpose its authority in thus allowing Mr. Mallory, or Mr. Anybody Else, to squander our public funds in such a wanton manner, consuming time, valuable materials, and guns which might be used to a better purpose....[4]

Since General Beauregard was distraught and displeased with the entire affair, he was most receptive when Captain Francis D. Lee disclosed his plans for a torpedo ram. After all, he deduced, wouldn't they fill a void in the harbor defenses already present?

As early as October 8, 1862, Beauregard sent a letter to Governor Francis W. Pickens of South Carolina, describing Lee's proposed attack vessel in detail, claiming that it "would be worth several gunboats." Furthermore, the General requested that the state's appropriations for gunboats be transferred to the construction of a prototype ram. In a later note he added:

> I believe an ordinary gunboat will effect but little against the enemy's new gigantic monitors ... we must attack them under water, where they are the most vulnerable if we wish to destroy them and the torpedo ram is the only probable way of accomplishing that desirable end.[5]

Such an innovative offensive vessel, according to Lee, would be constructed of iron plating, would measure 40 to 60 feet in length, and would be approximately seven feet in diameter at its center. Typically, the engine would be nestled in the rear of the boat, with the boiler situated at the forward end. In between would sit the captain, the engineer, and any number of able-bodied crew members able to squeeze into the limited space. All aboard would enter the belly of the ship through a hatchway from above.

The underwater explosive would be attached to a protruding spar that extended from the bow, and it could be lowered or raised by a line which was fed back through a tiny cubby-hole. A dual-bladed propeller would push the vessel through the water. When placed into operation, all that remained visibly above the surface would be the ship's short smokestack, her hatchway coaming, and the stanchion on which the torpedo line would be hoisted. In this way, Union lookouts would find it most difficult to spot the approach of their adversary; and, even if they did, it would be far too late to establish any sort of defensive maneuver.

General Beauregard, who was persistent to the very end, wasted no time in pressing the issue of the ram's needed construction. He dispatched Captain Lee to Richmond, Virginia, with the vessel's diagrams, a scale model, and a letter of introduction addressed to Adjutant General Samuel Cooper.

Lee arrived in the capital on October 16, 1862, and immediately hired a carriage to take him to the home of Congressman William Porcher Miles, an extremely influential politician. Although the state government had been impressed enough with Captain Lee's design to allocate $50,000 for its construction, Beauregard hoped to gain the support of the Confederate government as well.

The following day, Captain Lee visited the office of General Cooper, with not only the support of Beauregard, but with that of Congressman Miles.

A long spar torpedo boat beached at Charleston (courtesy of National Archives).

Slowly but surely, he worked his way up the political ladder to the office of Secretary Mallory, who made a "careful examination of the design." Despite Mallory's apparent dislike stemming from Beauregard's past criticism, he "expressed deep interest in the [torpedo ram] undertaking and his entire willingness to furnish everything in his power to make its accomplishment as early as possible."[6] Elated with the positive response, Captain Lee immediately returned to Charleston.

A few days later, General Beauregard wrote a letter to the Secretary of the Navy, easing the tension between them:

> I thank you for your prompt and favorable support you have given me in the desire to construct one of Capt. F. D. Lee's marine torpedo rams, which I think is destined ere long to change the system of naval warfare.[7]

On October 31, General Beauregard made the entire project official in Paragraph 3 of Special Orders No. 210, placing Captain Lee in charge of the construction phase of the ram, thus giving him permission to spend the allocated $50,000.

Work on the Lee torpedo ram began the following month, with the F. M. Jones Company hired to construct the hull, and Cameron & Company employed to install the machinery. Within seven days, the vessel began to take shape, with its rounded bare ribs protruding from the vessel's main body. Though Lee had hoped to secure strong oaken beams, he was forced to be content with the more easily available Carolina pine. In the meantime, he put in a huge order for materials from the Confederate Naval Department, which included 18,500 board feet of four-inch oak, 10,500 pounds of three-quarter-inch iron plating, 6,000 pounds of oakum, 5,000 pounds of eight-inch spikes, 5,100 pounds of ten-inch spikes, and 8,000 pounds of coal.

On February 17, 1863, while Cameron & Company was hard at work installing a used boiler and engine extracted from the steamer *Barton*, Captain Lee decided that construction was progressing far too slowly. In a letter written to Brigadier General Thomas Jordan, he requested that he be allowed to conduct experiments "with spar torpedoes with this view of using them on small boats against the Ironclads."[8]

Lee's reasoning was simple: not only was his work crew growing impatient waiting for the all-important iron plating, which had not yet arrived, but Cameron & Company had recently been taken over by the Confederate navy. Furthermore, Lee had become aware that official red tape was dictating that his project would take twice as long to complete as he had hoped.

By this point, the Federal blockading squadron had managed to reinforce their wooden vessels with stronger ironclad monitors, and the blockade of Charleston's coastline was becoming more and more effective as the days went by. The restless Captain was given the go-ahead to proceed with his test maneuvers.

Lee located a light-weight canoe-type boat, referred to as a "dugout," which measured approximately 20 feet in length. After careful calculations, he determined that one of his torpedoes, submerged a mere six feet below the water's surface and extending from a long spar, would have a devastating effect on an unsuspecting ironclad. To make absolutely certain that his estimations were indeed correct, he conducted a test run on an aging Confederate iron hulk:

> A torpedo made of copper, and containing thirty or forty pounds of gunpowder, having a sensitive fuze [sic], was attached by means of a socket to a long pine pole. To this weights were attached, and it was suspended horizontally beneath a row-boat, by cords from the bow and stern — the torpedo projecting eight or ten feet ahead of the boat, and six or seven feet below the surface. The boat was then drawn towards the hulk till the torpedo came in contact with it and exploded. The result was the immediate destruction of the old vessel and no damage to the [attack] boat.[9]

Looking on with great anticipation from the shoreline, General Beauregard was so taken with the successful demonstration that he recommended "at least one dozen (vessels) be fitted up at once with Captain Lee's spar-torpedo."[10]

Just after sunset, on March 18, 1863, Lieutenant William T. Glassell was dispatched, with a well-trained crew of seven, to attack the blockading fleet. With only a single spar torpedo on board, the Confederates would have no alternative but to ram the first vessel they chanced to encounter. Lieutenant Glassell later recalled the details of their mission:

> I started out with ebb-tide in search of a victim. I approached the ship [*Powhatan*] about one o'clock. The young moon had gone down, and every thing seemed favorable…. When they [the *Powhatan*'s crew] discovered us, two or three hundred yards distant from the port bow, we were hailed and immediately ordered to stop and not come nearer. To their question, "What boat is that?" and numerous others, I gave evasive and stupid answers; and notwithstanding repeated orders to stop, and threats to fire on us, I told them I was coming on board as fast as I could, and whispered to my men to pull with all their might….
>
> My men did pull splendidly, and I was aiming to strike the enemy on the portside, just below the gangway. They continued to threaten and to order us to lay in our oars; but I had no idea of doing so, as we were now within forty feet of the intended victim. I felt confident of success, when one of my trusted men, from terror or treason, suddenly backed his oar and stopped the boat's headway. This caused the others to give up apparently in despair….[11]

The tiny Confederate boat drifted aimlessly with the tide, passing the Federal ironclad's stern section, as an officer aboard continued to inquire as to who they were and exactly what they were doing. In the meantime, the USS *Powhatan* continued to float motionless in the calm waters, as the rowboat drifted off under a shroud of darkness. The man who had backed his oar threw his revolver overboard, and attempted to gain control of the gun of the man sitting next to him in order to accomplish the same with it. Quickly, Lieutenant Glassell drew his own weapon and regained the control of his men. Furthermore, he ordered his men to cut the torpedo line holding the explosive. Following the failed attempt to destroy the powerful Union ship, Glassell had this to say:

> I think the enemy must have received some hint from spies, creating a suspicion of torpedoes, before I made this attempt. I got back to Charleston after daylight next morning, with only the loss of one torpedo, and convinced that steam was the only reliable motive power.[12]

Captain Lee was tremendously disturbed and upset over the fact that the initial mission had failed. In a letter to the Chief of Staff, he wrote:

> As the inventor of the mode of attack, and consequently responsible in a greater degree than any other party for its successful operation, I would most respectfully protest against so unfair a test as the sending of a single boat unsupported against the [Federal] fleet.[13]

Although Lee indicated that the single-attack plan was totally insufficient to guarantee success, General Beauregard continued to support it. After all, he reasoned, Captain Lee's opinion might be exactly the opposite had Lieutenant Glassell and his crew been successful in their mission.

In the meantime, the arrival of the materials needed for Captain Lee's torpedo rams continued to be slow and sporadic. The Confederate government, which was certainly hard-pressed for weapons and other war materials, had decided against shipping the necessary iron plating for the armor. General Beauregard, who had by this time become totally incensed by the repeated delays, suggested that a number of the torpedo rams be constructed in Liverpool, England. Running out of patience, he ordered that spar torpedoes be installed on all gunboats, as well as on "every available steamer and small boat in the harbor."[14]

Though General Beauregard seemed anxious to outfit all existing vessels with underwater explosives, he was well aware of the risks involved. Adding to this keen awareness was the fact that Confederate ironclads such as the CSS *Palmetto State* were required to undergo periodic safety checks. Though a spar torpedo had, indeed, been installed, it was removed and examined every two weeks in order to make absolutely certain that it remained in perfect working order. Captain W. H. Parker, who had been given this dangerous job, had this to say of his duty:

> As executive officer I always attended to this with the gunner, and it was no joke to do it. In the first place we had to go out in a boat and take the torpedo off the staff, and in rough weather it was hard to keep the boat from striking it [the explosive].... A moderate blow was sufficient to break the glass phial inside the fuses and cause an explosion.[15]

Now totally convinced that Captain Lee's torpedo rams would be completed months behind schedule, General Beauregard proposed an innovative strategy to Captain John R. Tucker, a prestigious member of the Confederate States Navy in Charleston. He suggested that they tow out several rowboats equipped with spar torpedoes into the middle of the harbor. Then, they would commence a unified attack on the entire Federal blockading flotilla.

Captain Tucker, who had recently replaced Captain Duncan N. Ingraham as the major representative of the Confederate navy in Charleston, agreed. He ordered Lieutenant William G. Dozier, head of the Special Service Detachment, to make the necessary arrangements.

Dozier secured volunteer sailors from both Charleston and Wilmington, and then managed to locate ten small vessels to carry out the attack. A small side-wheeler known as the *Sumter* was given over to him to use as a command vessel for the expedition.

The men underwent rigorous training in preparation for the offensive mission, and they soon lost all fear of working with underwater explosives:

> It was not at all uncommon to see a sailor rolling down to his boat, when they were called for exercise, with a quid of tobacco in his cheek and a torpedo slung over his back; and when it is recalled that each [torpedo] ... had seven sensitive

fuses which a tap with a stick or blow with a stone was sufficient to explode and blow half the street down, it can readily be believed that we gave him a wide berth.[16]

Fifteen small boats were assembled near the steamer CSS *Stono* on the night of April 12, 1863. The *Stono* was anchored just behind Cummings Point at the mouth of Charleston Harbor. The step-by-step procedure had been practiced and repracticed until each crewman involved had learned every minute detail. In general, the plan called for:

> ...the parties to be divided into tens or twenties each under a leader. One of these parties to be prepared with iron wedges to wedge between the turret and the deck [in order to prevent the turret from turning]; a second party to cover the pilot-house with wet blankets; a third to throw powder down the smokestack or to cover it; another provided with turpentine or camphene in glass vessels, to smash over the turret, with an inextinguishable liquid to follow it; and still another to watch every opening in the turret or deck, provided with sulphuretted cartridges, etc., to smoke the enemy out.[17]

Each boat would depart from the front beach of Morris Island, making its way toward the blockading fleet. After the steps described above had been successfully carried out, the volunteers were to concentrate their next offensive maneuvers, attacking each individual Union vessel in pairs. Furthermore, they were ordered not to return to shore until their torpedoes had been exploded.

The well-outlined plan was cancelled however, when the Federal blockaders suddenly withdrew to other regions of the South without warning. During the next several months, the rowboats outfitted with spar torpedoes would only participate in occasional practice sessions. Eventually, their volunteer crews would each be assigned to other, unrelated duties. Finally, by September 1863, the flotilla would be completely disbanded.

Slowly, work continued on Captain Lee's prototype torpedo ram, and General Beauregard was forced to rely upon defensive mechanical underwater explosives for the protection of Charleston: "I multiplied the laying out of torpedoes in all navigable streams liable to be ascended by Federal gunboats and other craft...."[18]

One of these torpedoes, designed by Captain Lee, was detonated on April 7, 1863, during a Federal attack. At approximately 3:00 in the afternoon, the USS *Weehawken*, which was pushing a 50-foot "devil rake" designed to snare and explode the torpedoes, came upon a floating obstruction between Sumter and Moultrie. The threat of the ship's screw becoming entangled prompted her commander to turn the ship away from the unidentified object. As the *Weehawken* slowly rotated, an explosive collided with her hull, giving the crew a tremendous shock wave, yet there were no serious injuries.

During the spring of 1863, a patrol of Confederate soldiers waited patiently on shore near Charleston, hoping that one of the North's monitors would happen to position itself over their newly-planted electrical mine. Constructed of old boiler iron, it measured 18 feet long and three feet in diameter. Its fuses were made of a pair of carbon "pencils" wrapped tightly with copper wire and placed in a ten-inch-long glass phial. Their points were only a fraction of an inch apart, and positioned near the center. The explosive had been packed with nearly 3,000 pounds of gunpowder and then carefully submerged beneath the surface of the harbor.

Cables ran from the huge torpedo to a battery on shore, where Captain Langdon Cheves was stationed. Though he could not see the channel from his vantage point, signal scouts were positioned at both Battery Gregg and Battery Wagner on either side of him. They were ready to give him the go-ahead signal to detonate the explosive at a moment's notice.

Gradually, to the delight of the scouts, the mighty monitor, USS *New Ironsides*, dropped anchor. Though she was out of gunfire range from the fort, she "could not have been placed more directly over [the torpedo] if he [Cheves] had been allowed to [position her]." The contact between copper wiring and the battery cable was closed, and everyone on shore waited for the tremendous explosion. Over and over Cheves made the connection, yet "the confounded thing ... would not go off."

After a brief period of repeated attempts by Captain Cheves to set off the explosive, the *New Ironsides* weighed anchor and floated out away from the harbor. Later, after all Federal vessels had withdrawn to deeper waters, the mine was brought to the surface and thoroughly inspected for defects. When the cable leading up to the battery house was examined, searchers discovered a slice in it where it crossed the beach. Evidence indicated that a set of wagon wheels had done the damage, though the responsible party was never determined. Whoever had been at fault, the blunder had probably cost the Confederacy their best opportunity to destroy the most powerful enemy vessel afloat at that time.

The merchants of Charleston were thoroughly convinced of Captain Francis Lee's enterprise, but realized that it was fast becoming a lost cause. On June 6, 1863, John Frazer & Company, the city's largest exporting firm, sent a letter to the disgruntled Lee:

> The undersigned, in connection with other merchants in the city, propose the construction of a marine torpedo steamer abroad, and desire your services for carrying the work into effect. Arrangements have been made for placing the necessary funds at your disposal in Europe.[19]

Furthermore, it seems that those involved had already gone through the proper channels, and had subsequently received approval to dispatch Captain Lee overseas. However, Lee never went to Europe, perhaps due to international complications concerning the endeavor.

On July 11, 1863, Captain Lee wrote to General Beauregard, detailing his plans to launch his "completed" vessel at 3:00 P.M. that very afternoon. And, though the spar torpedo boat was, indeed, launched, it went off minus the fanfare and her iron plating.

Two weeks passed, as a close survey of the boat's seaworthiness was conducted by an entourage of naval personnel, who hoped "to ascertain if she was fitted to the services for which she was proposed." Apparently, she was, for finishing touches were subsequently pushed through the proverbial red tape: a cutwater was positioned over her bow, three torpedoes were placed on her spar, and Captain James Carlin, commander aboard the blockade runner CSS *Ella & Anna*, was placed at her helm.

Evidently, the Federal fleet must have had a dependable source of intelligence concerning her readiness, for on August 5, Admiral Dahlgren informed his men that "it is rumored that the enemy [Confederates] have a ram near Fort Johnson." Fifteen days later, on the night of August 20, 1863, Captain Carlin slipped quietly out into Charleston Harbor aboard the torpedo-laden ram, which had recently been christened the "CSS *Torch.*" His intended target was the USS *New Ironsides*.

At approximately 10:00 P.M., Captain Carlin reached Fort Sumter, where 11 soldiers, under the command of Lieutenant Eldred S. Flicking, came aboard. Continuing to make their way cautiously down the main shipping channel, Carlin spotted the *New Ironsides* at about midnight, lying at anchor just off of Morris Island. Within a quarter mile of his target now, the Captain ordered that the torpedo spar be lowered. When he was within 50 yards, Ensign Benjamin H. Porter, officer of the deck aboard the *New Ironsides*, demanded identification.

"The steamer *Live Yankee*," answered Carlin. Now only 40 yards away, the captain ordered that the engines of the *Torch* be shut down and the helm pushed hard to starboard. Apparently, the quartermaster in control was unable to hear the command, and though Carlin repeated it three more times, it was too late: the spar torpedo was heading in a direction that would miss the *New Ironsides*. By now, the ebb tide had gotten the *Torch* in its grip, and she was swept alongside the huge Federal monitor.

Acting quickly, Captain Carlin gave the command to restart the engine. Up above, Ensign Porter of the *New Ironsides* hailed him once again, inquiring where they were from.

"Port Royal," came Carlin's reply. In the tenseness of the situation, Carlin was informed that the tiny ship was about to be boarded. The *Torch* had come so close to the *New Ironsides* that the crewmen could see the faces of enemy sailors peering out from the ironclad's portholes. Wondering why his order to restart the engine had been ignored, Carlin ran to the engine room to discover that it had "caught upon the center" and stalled.

A flare was fired from the deck of the *New Ironsides*, warning five monitors anchored within 300 yards of a possible attack. Sailors lined the rails above the deck of the *Torch*, ready to shoot the Confederates. Finally, the balking engine was restarted, and the spar torpedo ram steamed away into the darkness, with rifles and cannon firing in her direction.

Two of the shots missed the CSS *Torch* by only 20 feet, as Captain Carlin refigured his strategy. Momentarily, he considered attacking one of the nearby monitors, but changed his mind due to the troublesome engine and the fact that his vessel had begun leaking badly.

Later Captain Stephen C. Rowan of the *New Ironsides* offered the following report concerning the Confederate attack: "A very low and apparently swift steamer came up under the stern of the ship, gave her name as the *Live Yankee* and made her escape."[20] And upon his return from the aborted mission, Captain Carlin offered the following explanation to General Beauregard:

> I feel it my duty most unhesitantly to express my condemnation of the vessel and engine for the purpose it was intended, and as soon as she can be docked and the leak stopped [I] would advise making a transport of her.[21]

Both General Beauregard and Captain Francis Lee were understandably disappointed at the failure, though Carlin was prevailed upon to remain in command of the CSS *Torch*. Shortly thereafter, Beauregard sent a brief note to Flag Officer John Randolph Tucker:

> It is my wish to turn over to you the torpedo ram steamer ... until it may be found convenient and judicious to mail armor and arrange her as originally designed.[22]

Though his hopes were still high, Francis Lee's initial torpedo ram had completed her service in the Confederate navy. She would never see action again.

Chapter 9

The *Little David*

As spring changed into summer in 1863, General Beauregard continued his dedicated attempt to defend the South Carolina coastline with unbending resiliency. By this point, torpedoes had been submerged in every major waterway throughout the state, and the Northern navy found itself literally blockaded by the South's ingenious weaponry. Growing impatient with the apparent stalemate, Northern muckrakers, who wrote titillating accounts of confrontations between the two sides, began to find fault with the seemingly incompetent Federal flotilla in and around Charleston:

> The ghosts of rebel torpedoes have ... paralyzed the efficiency of the [Northern] fleet ... and the sight of large beer barrels floating in the harbor ... [has] added terror to overwhelming fear.... The torpedo phantom has proved too powerful to be overcome.[1]

General Beauregard had employed every inventor available in the Charleston area in order to establish his underwater defense of the city. Experiments with electric torpedoes had thoroughly convinced him that such weaponry could be used quite successfully in most inlets throughout the region. One such explosive, designed by Engineer Captain M. Martin Gray, was used extensively.

Gray, a 42-year-old from Delaware, was placed in charge of the local electrical torpedo division in early 1863. Upon his arrival, he found that the department had most recently been under the direction of a civilian named M. J. Waldron. Working jointly, the two enterprising men concentrated their efforts on the design of compact electrical charges connected by a single cable. They hoped to replace the large majority of larger tanks already under construction.

Soon Gray and Waldron had managed to construct a number of self-detonating "tin-iron" containers. Each possessed a series of spreading armatures that completed a single circuit, thus setting off the explosive whenever it came in contact with a vessel. Such an arrangement relieved the Confederate lookouts of the responsibility for continually monitoring the movement of enemy ships.

Captain Gray was ordered by General Beauregard to escort a small

Illustration of one version of a *David*, a low-slung attack vessel deployed to attack Union ships. Resembling an early Northern ironclad, the majority of these *Davids* did not house cannons on board (courtesy of Valecia Bryner).

contingent of men to Skull Creek, a tiny inlet which wound its way into Charleston. Here he was to plant a few of his self-detonating electrical explosives. Gray soon learned that this would be no easy task, for his men were forced to move equipment and supplies across an area pocketed with numerous marshes and swamps. Yet after several weeks of tedious maneuvers, they succeeded in dropping the mines on Tuesday, May 18, 1863.

For the next several nights, Gray and his men attempted to entice the Union fleet into the area by using three small boats as bait. Yet, to their mutual disgust, the Federals refused to bite, choosing instead to remain anchored near Pope's Island. Finally, one of Gray's men suggested that a cannon be transported into the area and fired at the enemy in order to rouse their interest: "This would certainly bring a gunboat through Skull Creek of sufficient draft to explode our torpedoes...."[2] Despite the importation of the cannon, however, the Federal fleet remained at their stations, refusing to be attracted by the obvious ploy. The time was right, therefore, to employ more offensive measures. If the enemy wouldn't come to them, then they would go to the enemy.

On July 25, 1863, Captain Francis D. Lee sent a memo to Captain A. N. T. Beauregard, an aide to General Beauregard. It emphasized that "...the small torpedo steamer now building in Cooper River, is nearly complete, and we have good reason to expect will aid materially in the defense of this city."[3]

The "torpedo steamer" to which Lee was referring was the brainchild of

Ross Winan, from Baltimore, Maryland, who was an advocate of the Southern cause. Prior to the outbreak of war, Winan had concentrated on the design of numerous contrivances, most notably steam locomotives. More recently, he had turned his attention to the construction of offensive sea vessels, and he had managed to design a low-draft, cigar-shaped steamer.

Furthermore, Winan had secured a handful of wealthy investors residing in the Charleston area, including Theodore D. Stoney (who had contributed $25,000) and Theodore Wagner. The actual building of the vessel was being directed by Dr. St. Julian Ravenal, who had been given permission by General Beauregard to take leave from his job at Columbia Hospital. The "secret" construction area was nestled within a quiet district of Stony Landing, near the headwaters of the western branch of the Cooper River, some 30 miles from Charleston.

Work progressed slowly on the small steamer, which would measure approximately 54 feet long and slightly more than 5.5 feet in width. Samuel Masterby was employed as the master carpenter, D. C. Ebaugh as the chief mechanic, and John Chaulk was put in charge of installing the machinery. The actual work was being carried out by slave labor from nearby plantations.

Despite the fact that the entire Confederacy was still having difficulty securing adequate building materials, the persistent crew used what little they could lay their hands on. For example, the enterprising Dr. Ravenal obtained an aging steam locomotive engine from the Northeastern Railroad Company to be used as the primary mode of power, and iron plating was secured in a piecemeal fashion.

As their work continued slowly, General Beauregard was still planting mines throughout the region. To assist in this endless venture, Captain Gray was ordered away from the Skull Creek area to Light House Inlet, situated just south of Morris Island. There, on August 10, 1863, with the help of Stephen Elliott, he prepared to plant his explosives.

Stephen Elliott had long been interested in torpedo warfare. In fact, numerous historians would consider him a pioneer in the field. In April 1862 he had taken it upon himself to recruit several volunteers to drop crude mines of his own design into the waters of the Savannah River. Known as the "Beaufort Artillery Company," these brave men had risked a great deal, even though the torpedoes were never detonated. Elliott had continued to tinker with underwater explosives ever since.

It was around 8:00 P.M., and to Gray and Elliott August 10 seemed like an ideal night to begin their mission. The tide was high as a small contingent of men departed from Successionville, just south of Charleston, making their way down Light House Creek aboard three tiny rowboats. The night was unusually dark, with the moon and stars hiding behind a thick blanket of clouds. With them the men carried eight deadly torpedoes. They soon found themselves lost within the intricate network of creeks and inlets. Exasperated,

Gray ordered them to return to their base camp, where they arrived just before dawn. The following night was much lighter, and they were able to locate their destination: an area situated about 400 yards from the Federal fleet anchored off Light House Inlet.

Methodically, Gray and Elliott arranged four rows of explosives, using a total of 190 feet of rope to secure them all together in pairs. With floats spaced every 10 feet for support, the 50-pound torpedoes were attached at the extreme ends. However, they were like no other mines employed prior to this date, for each was fashioned from a pair of tin cans 15 inches in diameter, connected together by a slender 3.5-foot shaft.

The gunpowder for each of Gray's explosives was housed in the lower chamber, while the upper, air-filled can provided buoyancy. Running through the connecting rod was the barrel and firing mechanism of a sawed-off musket, loaded and ready to fire. A series of four long pins wired to the trigger projected from the top of the float. Theoretically, whenever a vessel's hull came in contact with any one of these pins, the musket's trigger would be released and the resulting shot would detonate the charge.

While making their way back to base camp, Gray and Elliott heard a reverberating explosion coming from the direction of their recently-planted torpedoes. At first, they suspected that one had been detonated by the strong currents. Later, they would learn that, instead, one of the highly-sensitive mines had floated against the hull of the USS *Pawnee*, the same Federal ship which had discovered the first Confederate torpedo in the waters of the Potomac River in 1861. The powerful *Pawnee* had not taken the brunt of the explosion, however, although her launch had been completely destroyed.

A few hours later, at approximately 4:00 A.M., another of these floating mines exploded near the *Pawnee*. Yet on this occasion, it had been detonated too far away to cause major damage to the 872-ton gunboat. Due to the close calls, however, the *Pawnee*'s commanding officer ordered the waters to be thoroughly searched for other explosives. On August 17 his crew found

> ...a torpedo made of three metallic cases, on the upper side of which were delicately arranged hammers connected with cords. The cords were to catch on a vessel, when the cases would swing against her, the hammers would fall on percussion caps, and thus the explosion would be caused in the powder chambers under the caps.[4]

Back at the construction site of the small torpedo steamer, both Winan and Ravenal agreed that she was ready for action. With every available plantation hand assisting, she was loaded onto flatcars and transported to Charleston, where she was promptly launched at Atlantic Wharf, on the eastern end of Broad Street.

To the delight of her designers and financiers, she floated upright and sat deeply submerged, with her smokestack and only a small section of her amidships above the surface. Furthermore, the engineers found that her ballast tanks worked well in bringing her down even deeper, so that when water was admitted even her curved deck was awash. At the suggestion of his wife, who had stood by him throughout this lengthy ordeal, Dr. Ravenal dubbed their creation the *David* (although the steamer would later become better known as the *Little David*).

The craft's torpedo explosive would be hoisted at the extreme end of a hollow, 14-foot iron shaft attached to the bow. The shaft could be either extended to its maximum reach, or positioned at an angle. This feature would allow the crew to strike their target at the optimal area of contact. The torpedo was an improved variety, designed by Captain Francis D. Lee and weighing approximately 100 pounds. It came fully equipped with four ultra-sensitive fuses.

When he heard of the *Little David*'s completion, Captain William T. Glassel, who had recently returned from Wilmington, volunteered to command her. On September 18, 1863, his offer was accepted, and he was placed in charge:

> On examination I determined to make a trial [run]. She was yet in an unfinished state. Assistant-engineer J. H. Toombs volunteered his services, and all the necessary machinery was soon fitted and got in working order, while Major Frank Lee gave me his zealous aid in fitting on a torpedo. James Stuart (alias Sullivan) volunteered to go as fireman, and afterwards the services of J. W. Cannon as pilot were secured. The boat was ballasted as to float deeply in the water, and all above painted the most invisible color [bluish]. The torpedo was made of copper ... I had also an armament on deck of four double-barrel shot guns, and as many navy revolvers; also, four cork life-preservers had been thrown on board, and made us feel safe.[5]

The *Little David* crept out of Charleston Harbor a little after dark on the night of October 5, 1863, and floated with the ebb-tide through the channel. A very slight breeze blew out of the north and the night was a bit hazy, but the crew could see the stars shining overhead. Glassel hoped to reach their intended target, the Federal monitor USS *New Ironsides*, at approximately the same time that the tide turned.

The tiny steamer made fairly good time through the calm waters. The *Little David* passed Fort Sumter and the line of Union picket boats beyond without detection. Moving silently along, just inside the bar, her crew had ample opportunity to reconnoiter the entire blockading Federal fleet at anchor. Beyond, Glassel could make out the flicker of the enemy campfires on shore at Morris Island, and, from time to time, could even pick up the faint echo of their voices as they talked. At approximately 8:30 P.M., the USS *New Ironsides* came into hazy view.

For the next half hour, Glassel and his crew floated back and forth, keeping a constant eye on the huge monitor as they waited for the tide. Just after the soothing music of the drum and fife had ceased, and the nine o'clock gun had sounded the signal for the Federal navy men to secure their vessels for the night, Glassel decided that the time had come to attack:

> Accordingly, having on a full head of steam, I took charge of the helm, it being so arranged that I could sit on deck and work the wheel with my feet. Then directing the engineer and fireman to keep below and give me all the speed possible, I gave a double-barrel gun to the pilot, with instructions not to fire until I should do so, and steered directly for the monitor. I intended to strike her just under the gang-way, but the tide still running out, carried us to a point nearer the quarter. Thus we rapidly approached the enemy. When within about 300 yards of her a sentinel hailed us: Boat ahoy! Boat ahoy! repeating the hail several times very rapidly. We were coming towards them with all speed, and I made no answer, but cocked both barrels of my gun. The officer of the deck next made his appearance, and loudly demanded "What boat is that?" Being now within forty yards of the ship, and plenty of headway to carry us on, I thought it about time the fight should commence, and I fired my gun. The officer of the deck [Ensign Charles W. Howard] fell back mortally wounded (poor fellow), and I ordered the engine stopped. The next moment the torpedo struck the vessel and exploded.... My little boat plunged violently, and a large body of water which had been thrown up descended upon her deck, and down the smokestack and hatchway.[6]

Aboard the USS *New Ironsides*, the crew was awakened by Glassel's shot, and then felt the mighty ship tremble beneath them. Next, her heavy rigging crashed violently to the deck, as cannons leaped from their moorings. Finally, the heavily damaged vessel rolled precariously to one side.

Glassel immediately sounded the order to reverse the *Little David*'s engine, in a maneuver intended to back away from the ailing monitor. However, Engineer Toombs informed him that the engine's fires had been doused by the huge spray of water that had washed over them. Furthermore, Toombs said, something had "become jammed in the machinery so that it would not move."[7]

Meanwhile, the navy men aboard the *New Ironsides* had raced up on deck, and a general alarm was sounded throughout the fleet. Without hesitation, Glassel ordered his men to abandon ship, and asked Engineer Toombs to cut the water pipes so that the *Little David* would sink to the bottom.

Glassel grabbed one of the cork floats, jumped into the water, and swam away as fast as he could. Meanwhile, Toombs and Sullivan had also gone into the water, with the former swimming in the direction of Morris Island and the latter clinging to the USS *Pawnee*'s anchor chains. Within a few moments, Toombs realized that Cannon was still aboard the *Little David*, choosing to remain with the ship because he could not swim. Toombs backtracked, making his way back to the small boat. Working together, Toombs and Cannon somehow managed to repair the *Little David*'s machinery and coaxed her engine to restart. As the enemy poured down a hail storm of rifle and pistol fire from the deck of the *New Ironsides*, they guided the torpedo steamer back toward Charleston.

A *David* torpedo boat found after the capture of Charleston (courtesy of National Archives).

Meanwhile, Glassel had disappeared into the watery shroud, still swimming for his life. Later he described his adventure:

> ...[I] found myself all alone in the water. I hoped that with the assistance of flood-tide, I might be able to reach Fort Sumter, but a north wind was against me, and after I had been in the water more than an hour, I became numb with cold, and was nearly exhausted. Just then the boat of a transport schooner picked me up, and found, to their surprise, that they had captured a rebel.[8]

James Sullivan (alias Stuart), the fireman aboard the *Little David*, was also taken prisoner by Federal navy men. Together, he and Glassel were put in irons and transported to New York. However, they were never put on trial for their attack on the *New Ironsides*. Instead, they were confined in prison at Fort Lafayette and Fort Warren, where they remained for nearly one year. Near the end of 1864, they would be exchanged for an imprisoned Federal captain and a sailor, both of whom were taken from the steamer USS *Isaac Smith* when she was captured in January 1863.

Back in Charleston, news spread quickly of the successful attack on the USS *New Ironsides*. By the early morning of October 6, it became apparent, however, that the 3,486-ton Northern monitor was still afloat. Yet appearances were deceiving, for it was later discovered that damage was, indeed, extensive, though it might have been much worse. Although Glassel had accurately calculated the perfect depth for his torpedo to be slightly more than eight feet, a flaw in the *Little David*'s flexible spar had subtracted more than a foot from this estimation. Hence, purely by further mechanical failure, the explosive had detonated against a strong structural bulkhead precisely where it met the hull, and the reinforced wall had absorbed the brunt of the shock.

Believing the USS *New Ironsides* to be in sound condition, the Federal commander ordered her to remain anchored in Charleston Harbor. However, nearly six weeks after the attack, Captain Rowan had the opportunity to examine his vessel more closely, since the coal was at an extremely low level in her bunker. He recommended to Admiral Dahlgren that she be given a thorough going over. In his own opinion, she was "very seriously injured, and ought to be sent home for repairs as soon as 'tis possible to spare her services."[9]

Eventually, the USS *New Ironsides* was towed to Port Royal, South Carolina, and, from there, was taken to her home port of Philadelphia. Engineers discovered that her hull plating and support beams had been drastically weakened by the blast, and that a huge deck beam had been completely driven "on end." The damage report, however, was kept totally secret from the Confederate government, in order that they might mistakenly continue to believe that the attack had been a failure. The once mighty monitor was destined to remain inactive for more than a year.

During the early weeks of January 1864, with Glassel a prisoner of war, command of the *Little David* was handed over to James H. Toombs. The following month, General Beauregard asked Flag Officer John Randolph Tucker his opinion as to whether or not the torpedo steamer could be used in the narrow waters of the Stono River. Evidently Beauregard hoped to attack the gunboats USS *Marblehead* and USS *Pawnee*, which had recently been sweeping up and down the waterway firing on Confederate batteries. It was decided not to take the risk, however, for two very good reasons: (1) there was a very real possibility that the *Little David* might run across one of the many Confederate torpedoes placed there; and (2) there was no trained pilot available who was familiar enough with the Stono's numerous mudbanks.

Instead, the *Little David* went through a face-lift, as quarter-inch steel was installed on her above-water decking in order to ward off any small arms fire. Furthermore, because her spar was found to be faulty, a new one was fitted, to be controlled from the pilot house. Finally, a thick shield was shaped to fit over her extending smokestack, in order to make more than certain that water would never again funnel down inside of her and put out her all-important fire.

On the night of March 4, 1864, the CSS *Little David* was once again called into action. Steaming slowly down the North Edisto River, she set her sights on the USS *Memphis* as her intended target. With Toombs at the helm, and J. Walker Cannon once again acting as pilot, she quietly approached the unsuspecting victim, getting close enough for her crew to spot the steamer's faint lights.

Without warning, however, the *Little David*'s pumps failed, and the bewildered crew was forced to limp back into port at Church Flats. The following night, at approximately the same time and place, the craft's pumps failed again. But this time the determined crew managed to repair them, and they continued on their mission.

The deck officer on duty aboard the USS *Memphis* spotted a low-floating form moving briskly through the water toward his ship, but when he hailed no one responded. Almost immediately, Federal navy men opened fire upon the mysterious object. The small arms fire bounced harmlessly off the *Little David*'s newly-fashioned armor, inflicting little damage, as she continued toward her target.

Moments later the *Little David* struck the USS *Memphis* on the port side with her submerged torpedo, about eight feet below the surface. Although it seemed to be a near-perfect strike, the explosive failed to detonate. By this time, the *Memphis* had gotten up enough steam to get under way. Acting instinctively, Toombs managed to turn the *Little David* sharply and strike the intended victim a second time, but again nothing happened. Just a few moments later, as she passed beneath the counter of the *Memphis*, a large piece of the *Little David*'s smokestack was sliced away. Leaving the Confederate torpedo ram severely damaged, the USS *Memphis* escaped into the night.

When the ailing *Little David* finally found her way back to Church Flats, the failed torpedo was closely inspected. It was discovered that the glass tube holding the acid had, indeed, shattered, but it was defective and had not managed to charge the 95 pounds of gunpowder packed into the warhead. Miserably, the crew realized that they had had a unique opportunity to blow a huge gash in the hull of the USS *Memphis*, which, more than likely, would have sent her plummeting to the bottom of the river.

The *Little David* was escorted back to home port in Charleston, where her smokestack was repaired and a new torpedo was fitted to the end of her spar. A few weeks later, she made her way out into the harbor's mouth once again, this time on a direct collision course with the USS *Wabash*. When she was less than 150 yards away, however, the tiny Confederate vessel was spotted.

Three times the *Little David*'s crew took aim to ram their target, and three times heavy swells rolled over her deck. Reluctantly, the crew was forced to return to port. Had Toombs and company been successful on this occasion, they would have earned the $100,000 reward being offered by John Frazer & Company for the *Wabash*'s destruction.

Though the Confederate steamer had failed on her last two outings, Federal officials were very much aware of the threat she posed to their blockaders. Admiral John Dahlgren, speaking on the subject of the attack of the *New Ironsides*, claimed, "It seems to me that nothing could have been more successful as a first effort, and it will place the torpedo among certain offensive means."[10]

Furthermore, Dahlgren believed that the "secrecy, rapidity of movement, control of direction, and precise explosion" made the *Little David* an extremely effective weapon.

During the final week of January 1864, Theodore D. Stoney sent a letter to his chief of staff, explaining that the Southern Torpedo Company would have "two more steamers afloat tomorrow or next day."[11] On January 27, Lieutenant Colonel A. L. Rives contacted Captain Francis Lee, saying, "Inclosed [*sic*] I send you orders placing you in charge of the construction of torpedo-boats...."[12] Rives further stated that as soon as sketches were forwarded to him, he would place Lieutenant Colonel Victor von Sheliha in charge of the construction of these vessels in Mobile, Alabama.

Meanwhile, as time passed, the Northern government was gaining more and more respect for all Confederate torpedo ram vessels. In a letter from Admiral Dahlgren to Secretary of the Navy Gideon Welles, Dahlgren suggested that

> ...[we should pay] a large reward of prize money for the capture or destruction of a "David." I should say not less than $20,000 or $30,000 for each. They are worth more than that to us.[13]

In Mobile, work on similar vessels had been going on for quite some time. During the early months of 1863, a small torpedo ram was outfitted with a spar torpedo and christened the CSS *Gunnison*. Her 20-foot-long pole could easily be raised and lowered by a windlass, and the explosive itself was equipped with three sensitive fuses. As she cruised the waters of Mobile Bay, Federal officials quickly became aware of her menacing presence. Northern vessels anchored near Ship Island, just below the Mississippi coastline, were warned to be on the lookout for other *Davids*.

On November 9, 1863, Midshipman E. A. Swain was placed in command of the CSS *Gunnison*, and was instructed to "destroy, if possible, the USS *Colorado* or any other vessel of the blockading squadron...."[14] However, to the chagrin of Confederate officials, the opportunity never materialized.

Back in Charleston, on May 1, 1864, General Beauregard dispatched detailed instructions to Brigadier General Henry A. Wise, explaining that newly-constructed *Davids* were being shifted to his command:

> ...three army torpedo boats under the control of Mr. Theodore Stoney, [are] leaving this city tomorrow by inland navigation for operation against the enemy fleet in the waters of Port Royal.[15]

Evidently, two of these attack vessels had just recently been completed, with the third being the original *Little David*. However, the trio of torpedo rams never made it to their Port Royal destination, for they were forced to return to Charleston with engine problems.

Discouraged by their lack of success in reaching Port Royal, General Beauregard wrote a letter to General W. H. C. Whiting in Wilmington, North Carolina:

> The navy has the real [*Little*] *David* in its possession, but it seems to have exhausted itself in its attack on the *Ironsides*. It now keeps company with the gunboats.[16]

Although a lack of suitable machinery and iron plating greatly delayed the building phase, construction of similar vessels had commenced throughout much of the South. Two more were commissioned in Charleston; still others were under construction elsewhere in piecemeal fashion, with parts being assembled in both Savannah and Augusta. Exactly how many of these ever reached completion is difficult to ascertain, but apparently there were several dozen.

On February 16, 1865, just one day before Charleston was evacuated, Confederate President Jefferson Davis sent a wire to General Beauregard, inquiring "What's to be done with the torpedo-boats?"[17]

When Charleston did finally fall, Admiral Dahlgren wrote to Commodore George S. Black disclosing that

> ...a torpedo boat, being one of nine found here [Charleston], and of two that were raised by the squadron divers from the bed of the Cooper River, where they had been sunk just before we entered. It was such a boat as this that exploded a torpedo under the *New Ironsides*.[18]

Chapter 10

A Pioneer in Southern Waters

The initial attempt to construct a vessel which would be totally submerged beneath the surface occurred in New Orleans, Louisiana, a strategic port situated at the mouth of the Mississippi River. In this region, with its rich French tradition, privateering ventures quickly became prevalent. The possibility of a Confederate citizen sinking an enemy ship made the headlines in local newspapers; it was discussed in depth down on the wharfs; and it was the major interest aboard the extravagantly outfitted horsedrawn carriages which had recently been installed in the city.

Just a few days after President Jefferson Davis' proclamation explaining the South's willingness to grant letters of marque, a variety of periodicals began filling up with articles concerning privateering ventures. On April 22, 1861, the New Orleans *Daily Crescent* carried a story informing its readers that "...there are two large and fast sailing schooners fitting out at this city for the privateering business."[1] The article went on to explain that Walter H. Peters, a notary public whose office was located at 50 Camp Street, had in his possession blank applications for letters of marque. Soon the entire city seemed to be intrigued with the work being conducted down at the docks in Algiers, on the opposite side of the river.

A meeting of interested parties who might enter the business of outfitting privateer vessels was scheduled for May 18, 1861, at 12 noon. It was to be held in the former Circuit Courtroom above the New Merchant Exchange Building. Evidence indicates that two young men interested in constructing a Confederate underwater vessel were present, choosing to remain somewhat tight-lipped about their ideas. After all, who knew what spies might be listening, ready to steal the plans for their unique ship?

The designers were James R. McClintock and Baxter Watson, two experienced marine engineers who jointly owned a firm at 31 Front Levee. The company was currently engaged in the manufacture and sale of steam gauges, and the pair were local celebrities of sorts. Just weeks earlier, they had invented a machine that could produce the rapid pressing of minié balls, hollow-based conical bullets which expanded when they were fired. Such innovative weaponry would remain in great demand throughout the entire war.

McClintock and Watson engaged a local manufacturer, the Leeds Foundry, located on the corner of Delord and Fourcher streets, to construct the vessel. Leeds, which was owned and operated by the Confederate government, was already heavily involved in the Southern war effort casting field cannons for the army. Yet, despite the fact that they were behind in filling orders, they agreed to put the submersible design into physical form.

As the work began in the autumn of 1861, McClintock and Watson worked toward securing financial backing for their project. Contributors included Horace Lawson Hunley, H. J. Leovy, Robbin R. Barron, and John K. Scott. Aside from money, each also contributed ideas as to where and when they would begin testing their craft.

The McClintock and Watson submarine began to take shape during December of that year, as huge sheets of quarter-inch iron, intended for use in the construction of steam boilers, were bolted into place with five-eighths-inch rivets. The Leeds Foundry seemed to be working around the clock, as employees took the time to counter-sink each individual bolt head, making certain that the completed vessel would be as streamlined as possible.

Of course, Leeds could not devote all of its time and effort toward the creation of this "new-fangled" invention. The foundry was also involved in numerous other privateering projects, the most notable of which was the transfer of a pair of hefty steam engines from the CSS *Ingomar* into the hull of a newly-constructed ironclad, the CSS *Louisiana*.

By January of 1862, the one-of-a-kind underwater craft began to take on the characteristics of an oversized porpoise. She measured 19 feet in length (although her license would officially place it at 34 feet), six feet wide and four feet deep. Her sides, deck, and keel were all rounded off in near-perfect curves. Instead of possessing a superstructure and funnel like other vessels of the day, she had a compact, 18-inch round hatchway situated amidship, along the topmost portion of her curvature. This opening was reinforced with a three-eighths-inch by two-inch iron collar.

Jutting outward from the craft's stem were a pair of iron fins, each of which measured 35 inches long and 16 inches wide. These "flippers" were attached to a shaft which would be controlled from within. In theory, such an arrangement would be used to submerge at a moment's notice, enabling the crew to return to the surface whenever they so desired. For still further mobility, and to avoid any sideways swaying, she sported wooden rudders at either end.

Workmen at the Leeds Foundry quickly began to realize that the top-secret vessel would not be equipped with a pilot-house for directional observations. Instead, they drilled two groupings of eight three-quarter-inch holes arranged in one-foot circles which held glass-covered portholes. Her power did not originate from a coal-burning, steam-powered engine, either, as was the case with the CSS *Little David*. Rather, she was outfitted with a small propeller fastened to the extreme end of a shaft extending from the stern. This propeller would be hand-operated from inside, with the crew turning a large crank fashioned with hand grips.

The craft also housed a crude snorkeling device, designed to take in fresh air while she was relatively close to the surface. This "breather," fashioned from flexible rubber tubing, extended from a cuff five inches in diameter to the ocean's surface by incorporating a wooden float attached to one end. A stop-cock on the inside of the hose would ensure that sea water did not enter the vessel once she was fully submerged.

Other interior features included U-shaped brackets bolted to the floor section, which would serve as seats for the captain and his crew; candles, which would provide adequate light for the men whenever they were submerged; a hand-operated pump, situated next to the sea-cock, which would empty the ballast tanks when the crew wished to resurface; and a small directional compass, which would be the only piece of equipment attached to the instrument panel at the front of the vessel. Finally, and perhaps most important, located at the extreme nose of the craft, there was a two-inch-wide circular crevice, to which the torpedo spar would be attached.

The underwater craft was finally completed in early February 1862, and she was aptly dubbed the *Pioneer*. To her owners and designers, she was nothing less than sheer beauty; yet, to the men who had built her, she looked more like an "oversized cigar."

Only McClintock and Watson, along with the *Pioneer*'s four financiers, were present for her launching, which took place at the Government Navy Yard at New Basin. As she was slowly lowered into the water, the men congratulated one another for their accomplishment. Next, they prepared their hand-picked crew for a brief yet all-important test run. It was time to prove to themselves that she could, indeed, withstand the immense water pressure below the surface. John K. Scott took the helm, as three other crew members prepared themselves to operate the hand-cranked propeller. All went well on this, their first outing, and those involved decided to conduct more extensive tests in the weeks ahead.

A few days later, while out on one of several deep practice dives, Scott decided that the *Pioneer*'s compass was, for all intents and purposes, quite worthless. The needle was highly unsteady, wavering in all directions, and the crew had no idea at what reading they were headed at any given time. McClintock later reported that:

> At times [the compass] acted so slow, that the Boat would ... alter her course for one or two minutes, before it would be discovered, thus losing her direct course, and ... compel the opperator [sic] to come to the top of the water, more frequently then [sic] he would otherwise.[2]

In an attempt to solve the problem, other directional devices were installed and tested; but none operated satisfactorily. Finally, convinced that a solution did not exist, Scott decided that he would be forced to take a bearing prior to submerging, and then to resurface occasionally for a more accurate visual sighting. This method, however, would certainly have some effect on any future surprise attacks. Still, it was far better than becoming helplessly lost while out on a dangerous mission.

Over the course of the next several months, the *Pioneer* proved herself quite seaworthy, with only a few slight leaks which were easily sealed with tar and beeswax. It was her inability to remain underwater for a lengthy period of time that caused worry among the owners — due to her extremely limited air supply and a breathing apparatus that could only function near the surface. Furthermore, her faulty directional compass, coupled with a quickly exhausted crank-operating crew, made the craft's practicality seem even more suspect. Despite these problems, however, in March 1862 the *Pioneer* was prepared to submerge for a full-scale test attack on a predesignated anchored vessel.

The target would be an old wooden barge which sat idle in the middle of Lake Ponchartrain, just north of New Orleans. The submarine's weapon was a torpedo with extremely sensitive fuses, similar to the explosive designed by Francis D. Lee of Charleston.

As the owners and builders sat in anxious anticipation along the shoreline, the *Pioneer* cruised slowly at surface level toward her prey. The explosive which Captain Scott hoped would destroy the barge was being pulled along behind with a length of strong rope. Captain Scott took one final look through the vessel's porthole before ordering his crew to open the ballast tanks, and the *Pioneer* quickly vanished beneath the water. As tense moments went by, nothing happened, and the onlookers began to believe that they had somehow failed in their calculations.

Suddenly, without warning, the *Pioneer*'s torpedo came in contact with its target, setting off the deafening charge, and the barge was blown "so high that only a few splinters were heard from."[3]

Captain John K. Scott, who had now been officially selected to hold the proud post of Captain of the *Pioneer*, made formal application for a letter of marque in late March 1862.

To the Hon. Secretary of the Confederate States of America.
Sir:
   Application is hereby made for a commission of authority in the name of the Government of these States, to issue to the undersigned as commander of the submarine boat called the *Pioneer* for authority to cruise the high seas, bays, rivers, estuaries, etc., in the name of the Government, and aid said Government by the destruction or capture of any and all vessels opposed to or at war with said Confederate States, and to aid in repelling its enemies.
   Said vessel is commanded by John K. Scott, who is a citizen of New Orleans and of this Confederacy. Said vessel was built at New Orleans in the year 1862; is a propeller; is 34 feet in length; is 4 feet breadth; is 4 feet deep. She measures

about 4 tons; has rounded conical ends and is painted black. She is owned by Robert R. Barrow, Baxter Watson, and James R. McClintock, all of this city of New Orleans. She will carry a magazine of explosive matter, and will be manned by two men or more.

And I hereby promise to be vigilant and zealous in employing said vessel for the purpose aforesaid and abide by all laws and instructions and at all times acknowledge the authority of the Government of said States and its lawful agent and officers.

Considering his bond the undersigned prays for the issuance of a commission or letter of marque.

(signed) John K. Scott[4]

The official letter of marque was granted by the Confederate government on the financial security of Horace Lawson Hunley and H. J. Leovy on March 31, 1862, legally making the *Pioneer* submarine a privateering vessel. In the license, the amount of bond was listed at $5,000, and the number of her crew was set at three. The actual commission read:

Confederate States of America
    State of Louisiana,
    City of New Orleans.

Be it remembered that on this 29th day of the month of March in the year 1862, before me, Walter Hicks Peters, notary public, in and for this city and parish duly commissioned and qualified:

Personally came and appeared the above-named John K. Scott, applicant for the issuance of a letter of marque or commission to him as commander or captain of the vessel called the *Pioneer*, which appearer being known to me, and being by me duly sworn, says that he has accurately described the said vessel, her armament, number of crew, and the object and purpose in which said vessel is to be engaged, and that he will support the laws and constitution of said Confederate States, and obey all lawful commands of said Government and its officers.

So help me God.

(signed) John K. Scott

Sworn to me and subscribed to before me this 29th March, A.D., 1862.
                            (signed) Walter Hicks Peters.[5]

The construction of the *Pioneer* proved undoubtedly that not all privateersmen were motivated by the right to secure cargo for profit from defenseless merchant ships. Not only was she incapable of taking on merchandise of any sort, but she would only be able to cruise through harbor and coastal areas — she would never be equipped to travel far out to sea.

Still, one important question remained: would the *Pioneer* be capable of destroying a Union warship during the heat of battle? Only time could tell.

While the *Pioneer* underwent further extensive experimental testing, the Federal navy, under the command of Admiral David G. Farragut, was preparing to invade New Orleans. During the winter and spring of 1861–1862, the North had assembled the strongest naval fleet that had ever been brought together under the Stars and Stripes. It consisted of a total of 46 vessels, transporting 348 guns and 21 mortars, and they were ready to begin their heavy assault on April 16, 1862.

At that time, the shore defenses of New Orleans consisted of only two forts, situated almost opposite of one another at the first 90-degree bend of the Mississippi River. They were 25 miles north of the waterway's gaping mouth, with the aging French settlement lying nearly 75 miles farther upstream.

One of these defense installations, known as Fort Jackson, had been constructed in the shape of a star and was nestled almost 100 yards off the levee. Its inadequate defenses consisted of 42 heavy guns in babette and 24 in casemates. Fort Jackson's sister installation, Fort St. John, stood on the opposite side of the Mississippi, nearly one-half-mile to the north. Though it covered a wider geographic area, it housed only 52 guns total. Jointly, the two forts had about 1,400 men at their disposal. To back them up in an emergency, the Confederate naval force at New Orleans consisted of just 13 vessels, armed with a total of 40 guns.

The sister forts also had a battery of auxiliary defenses which could assist them. Aside from the 13 warships at New Orleans, they depended heavily on a floating barrier of logs and other obstructive materials, which had been interconnected across the channel with powerful iron chains. This obstacle course was situated one-half-mile below Fort Jackson, and was intended to damage and, ultimately, detour any approaching enemy vessels.

Admiral Farragut had no ironclad vessels under his command as he prepared for the invasion of New Orleans. He had always claimed, from the very early planning stages of the assault, that a fleet of wooden ships, if properly commanded, would be able to pass the two forts and their accompanying river jam successfully: "I would as soon have a paper ship as an ironclad; only give me men to fight...."[6]

Despite the apparent lack of adequate Confederate defense, New Orleans was vitally important to both sides during the war. It was said by more than one expert that whoever controlled her also controlled the Mississippi River. And as the spring weather began to roll across the Gulf of Mexico, townspeople residing along Grange, Race, and Constance streets looked on as local men in uniforms practiced their drills. They understood that a Northern invasion was inevitable.

Very few businesses throughout the region, other than shipbuilding firms, were still in peacetime operation. Factories had turned their attention to the sport of war, with the spoils of enemy vessels making it well worth their time and effort. The majority of sea-going tow boats had been covered with tarpaulin, and were crowded together near Slaughterhouse Point, silently crumbling away against the incessant tide. Still, some of the larger vessels had been moved to the lengthy wharf once controlled by the now-defunct Morgan's Texas Steamship Company. There they were undergoing massive transformations, being turned into strong ironclad blockade-runners. In essence, only the foundries, dry docks, and shipbuilding establishments were actively employing able-bodied men.

Recently, the city had been placed under martial law, yet not much had changed in preparation for the inevitable invasion. The school children were no longer singing "The Star Spangled Banner"; instead, it was "Dixie" and "The Bonnie Blue Flag." Yet basic education remained the same. One frightening fact that the students had learned, however, was, perhaps, the most important lesson of all: war was coming soon.

By mid–April, Admiral Farragut had managed to move 17 warships boasting a total of 177 guns into the lower Mississippi. To back him up he had Commander David D. Porter, who had been placed in charge of a mortar flotilla consisting of half-dozen armed steamers and 19 schooners. Furthermore, on land, New Orleans would be simultaneously invaded by the forces of General Benjamin P. Butler, who commanded an army of 6,000 men. The stage was now most definitely set.

Before proceeding, Admiral Farragut offered final instructions to the men in his squadron:

> ...I wish you to understand that the day is at hand when you will be called upon to meet the enemy in the worst form for our profession. You must be prepared to execute all those duties to which you have been so long trained.... I expect every vessel's crew to be well exercised at their guns ... but they must be equally well trained for stopping shot holes and extinguishing fire. Hot and cold shot will, no doubt, be freely dealt to us, and there must be stout hearts and quick hands to extinguish the one and stop the holes of the other....[7]

Porter's flotilla of 19 vessels carried two mortars apiece. Anchored just below the Confederate forts for several days of preparation, they began their assault on April 16, 1862, and maintained a heavy bombardment for five straight days. This in turn paved the way for a full-scale attack by Farragut's fleet, which began on April 20. It was on that particular night that a pair of the admiral's gunboats managed to slice their way up the river, cutting a thin pathway through the debris for advancement by the remainder of the fleet.

Then, on the morning of April 24, Admiral Farragut gave the command, and the first division of ships moved forward. Eight vessels, led by Captain Theodorus Bailey, succeeded in skirting the weakened forts. Next came the second wave of ships, but these nine vessels were not as fortunate: three of them did not make it. The others, however, commanded by Farragut himself, continued to advance.

After stopping briefly to estimate casualties at the city of Quarantine, located six miles north of the forts, the Federal fleet pushed forward, covering the remaining 70 miles in less than 24 hours. And by midday of April 25, New Orleans was helpless under the guns of the Union ships.

It is quite clear that the *Pioneer*'s owners decided not to do battle against Farragut and his mighty flotilla. Understandably, the prototype submarine was purposely sunk just a day before the fall of New Orleans. And as the Union forces humbled the Confederate forts and naval fleet, capturing the city, Admiral Farragut never realized how close he had come to an underwater torpedo attack.

Numerous local stories concerning the sinking of the *Pioneer* were told in the weeks and months that followed. Few, if any, were accurate enough to accept as fact, with one such tale, as retold by writer Simon Lake, seeming to be the most unlikely:

> ...it appears that this submarine was the conception of a wealthy planter who owned a number of slaves. He thought that it would add considerable interest to the occasion of her launching if, when the vessel left the ways, she would disappear beneath the waves and make a short run beneath the surface before coming up. So he took two of his most intelligent slaves and instructed them how to hold the tiller when the vessel slid down the ways, and in which way to turn the propeller for a time after she began to lose her launched speed. He told them when they got ready to come up they should push the tiller down and the vessel would come to the surface to be towed ashore.
>
> A great crowd assembled to see this novel launching.... Well, it seems that the boat slid down the ways and disappeared under the water just as had been planned. The crowd awaited expectantly, but the vessel did not reappear. Eventually they got into boats and put out grappling lines, but she could not be found. The designer of the craft stated that ... he was willing to bet that they [the two slaves] had taken the opportunity to steal the vessel and run away. He asserted that very likely they would take the boat up North and give it to the Yankees, and that they could expect to hear of the "Yanks" using it to blow up some of their [Confederates'] own ships....[8]

It was a mistake to believe that the builders and investors of the *Pioneer*, with so much money, time, and interest at stake, would allow anyone but those directly involved in the craft's construction to take her down for a test run. In fact, only men well-trained in such maneuvers would have been trusted.

To gain a truthful portrait of what transpired leading to the demise of the *Pioneer*, we must piece the entire puzzle together from fragmented historical sources. In a letter written by James R. McClintock to Matthew Fontaine Maury during the early 1870s, the designer of the *Pioneer* speaks of events surrounding her sinking. McClintock explained:

> ...[the Pioneer] demonstrated to us the fact that we could construct a Boat, that would move at will in any direction desired, and at any distance from the surface. The evacuation of New Orleans lost this Boat before our experiments were completed.[9]

Since McClintock wrote nothing of an attack on a Federal vessel, it can be assumed that the *Pioneer* was not yet ready for battle. Such an explanation is further reinforced by W. A. Alexander, who would later assist in the construction of a second submarine model:

> Shortly before the capture of New Orleans by the United States troops, Captain Hunley, Captain James R. McClintock and Baxter Watson were engaged in building a submarine torpedo-boat in the New Basin of that city. The city falling into the hands of the Federals before it was completed, the boat was sunk, and these gentlemen came to Mobile....[10]

The *Pioneer*, which would prove to be the forerunner of the first successful underwater attack vessel, showed herself to be quite seaworthy. Much later, in 1879, she was accidentally recovered by the crew of a channel dredge. Her historical significance unrecognized, the craft was deposited along the banks of the Mississippi, to corrode in the mud and weeds for the next 30 years.

During an attempt to make further renovations along the channel, she was eventually rescued by the Beauregard Camp of the United Sons of the Confederate Veterans. And on April 10, 1909, the 53-year-old submarine was mounted on a cement base at Camp Nicholls, on the bank of the Bayou Teche. She would later be relocated to Jackson Square, just outside the Louisiana State Museum.

The *Pioneer* was, indeed, way ahead of her time. And, though she failed to accomplish what she had originally been designed to do, her promoters continued their experiments. With the fall of New Orleans, they transferred their designs and hopes to the nearby city of Mobile, Alabama.

Chapter 11

The *H. L. Hunley* Submarine

As assaults on Federal vessels continued during the latter portion of 1863, Confederate navy men had only mild success at destroying enemy ships. By and large, this was not due to Southern incompetence, but rather to the Federal navy's reluctance to venture into regions thought to be mined with deadly explosives. The USS *John Farron*, a 250-ton army transport, was seriously damaged by an electrically-charged torpedo in late September 1863, but the isolated incident only briefly renewed the hopes of Confederates attempting to break up the blockading Union fleet.

During the fall of that same year, the Northern flotilla pressed onward in their search-and-destroy tactics along most Southern river and harbor regions. Soon after the *John Farron* attack, a series of mines were discovered in the James River. They were described as:

> Tin cylinders in wooden cases, with long tin chimneys extending above the water and fitted for ventilation. In this chimney is a piece of slow match, extending down to the magazine. These torpedoes contain from 50 to 100 pounds of powder and are evidently extended to float down the stream. Tin cylinders of the same size as above, to be exploded by means of a friction primer pulled from the shore or by a vessel's wheels or propeller getting foul of the lanyard. These torpedoes have a board float and are suspended some 6 or 8 feet below the surface. Cylindrical tanks with conical ends, [they are] made of half-inch boiler iron and securely riveted. These are anchored at the bottom in the deepest water (7 and 8 fathoms), and each has two insulated copper wires running from the center of the torpedo through a composition plug screwed into one end and connecting with a galvanic battery on shore, by means of which they are exploded....
> ...[These] torpedoes are constructed with great ingenuity and scientific skill, and when taken from the water were in as good a state of preservation as when first put down....[1]

Further south, in Mobile, Alabama, a much different strategy was being pursued by the men who had designed and built the *Pioneer*. Though their prototype submarine had, in fact, been scuttled near New Orleans, they were quite determined to continue their highly-secretive endeavors. It seems, however, that they had competition in building such an innovative submersible vessel.

One Spanish inventor named Narciso Monturiol had even completed work on his underwater craft, which he aptly dubbed *Ictineo* (meaning fish-like vessel). In a letter sent from Monterey on April 9, 1863, to J. P. Benjamin, an official of the Confederate States government, the *Ictineo* was described as being

> ...a man-of-war ... [which] can prevent not only the bombardment of the ports, but also the landing of the enemy. If ... the necessary number of vessels [are] built, no Federal squadron would dare to approach our coasts, since an unseen enemy can leave our harbors and destroy their ships. The "Ictineos" have guns which fire under water and also rams and torpedoes. They can navigate in a depth of about twenty-five fathoms.
>
> The want of atmosphere to support animal life in the depth of the seas, which has been the great drawback to submarine navigation, has been obviated. The inventor creates an artificial atmosphere and shutting himself up, like a larva, carries with him the elements of existence.[2]

Though the correspondence did, indeed, reach its intended destination, nothing more is known of the *Ictineo*'s eventual fate.

Though the loss of their initial craft had been discouraging, the designers of the *Pioneer* contacted local Mobile machine shops, inquiring as to whether or not they might be interested in constructing a second model. Thomas Parks and Thomas B. Lyons, owners of a foundry engaged in the manufacture of artillery engines, along with a variety of other machinery for the Confederate States government, willingly accepted the offer. Initially, the craft's keel was laid out in a small building on Water Street, and then she was moved to the Parks & Lyons Foundry for completion.

Here an expert British-born machinist named William A. Alexander, who had come to the United States in 1859, was hired to oversee the entire project. Recently, Alexander had been an active member of the Twenty-first Alabama Regiment, and had fought under the command of Captain Charles Gage.

The newer submarine was a bit larger than her predecessor, and she possessed numerous sophisticated devices. Constructed of boiler iron, her ends were longer than those of the *Pioneer*, and she was more streamlined. A single rudder was positioned aft, and two pairs of fins located at the bow would control her ability to dive and resurface.

Since manpower had proven to be an inadequate source of propulsion, James R. McClintock, Baxter Watson, and Horace Lawson Hunley searched for an alternative source. Eventually, the inventors turned toward a revolutionary concept — the use of electricity for power. Though the mode was not widely employed aboard water-bound vehicles of the times, it would meet with great approval in future generations of sea-going ships.

Several weeks were spent in an attempt to design an electro-magnetic engine, but with the limited resources available, the venture failed. Subsequently, the builders were forced to return to their original mode of power, and an ample amount of room was made ready for a hearty crew of crankers. In addition, two hatchways were installed, fitted with glass viewports for improved vision and lighting, along with a crude mercury gauge to be used for depth-perception.

Although the *Pioneer II* was somewhat successful on trial runs, the inventors were still forced to deal with a number of shortcomings. The speed of the improved version remained turtle-like; the crew felt cramped in its belly; and the air supply was depleted after only a brief period of being submerged. After a number of trial runs in the harbor area surrounding Mobile, with the men becoming increasingly dissatisfied, the vessel was outfitted with a torpedo and made ready for her initial assault:

> The cross section was oblong, about 25 feet long, tapering at each end, 5 feet wide, and 6 feet deep. It was towed off Fort Morgan, intending to man it there and attack the blockading fleet outside, but the weather was rough, and with a heavy sea the boat became unmanageable....[3]

As huge, choppy waves broke over her deck, water gushed into the *Pioneer II*'s hatchways, which had been left open for ventilation purposes. Her owners tried frantically to empty her, but the swells were too high and the vessel slowly settled deeper and deeper. Eventually, she filled up with water, rolled over, and sank to the bottom of the bay.

Though "there was much time and money lost," McClintock, Watson, and Hunley did not give up. Instead, they took "more pains with the model, and the machinery," and even sold part interest in yet a third vessel, hoping to more adequately finance it. Within weeks, the relentless trio had managed to raise a total of $15,000 for the project. William A. Alexander described the latest vessel in detail:

> We ... took a cylinder boiler which we had on hand, 48 inches in diameter and 25 feet long.... We cut this boiler in two, longitudinally, and inserted two 12-inch boiler iron strips in her sides; lengthened her by one tapering course for and aft, to which were attached bow and stern castings, making the boat about 30 feet long, 4 feet wide, and 5 feet deep. A longitudinal strip 12 inches wide was riveted the full length on top. At each end a bulk-head was riveted across to form water-ballast tanks ... they were used in raising and sinking the boat. In addition to these ... the boat was ballasted by flat castings, made to fit the outside bottom of the shell and fastened thereto by "Tee" headed bolts passing through stuffing boxes inside the boat, the inside end of [each] bolt squared to fit a wrench, that the bolts might be turned and the ballast dropped, should the necessity arise.
>
> In connection with each of the water tanks there was a sea-cock open to the sea to supply the tank for sinking; also a force pump to eject the water from the tanks in the sea for raising the boat to the surface. There was also a bilge connection to the pump. A mercury gauge, open to the sea, was attached to the shell near the forward tank, to indicate the depth of the boat below the surface. A one and a quarter [inch] shaft passed through the stuffing boxes on each side of the boat, just forward of the end of the propeller shaft. On each end of this shaft,

outside the boat ... fins, five feet long and eight inches wide, were secured. This shaft was operated by a lever amidships, and by raising or lowering the ends of these fins, operated as the fins of a fish, changing the depth of the boat below the surface at will, without disturbing the water level in the ballast tanks.

The rudder was operated by a wheel, and levers connected to rods passing through stuffing boxes in the stern castings, and operated by the captain or pilot forward. An adjusted compass was placed in front of the forward tank. The boat was operated by manual power, with an ordinary propeller. On the propeller shaft there were forward eight cranks at different angles ... the men sitting on the port side turning on the cranks. The propeller shaft and cranks took up so much room that it was very difficult to pass fore and aft, and when the men were in their places this was next to impossible. In operation, one half of the crew had to pass through the fore hatch, the other through the after hatchway. The propeller revolved in a wrought iron ring or band, to guard against a line being thrown in to foul it ... [The] two hatchways ... [were] 16 inches by 12, with a combing [sic] 8 inches high. These hatches had hinged covers with rubber gaskets, and were bolted from the inside. In the sides and ends of these combings [sic] glasses were inserted to sight from. There was an opening made in the top of the boat for an air box, a casting with a close top 12 by 18 by 4 inches, made to carry a hollow shaft ... on the outside was a lever with a stopcock to admit air.[4]

The type of explosive chosen was a cylinder made of copper which housed approximately 90 pounds of gunpowder. In theory, it would be floated upon the surface, with its percussion and friction primer mechanism prepared to be set off by lengthy, flair triggers when rammed against the hull of an enemy vessel. This deadly torpedo was attached to the submarine at the end of a 200-foot rope, being dragged in her wake.

Experiments were conducted on several old flatboats anchored in the Mobile River, and the "dragging" concept worked well. Each successive attempt created an atmosphere of increased security for the crew, as they gradually began to feel comfortable during such operations.

However, when they transferred their tests from the relatively calm waters of the river to those of Mobile Bay, which was far more unsettled, near catastrophe struck. On one test run the winds seemed to be pushing the torpedo along the surface at a much quicker pace than the crankturners could power their craft. Finally, fearing that the explosive would strike the submarine, the captain cut the line and allowed the torpedo to float away. Obviously, an alternative to the "dragging" method was needed.

Horace L. Hunley, who seems to have taken charge of the submarine's operations at about this time, suggested that a spar be attached to the front of the boat: "We then rigged a yellow-pine boom, 22 feet long and tapering; this was attached to the bow, banded and guyed on each side. A socket on the torpedo secured it to the boom."[5]

Thus, instead of passing totally beneath the target ship, the submarine would now only need to submerge a few feet and ram its victim. When this new approach was tested, crew members noticed a slight jolt from the explosion, but the submarine seemed to survive in one piece.

Two men were trained to handle the command post, along with a total of seven crew members. The first officer was placed in charge of directing the assault from the forward section, while the second attended to the after-tank, pumps, and air supply. With all other available hands operating the cranks, the two commanders would be able to "stand in their places with their hands in the hatchways and take observations through the lights of the combings [sic]."[6] Soon, with a good deal of practice, operating the vessel became almost routine:

> All hands aboard and ready, they would fasten the hatch covers down tight, light a candle, then let the water in from the sea into the ballast tanks until the top of the shell was about three inches under water. This could be seen by the water lever showing through the glasses in the hatch combings [sic]. The sea cocks were then closed and the boat put under way. The captain would then lower the lever and depress the forward end of the fins very slightly, noting on the mercury gauge the depth of the boat beneath the surface; then bring the fins to a level; the boat would remain and travel at that depth. To rise to a higher level in the water he would raise the lever and elevate the forward end of the fins, and the boat would rise to its original position in the water.
>
> If the boat was not under way, in order to rise to the surface, it was necessary to start the pumps, and lighten the boat by ejecting the water from the tanks onto the sea. In making a landing, the second officer would open his hatch cover, climb out and pass a line to the shore....[7]

General P. G. T. Beauregard, still quite intent on breaking up the Federal blockading squadron in Charleston Harbor, had the craft sent from Mobile. Now known as the "Whitney Submarine Boat," after one of her investors, B. A. Whitney, the submersible was shipped by flatcars to South Carolina in early August of 1863. In the event that she was successful in destroying the USS *New Ironsides* or the USS *Wabash*, then threatening the Charleston region, the co-owners would receive a $100,000 reward being offered by John Frazer & Company; any other Federal monitor would be worth half that amount. Brigadier General Thomas Jordan, chief of staff, outlined other compensations in case of failure:

> Steps are being taken to secure a large sum to be settled for the support of the families of parties, who ... shall fail in the enterprise, and fall or be captured in the attempt.[8]

Apparently, naval officials in and around the Charleston area soon became disgruntled with the Whitney submarine. On August 23, 1863, within a few short weeks of her arrival, Brigadier General Thomas L. Clingman sent a letter to Captain William F. Nance, describing his disappointment:

> The Torpedo-boat started out at sunset, but returned, as they [the crew] state, because of an accident. Whitney says that though McClintock is timid, yet it shall go tonight unless the weather is bad.[9]

With McClintock now at the helm, the situation quickly went from bad to worse. On August 30, Theodore A. Honour wrote from Legare Point on James Island:

> You doubtless remember and perhaps you saw while in the City the iron torpedo boat which certain parties brought from Mobile to blow up the *Ironsides*. They have been out three times without accomplishing anything, and the government suspecting something wrong, proposed to them to allow a Naval Officer to go with them on their next trial, which they refused. The boat was therefore seized and yesterday nine men from one of the gunboats were placed in her to learn how to work her and go out and see what they could do....[10]

This newly-implemented crew included Lieutenant John Payne, along with eight others, who had been more than willing to volunteer their services. Just a single day after taking charge of the submarine, on August 30, disaster struck. After overseeing the lowering of the craft from the dock, the crew was ordered to commence their attack on the USS *New Ironsides*. Following one or two practice dives earlier in the day, the submarine was moved to a more strategic wharf located at old Fort Johnson, on the southern end of the bay. As it prepared to go into actual combat action, the steamer CSS *Etiwan* was ready to shove off.

Lieutenant Payne, along with six of his volunteer crewmen, climbed aboard the Whitney submarine. Suddenly, without warning, the *Etiwan* began to move swiftly away from the dock. The steamer's ropes fell into the water and became entangled with the submarine, whose hatches were still open. Almost immediately, the submersible was capsized, and her limited buoyancy was weighted down by the torrent of the sea water that gushed inside.

Acting instinctively, Lieutenant Payne ordered his crew to abandon ship, and he dove overboard. But it was too late: five of his crewmen were sent to the bottom with the submarine, unable to escape. The Charleston *Daily Courier* printed an account of the mishap:

> UNFORTUNATE ACCIDENT, on Saturday last, while Lieutenant(s) Payne and Hasker, of the Confederate Navy, were experimenting with a boat in the harbor, she parted from her moorings and became suddenly submerged, carrying down with her five seamen, who were drowned. The boat and bodies had not been recovered up to a late hour on Sunday. Four of the men belonged to the gunboat *Chicora*, and were ... Frank Doyle, John Kelly, Michael Cane, and Nicholas Davis. The fifth man, whose name we did not learn, was attached to the *Palmetto State*.[11]

It is quite apparent from the article that no accurate details were given to the press concerning the type of ship involved in the accident.

One of the fortunate survivors, Lieutenant Charles H. Hasker, came close to being the sixth victim of the sinking. As the submarine began its downward descent, he was momentarily trapped inside with the others. He fought hard against the geyser of water pouring in through the open hatchway.

Instinctively, he crawled over the bars that controlled the diving fins and inched his way toward the opening. Just as he began to climb through, the heavy iron hatchway came down heavily on his back. Using all of his strength, he forced it open once again, only to be caught by his leg when it swung shut a second time. Hooked, he was carried to the very bottom, struggling beneath 24 feet of sea water.

As soon as the fallen vessel had settled, however, water pressure suddenly became equalized, and he was able to pull himself free. With the bones in his leg painfully shattered, he managed to swim to the surface, and was quickly pulled safely onto the dock. He reported: "I was the only man that went to the bottom with the 'Fishboat' and came up to tell the tale."[12]

Within two weeks' time the submarine had been raised, dried out, and repaired. Horace Lawson Hunley, who had put up most of the money to build her, traveled from Mobile to Charleston to offer his expert assistance. On September 19, 1863, he contacted General Beauregard, suggesting that a crew from Mobile be placed in charge of the submarine. As he saw it, they would be "well acquainted with the management and make the attempt to destroy a vessel of the enemy as early as practicable." Beauregard agreed:

> Captain Hunley and Thomas Parks (one of the best of men), of the firm of Parks & Lyons, in whose shop the boat had been built, were in charge, with Messrs. Brockbank, Patterson, McHugh, Marshall, White, Beard, and another [Sprague], as the crew....[13]

The submarine, now referred to in local Charleston circles as the "H. L. Hunley torpedo-boat," became quite a common sight in both the Ashley and Cooper rivers. Often in command, Captain George E. Dixon would take the craft down for as long as a half hour at a time, but he hesitated to keep her submerged much longer. On October 15, 1863, the weather was relatively calm, and Dixon was dispatched from Charleston on another assignment. In his absence, Captain Hunley assumed command, and ordered the crew to assemble for a practice dive. As usual, he planned to conduct a mock-attack upon the CSS *Indian Chief*, anchored in the inner harbor.

Everything went as planned, as the well-trained crew made their way toward the Confederate vessel. Approximately 300 yards distant from the CSS *Indian Chief*, Captain Hunley ordered the hatches closed. Before submerging, he took one final sighting of his target, checked his compass, and opened the ballast valve.

Apparently, however, he opened the valve too abruptly, for the submarine plummeted like a rock, angling into the sea bottom sharply and sending the crew members tumbling. Quickly, the forward ballast filled with water, eventually spilling over into the cabin. As the water began to rise around his men, Hunley grasped the handle of the pump and worked it frantically until he was nearly exhausted. In desperation, he then ordered the crew to release the heavy iron ballast bars affixed beneath the ship's keel. But before this could be done they found themselves almost totally submerged in water.

As a last-ditch effort, both Hunley and Parks unscrewed the bolts holding the hatches and pushed on them with all of their might. Unfortunately, however, the weight of the water above them held the hatchways firmly in check, and the men realized that they were hopelessly trapped in their iron coffin.

Up above, aboard the CSS *Indian Chief*, the crew members were becoming increasingly worried. As the minutes rushed by, they saw clusters of bubbles rising to the surface, but no submarine. Finally, at approximately noon, they were forced to accept the awful truth: another crew had perished aboard the ill-fated H. L. *Hunley* torpedo-boat. A few days later, the following disclosure appeared in a local journal:

> October 15, 1863 — an unfortunate accident occurred this morning with the submarine boat, by which, Capt. H. L. Hunley and 7 men lost their lives, in an attempt to run under the Navy receiving ship. The boat left the wharf at 9:25 A.M. and disappeared at 9:35. As soon as she sunk, air bubbles were seen to rise to the surface of the water, and from this fact it is supposed the hole in the top of the boat by which the men entered was not properly closed. It was impossible at the time to make any effort to rescue the unfortunate men, as the water was some nine fathoms deep....[14]

Everyone involved with the submarine project was deeply interested in discovering precisely what had gone wrong aboard the H. L. *Hunley*. William A. Alexander, one of the builders who had stayed behind in Mobile, came to Charleston to head the investigation. With the help of Lieutenant Dixon, the boat was found resting on the bottom with her bow buried deep in the mud. Engineers dispatched a salvage crew to the area, and just nine days after she had gone down, the craft was brought onto dry land.

Tensely, Alexander, Dixon, Beauregard, and the others crowded around the compact iron hull, as her hatchways were opened. As the lids were lifted away from the vessel, fetid gas escaped. Just below the forward cover, they discovered the body of Horace Lawson Hunley, with his face depicting an expression of "despair and agony." His right hand was extended up over his head, obviously pressing up against the immovable hatchway cover. In his left hand he gripped an unlighted candle.

At the opposite end of the submarine, the investigators discovered the body of Thomas Parks; below, the bodies of the rest of the crew were "tightly grappled together." Examinations indicated that Hunley and Parks had both succumbed to suffocation, while the others had drowned. Later, Alexander offered a graphic account of what had most likely occurred during those agonizing final moments:

Captain Hunley's practice with the boat had made him quite familiar and expert in handling her, and this familiarity produced at this time forgetfulness. It was found in practice to be easier on the crew to come to the surface by giving the pumps a few strokes and ejecting some of the water ballast, than by the momentum of the boat operating on the elevated fins. At this time the boat was under way, lighted through the dead-lights in the hatch-ways. He [Hunley] partly turned the fins to go down, but thought, no doubt, that he needed more ballast and opened his sea cock. Immediately the boat was in total darkness. He then undertook to light the candle. While trying to do this the tank quickly flooded, and under great pressure the boat sank very fast and soon overflowed, and the first intimation they would have of anything being wrong was the water rising fast, but noiselessly, about their feet in the bottom of the boat. They tried to release the iron keel ballast, but did not turn the keys quite far enough, therefore failed. The water soon forced the air to the top of the boat and into the hatch-ways, where Captains Hunley and Parks were found. Parks had pumped his ballast tank dry, and no doubt Captain Hunley had exhausted himself on his pump, but he had forgotten that he had not closed his sea-cock.[15]

Engineers worked to refit and dry out the submarine once again, making her ready for active service. Soon, Alexander reported to General Thomas Jordan that the boat was ready to conduct further dives, and he requested an able-bodied crew to man her. However, after so many accidents, General Beauregard questioned whether or not the submarine was too dangerous for such a mission, and he adamantly refused to give his approval. Finally, though only after a good deal of persuasion, the general relented. Thus, Alexander and Dixon were allowed to recruit volunteers from the Confederate navy's receiving ship, CSS *Indian Chief.*

Following a thorough briefing concerning the hazardous nature of the service solicited, and after offering a complete history of the seemingly ill-fated craft, an ample crew was secured. The *H. L. Hunley* was then taken to a new mooring site just off Battery Marshall, on Sullivan's Island, and the new volunteers were instructed to carry out extensive training maneuvers from their base camp at Mount Pleasant:

In comparatively smooth water and light current the Hunley could make four miles an hour, but in rough water the speed was much slower. It was winter, therefore necessary that we go out with the ebb and come in with the flood tide, a fair wind, and dark moon. This latter was essential to our success, as our experience had fully demonstrated the necessity of occasionally coming to the surface, slightly lifting the hatch-cover, and letting in a little air. On several occasions we came to the surface for air, opened the cover, and heard the men in the Federal picket boats talking and singing. Our daily routine, whenever possible, was about as follows:

Leave Mount Pleasant about 1 P.M., walk seven miles to Battery Marshall on the beach (this exposed us to fire, but it was the best walking), take the boat out and practice the crew for two hours in the Back Bay. Dixon and myself [Alexander] would then stretch out on the beach with the compass between us and get the bearings of the nearest vessel as she took her position for the night; ship up

the torpedo on the boom, and, when dark, go out, steering for the vessel, proceed until the condition of the men, sea, tide, wind, moon, and daylight com-
pelled our return to the dock; unship the torpedo, put it under guard at Battery
Marshall, walk back to quarters at Mount Pleasant, and cook breakfast.[16]

The *H. L. Hunley*'s crew continued this daily routine all through the
month of November and into December. As the days rolled by, the increas-
ing headwinds became almost unbearable, which, in turn, made progress
extremely slow. All through January, as well as the early portion of February
1864, they ventured into the water an average of four times per week, determined to increase their stamina. Gradually, the crew became physically con-
ditioned for the arduous task, and their average range increased from four to
five, to six, and finally seven grueling miles one way. On numerous return
trips, they would have to tax themselves with their "utmost exertions" in order
to keep the *H. L. Hunley* from drifting far out to sea.

Eventually it came time to conduct an endurance test, to see exactly how
long they might be able to remain submerged without coming up for air:

> It was agreed by all hands to sink and let the boat rest on the bottom in the
> back bay off Battery Marshall, each man to make equal physical exertion in turn-
> ing the propeller. It was also agreed that if anyone in the crew felt he must come
> to the surface for air and he gave the word "Up," we would at once bring the boat
> to the surface.
>
> It was usual when practicing near the bay that the banks would be lined with
> soldiers. One evening after alternately diving and rising many times, Dixon and
> myself and several of the crew compared watches, noted the time and sank for
> the test. In twenty-five minutes after I had closed the after manhead and excluded
> the outer air, the candle would not burn. Dixon forward and myself aft turned
> on the propeller tanks as hard as we could. In comparing our individual experi-
> ences afterwards, the experience of one was found to be the experience of all.
> Each man had determined that he would not be the first man to say "Up." Not a
> word was said except an occasional "How is it?" between Dixon and myself until
> the "Up!" came from all nine.
>
> We started the pumps. Dixon's worked all right but mine was not throwing
> (water). From experience I guessed the cause of the failure, took off the cap of
> the pump, looked at the valve and drew out some chunks of seaweed that had
> choked it.
>
> In the time that it took to do this the boat was considerably by the stern. Thick
> darkness prevailed. All hands had already endured what they felt was the utmost
> limit. Some of the crew almost lost control of themselves. It was a terrible few
> minutes, better imagined than described.
>
> We soon had the boat to the surface and the manhead opened. What an expe-
> rience! While the sun was shining when we went down and the beach lined with
> soldiers, it was not quite dark with one solitary soldier gazing on the spot where
> he had seen the boat before going down the last time. He did not see the boat
> until he saw me standing on the hatch coaming calling for him to stand by to
> take the line.
>
> The line was struck and the time taken. We had been on the bottom two hours
> and thirty-five minutes. The candle ceased to burn twenty-five minutes after we

went down, showing that we had remained on the bottom two hours and ten minutes after the candle went out. The soldier informed us that we had been given up for lost and that a message had been sent to General Beauregard that a torpedo boat had been lost off Battery Marshall with all hands.[17]

The following morning, the crew, alive and rested, visited the headquarters of General Beauregard, who congratulated them for their accomplishment. Apparently, the endurance test had revived his failing confidence in the *H. L. Hunley* project, for he insisted that they continue to prepare for an inevitable attack on the Federal blockaders.

On February 5, 1864, William A. Alexander received some disheartening news: he was ordered to report to Mobile, Alabama, to oversee the construction of a breach-loading repeating gun. Obviously, it was a terrible blow to his hopes of being included among those who would one day take part in the attack. Despite his disappointment, however, he did not argue with his commanding officer concerning the new assignment, and he left that very evening for Mobile.

Soon after, Captain Dixon had managed to secure a pair of German-born volunteers to replace Alexander. Although he had lost a valuable assistant, Dixon was determined to carry out his orders to initiate an offensive at the earliest possible opportunity. His chance came on the night of February 17, 1864.

At dusk, with "the bay as smooth as a small pond," Captain Dixon and crew slipped away from the dock at Battery Marshall, drifting with the ebb tide. Carefully, he guided the *H. L. Hunley* through the intricate Breach Inlet channel, heading out to sea toward the nearest Northern blockading vessel. Just a few miles south of Charleston Harbor, the USS *Housatonic*, a 1,240-ton wooden corvette, mounting 23 guns, guarded the waterway against outgoing and incoming blockade runners:

> The *Housatonic* was a new vessel on the station, and anchored closer in than the *Wabash* or others. On this night the wind had lulled, with but little sea on, and although it was moonlight, Dixon, who had been waiting so long for a change of wind, took the risk of the moonlight and went out....[18]

To her southwest was anchored the USS *Canandaigua*, and, within a narrow radius, the USS *Paul Jones* and USS *Mary Sanford* sat idle.

Aboard the *Housatonic*, all was quiet, as officer of the deck Master J. K. Crosby secured quarters. The night was calm, there was no wind, and the moon seemed to become brighter as the hours passed. At just before 9:00 P.M., Crosby's watchful eyes detected something mysterious lurking a few feet beneath the dark waters approximately 100 yards off. From his quarterdeck position, Crosby thought that the strange object, moving closer now, must be a porpoise. Others walking the deck, viewing the unidentified object through a glass scope, believed it to be nothing more than a school of fish.

As the Confederate submarine drew nearer, the officer of the deck became somewhat alarmed. Then, taking the necessary precautions, he acted quickly, sounding the horn ordering a beat to quarters, slipping the anchor chain, and calling the captain:

> The lookout on the ship [*Housatonic*] saw him [Captain Dixon] when he came to the surface for his final observation.... He [Dixon] of course, not knowing that the ship had slipped her chain and was backing down upon him, then sank the boat [*H. L. Hunley*] a few feet, steered for the stern of the ship and struck with the torpedo. The momentum of the two vessels brought them together unexpectedly. The stern of the ship *Housatonic* was blown off entirely....[19]

Several men aboard the injured Federal vessel had fired their muskets and rifles at the approaching submarine, but it was already too late. The massive explosion shook the mighty Northern blockader back and forth; timbers and splinters flew through the air; and there was a "fearful rush of water." Moments later, heavy black smoke lingered above, as the *Housatonic* began to lurch forcefully forward. Slowly, she began to settle and sink.

Certainly, thought the Federal crewmen, there must be casualties, though they were not overcome with panic. Instead, they quickly lowered their lifeboats into position and prepared to abandon ship. However, at that precise moment, the *Housatonic* shifted violently once again, swamping the small lifeboats as the fleeing crewmen were ready to shove off. Most found themselves in the chilly waters of Charleston Harbor, swimming for their lives.

Next, the *Housatonic*'s starboard lifeboats were made ready, and the crewmen and officers who had fallen overboard were rescued one by one. Just moments later, they would be picked up by the USS *Canandaigua*. From just yards away, they looked on as the once mighty Federal blockader sank to the bottom of Charleston Harbor. At daybreak the following morning, heads were counted. Five Northern navy men were reported to be still missing.

The *H. L. Hunley* submarine never made it back to home base. Not until the war was over would anyone truly know the fate of her heroic crew. While attempting to locate the fallen USS *Housatonic* beneath 27 feet of water, salvagers spotted the submarine lying nearby. One diver even took the time to approach her, and laid his hands on her bent propeller. She was not raised, however, and though her location was well documented, she has not been found by modern-day searchers.

There was little agreement at the time of her demise exactly how many times the innovative submersible sank, or precisely how many Confederates lost their lives. On March 3, 1864, J. D. Breaman wrote a letter to his wife from Mobile, Alabama. In a few paragraphs, he summed up the total history of the Hunley submarine:

> ...among the number, however was a submarine boat, built in this place, of which Whitney and myself bought one-fifth for $3,000.

We took her to Charleston, for the purpose of operating there, and a few days after her arrival there, she sunk through carelessness and her crew of 5 men drowned.

Another crew of 8 men went on from here, raised her, and while experimenting with her in the harbor, sunk her and all 8 were drowned.

Lieutenant Dixon then went on from here and got another crew in Charleston. A few nights ago he went out, attacked and sunk the steam sloop of war *Housatonic,* but unfortunately (like his predecessor in this desperate and untried adventure), [I] fear that he and his crew were all lost....[20]

Though some Civil War experts place the number of deaths during the *H. L. Hunley* expeditions as high as 40, it is likely that Breaman's account is more accurate.

In summing up the fate of the *Hunley* during the early 1870s, James McClintock offered some hint at what the future would hold for underwater warfare:

The boat and machinery was so very simple, that many persons at first inspection believed that they could work ... without practice ... and although I endeavoured to prevent inexperienced persons from going under water ... I was not always successful....

Since the war, I have thought over the subject considerable, and am satisfied that the Power can easily be obtained ... to make the submarine Boat the most formidable enemy of Marine warfare ever known....[21]

Chapter 12

A Flurry in Northern Florida

Though Confederate naval operations along the coastline and within inland waters of Florida were not, perhaps, as strategically important as those in numerous other portions of the South, they did, indeed, hold a good deal of historical significance. In fact, the struggle for control of Florida's northern-most waterways was not unlike that in South Carolina and Georgia, and certainly prompted the Confederates to incorporate new types of underwater warfare.

During October and November of 1863, the St. John's River in the north-eastern part of the state suddenly became a hotly contested area. This wide, deep passageway, which had seen little fighting during the first two years of the war, was of vital importance to both sides for transportation and communication purposes. Hence, it should have come as no surprise to the Federals, whose warships constantly patrolled the area looking for Confederate installations, when they stumbled upon a small contingent of Rebels actively planting underwater explosives. In fact, a continual line of top-secret information concerning such activities had flowed into Northern intelligence circles throughout the summer of 1863, offering the Federals ample warning of Southern river assaults.

Northward, in Charleston, not a single confrontation took place on New Year's Day, 1864. Strangely enough, after nearly five months of continual bombardment of the forts, there was an eerie silence throughout the region. Yet just as quickly as it had ceased, it began once again, building to a gradual crescendo of exploding shells. During a single nine-day period in the middle of January, more than 1,500 shells were fired by Union troops at the almost-defenseless city. Then, once more, the fighting came to a halt.

At first, General Pierre G. T. Beauregard believed that the distinct lull in Federal naval activities along the entire coastline meant that Union ammunition supplies had been depleted, or that the majority of their weapons had become inoperable. Little did he realize, however, that large numbers of Federal troops had recently been relocated out of the area to the "Sunshine State," in order that they might take part in the so-called "Florida Expedition." The major reason for this move was to dissolve the Confederate stronghold along

Horological torpedo, found hidden in some bushes near the St. John's River in Florida in February of 1864. It housed a clockwork mechanism designed to remain harmless until a spring activated a hammer, thus detonating the torpedo. Believed to have been invented by Thomas L. Buckman, Confederate ordnance officer (courtesy of West Point Museum Collection).

the eastern shoreline of Florida, and to capture the strategic port city of Jacksonville. Whoever controlled this would also control the St. John's River.

In order to keep General Beauregard off balance, mock attacks were conducted in and around Charleston. During one such incident, on February 9, 1864, Federal forces under the direction of General Alexander Schimmelfennig attacked John's Island, just to the south of Charleston harbor. Though his 3,000 to 4,000 troops, with their six-piece artillery unit, were repulsed by General Henry A. Wise's brigade, the ploy seemed effective: General Beauregard continued to concentrate defenses in the South Carolina region.

Soon, however, when the Confederate general finally realized that he had been tricked, Southern troops were transferred from Charleston and Savannah into Florida. As both sides rushed men to the newly-anointed battleground, Charleston's reputation of being the center of the action quickly became a thing of the past. In fact, by the end of February, even Beauregard himself traveled south, taking command of the Florida operations. And along with him went his strategic plans for underwater warfare.

The first proof that Southern torpedoes would be effective in the Florida region came on March 6, 1864, when Federal General Truman Seymour sent his mighty flotilla down the St. John's River. To his apparent surprise, the fleet discovered a band of Confederates carefully launching mines from the waterway's high banks. After several rounds of gunfire had been exchanged, the Confederates vanished into the brush, leaving behind two prime samples of a new type of explosive. They were found hidden beneath some bushes near Sisters Creek, and, later, two others were discovered. However, the Federals could not be sure how many explosives had been planted.

Obviously, General Beauregard continued to value the use of torpedoes as a primary means of defense:

> It is suggestive to think what might have been the influence on the Union cause if the Confederate practice of submarine [torpedo] warfare had been nearly as efficient at the commencement as it was at the close of the war. It is not too much to say, respecting the blockade of Southern ports, that if not altogether broken up, it would have been rendered ... inefficient ... while the command of rivers all important to the Union forces as bases of operation, would have been next to impossible.[1]

The type of torpedo discovered in the St. John's River by General Seymour's men housed a clockwork mechanism designed to be idle for a specific period of time. Such explosives would remain harmless until a spring activated a hammer, thus detonating the torpedo. In this way, the Confederates were able to plant mines which would go off after a predetermined time-lapse.

Credit for the invention of this ingenious weapon goes to Thomas L. Buckman, the Confederate army ordnance officer in Florida. As supervisor of the Florida, Atlantic & Gulf Central Railroad, Buckman had long ago become interested in clockwork explosives. In an attempt to repel the Federal invaders from the St. John's River basin, he had planted torpedoes constructed of copper, containing approximately 70 to 80 pounds of gunpowder each. They were set to explode just one hour and 40 minutes after they were discovered by Seymour's men.

Over the course of the next few months, Federal river traffic was on the rise between Jacksonville and Palatka, several miles to the south. Realizing that this continual flow of Union ships was the very lifeline for Northern troops stationed along the St. John's, General Beauregard opted to implement a blockade of his own, in the hopes of cutting off Federal supplies and reinforcements. To this end, he appointed Captain E. Pliny Bryan as the man in charge of Florida's torpedo program. Just a few months earlier, in October 1863, Bryan had used his own variety of explosives (outfitted with Rains fuses) against the Federal blockading squadron in Charleston. Known as "buoy torpedoes," they contained approximately 150 pounds of gunpowder.

> ...the Federals would sometimes pick up floating torpedoes sent against the fleet, at the rate of a hundred a day. These torpedoes were suspended in pairs to wooden buoys, and were connected by trigger-lines which would explode them on contact with a ship; but the Federals guarded against them by putting out booms and nettings in such a way that the torpedo floats were sheered off and passed harmlessly by.[2]

Captain Bryan had been totally unsuccessful in destroying Federal blockaders in Charleston waters, through his men had reported "hearing at least one loud explosion." Since Union records did not mention any damage to their vessels during this particular time period, Bryan could only surmise that his torpedo had been detonated by driftwood.

Captain Bryan's initial request for supplies during his Florida assignment included one dozen 40-pound-keg torpedo jackets, 300 Rains fuses, several anchors, and nearly a half-ton of gunpowder. The order was promptly filled by Captain M. Martin Gray, who was stationed in Charleston, on March 12, 1864, with the shipment being dispatched by rail to its destination. Within three weeks, Bryan's men were ready to plant a number of these weighted torpedoes near an area known as Mandarin Point. Situated just a few miles south of Jacksonville, it was an extremely narrow length of river: one which would almost guarantee that any Federal vessel which dared to venture into the region would be destroyed. Now all that Bryan and his cohorts could do was to wait.

The enterprising captain's wait was brief, for just a few days later a contingent of Federal vessels passed Mandarin Point on their way to Palatka. At precisely 4:00 P.M. on the afternoon of April 1, 1864, the USS *Maple Leaf*, USS *General Hunter*, and USS *Harriett A. Weed* were spotted steaming steadily southward by Confederate lookouts. Miraculously, however, all three vessels managed to safely bypass the submerged explosives. Yet, within a matter of hours, Bryan would get a second chance, when the Union ships passed on their return voyage.

The USS *Maple Leaf*, a 508-ton army transport, would be the unfortunate victim of Bryan's invention. The captain and his men could not have been more elated, since they were well aware of the Northern vessel's colorful history:

> She [USS *Maple Leaf*] was chartered from the U.S. government from her owner, who was also her captain, and on July 7th started from Fortress Monroe for Fort Delaware, with 93 Confederate officers who had been taken prisoners on the Mississippi, and sent east for confinement. The ranking officer ... and others of the

prisoners, had conceived a scheme to take possession of any vessel upon which they might be placed.... After getting out to sea at night, the lieutenant arranged his guard in three reliefs, the men not on duty stacking their arms, and he retired to rest. [The Confederates] had arranged that one of their men should be on the upper deck, and at a given signal tap the bell.... When the bell struck, the stacked muskets were seized by the [prisoners] ... in the secret, the guard was overpowered without a shot being fired, and in five minutes ... [they were] in command of the *Maple Leaf*, and the Federal soldiers became the prisoners.[3]

Later, 70 of the escaped Confederate prisoners managed to leave the ship, which was subsequently recaptured by the Federals. The remaining 23 Southerners, who had been wounded, were transported to Federally-controlled Fortress Monroe, despite an adamant promise by the ship's captain to carry them safely to a Confederate installation. And now, here was Captain Bryan's opportunity to repay the USS *Maple Leaf*'s owner/commander for his blatant lies.

As the afternoon shadows hung low over the river bank, the three Federal army transports came past Mandarin Point. Suddenly, the USS *Maple Leaf* was violently rocked by an immense explosion from beneath her bow. Slowly, the vessel leaned heavily to one side and, within minutes, she sank to the muddy bottom of the river.

In an attempt to pinpoint her exact location, Federal navy men looked on as she plummeted beneath the rippling blue waters near an area known as Beauclerc's Bluff. They recorded it as being approximately 12 miles south of Jacksonville, and also noted that she took four Federal seamen and the combined supplies of three army regiments down with her. The remaining two army transports, whose men were somewhat fearful that they might meet a similar fate, continued to steam on their route northward.

Immediately after the successful destruction of the *Maple Leaf*, Captain Bryan sent a message to Major General Patton Anderson, commander of the Florida district, describing the attack in graphic detail. Furthermore, explained Bryan, he planned to search the wreck at the earliest possible convenience, in order to retrieve all contraband that had managed to survive the destruction. Evidently, however, he was unable to do this on that very same day, due to foul weather.

On the evening of April 1, a Federal gunboat arrived in the area, planning to conduct a thorough investigation of the entire affair. This caused Bryan to delay his salvage operations even longer. The Union vessel lingered in the general vicinity until late the following afternoon.

Meanwhile, a battalion of the First Georgia Regular Infantry, along with a small support group from the Florida Light Artillery Brigade, had been dispatched to the scene by General Anderson. They were given instructions to destroy whatever remained of the sunken transport. Arriving at Mandarin Point at just before daybreak on April 2, they prepared their hefty brass 12-pounder howitzer, a pair of six-pounder smoothbore cannon, and an iron three-inch rifle.

After firing off a few decoy rounds, with intentions of giving the Federal contingent "the idea that a battery is located there,"⁴ Bryan and two foot soldiers went aboard the plundered USS *Maple Leaf*. They discovered that river water ran two feet deep across the upper deck, and in cabins below they found "a few mattresses, sofas, washbowls, and other unimportant items."⁵

Much of the remainder of the haul could not be reached by the Confederates, who discovered that it was locked tightly away in the holding section of the vessel. Deciding that he could retrieve nothing more of significant value, Captain Bryan ordered his men to set fire to the dry mattresses. Soon, whatever was left of the fallen USS *Maple Leaf* went up in flames.

From that day forward, Federal navy men became far more careful while operating on the St. John's River. In fact, they were instructed to travel in single-file fashion whenever they came near the spot where the ill-fated army transport had been destroyed.

Early in the morning on April 16, 1864, a trio of Union vessels made their way toward Jacksonville, on their return voyage from Picolata. Led by the screw gunboat USS *Norwich*, two army transports, the USS *Cosmopolitan* and USS *General Hunter* followed close behind. As they slowly approached the blackened wreck of the USS *Maple Leaf*, whose vacant timbers reminded them of possible tragedy, the Northern navy men grew silent. For the men aboard the USS *General Hunter*, the eeriness was especially intense: after all, they had been here when she had been struck down, and fears of further Rebel attacks plagued their thoughts.

As she floated close to Mandarin Point, the *General Hunter* began to have difficulty staying on the intended course. She was being pushed off to one side by a sudden gust of wind, and she zig-zagged back and forth briefly before her rear section swayed ominously toward the sunken *Maple Leaf*.

Suddenly, the USS *General Hunter* was pushed upward by a huge column of water, which managed to smash "the forward part of the hull to fragments."⁶ It was obvious to her crew that she was doomed, and they scrambled to get overboard. Within three minutes, she sank out of sight, as men from the other two ships looked on in horror. Apparently, however, moments were all that were required to save the majority of Federal seamen who had been aboard the *General Hunter*. Only a single man, the quartermaster, was drowned, while a second suffered a fracture of his left leg.

During the next several weeks, Federal navy men concentrated their efforts on locating and destroying all Confederate torpedoes in the St. John's River. However, although a number were subsequently discovered, Captain Bryan simply replaced them with a fresh supply shipped in from Charleston.

It was now quite apparent that both Union and Confederate forces would maintain their persistent efforts to control Florida's waterways. On the Northern side, this strong desire was held at all levels of government, right on up to President Abraham Lincoln himself:

> I understand an effort is being made by some worthy gentlemen to reconstruct a loyal State government in Florida.... It is desirable for all to cooperate.... I wish the thing done in the most speedy way possible....[7]

Headlines in newspapers throughout the North, reporting on the incidents occurring in Florida's inland waters, soon became somewhat sarcastic. One editor, whose *Norfolk New Regime* supported the Federal forces in the conflict, had this to say following the destruction of the *General Hunter*:

> If the United States desire(s) to pay a round sum for pasteboard boats, and to have them used up at an early day, let them duplicate the General Hunter....[8]

On May 9, 1864, a third Federal army transport was destroyed by a Bryan torpedo. On that day, the 290-ton USS *Harriett A. Weed*, which had also been present when the USS *Maple Leaf* had been sunk, struck an underwater explosive in the vicinity of Cedar Creek, just south of Jacksonville. The attack caused the deaths of five Union navy men, with the remainder of the crew being "more or less injured."

One of the 13 officers on board when the explosive was detonated was tossed more than 20 feet into the air, and the ship's captain was jostled overboard. When he was later pulled from the river's waters by a schooner, which had been towed to the region by the ill-fated vessel, the skipper seemed to be in shock. Brigadier General George Henry Gordon attempted to settle the captain's nerves, but the immense strain was more than evident. Clasping his hands together tightly, and continually rubbing his forehead, the captain broke down in tears, moaning: "Who will come next? How are we to navigate these waters?"

Taking a deep breath, and attempting to be understanding of his stress, Gordon answered by explaining that strong-willed navy men must "take ... chances, with the [un]pleasant feeling that at any moment we might find ourselves blown high in the air...."[9]

Throughout the South, stories of these successes with underwater explosives sparked new hope for victory, and prompted their continued deployment. One expert in the design of torpedoes had this to say in their support:

> Could a piece of Ordnance be made to sweep a battle field in a moment of time, there soon would be no battle field, or could a blast of wind loaded with deadly mephitic malaria in one night, sent like the destroying angel in Sanacherib's [*sic*] army, or the earth be made to open in a thousand places with the fire of death for destruction, as in the days of Korah, Dothan and Abiram, to which this [torpedo] system tends, then and then only may we beat the sword into the ploughshare, the spear into the pruning hook....[10]

On May 11, 1864, Charles B. Boutelle, a member of the United States Coastal Survey team, made his way down the St. John's River aboard the USS

Vixen. His mission was to seek out and destroy any detectable Confederate torpedoes that remained in the area. Near the spot where the USS *Harriett A. Weed* went down, Boutelle noticed a series of strange ripples being pushed across the surface, which seemed to indicate objects submerged at shallow depths. With further investigation, a pair of cutters latched on to one of Captain Bryan's keg explosives, held down by an iron anchor. In an attempt to disarm it, crewmen fired their rifles in its direction: but efforts to pierce it failed. Robert Platt, one of the men involved, then proceeded to tow the foreign object toward the waiting *Vixen*.

With great care and agility, the torpedo was transferred onto the dry shore, where its powder was safely wetted down through a series of newly-drilled holes. Later, the now-harmless weapon was shipped off to Washington, D.C., for a more thorough inspection.

On June 19, still another unsuspecting Federal army transport was devastated by the persistent activities of Captain Bryan's men. The USS *Alice Price*, on her way to Jacksonville, lost a good portion of her underside near Beauclerc's Bluff. This brought the total number of Union vessels destroyed by torpedoes in the St. John's River to four.

Much later, after the war had ended, an East Coast newspaper reported the events which took place in this, the southernmost state along the eastern border of the Confederacy:

> In the experiments with the torpedo lately in the Florida channel, the country has been furnished with a more complete exhibition of the destructive capacities of this submarine projectile, than is now known to military and naval science....[11]

And as the battle for the control of Southern waterways progressed, each success with submerged torpedoes brought with it newfound hopes that perhaps the Confederacy might one day win the respect it well deserved.

Chapter 13

Attack of the *Squib*

During the spring of 1864, the Union Navy continued its search for underwater explosives in most rivers and harbors throughout the Confederacy. The details surrounding a typical search and destroy operation in the James River, for example, were reported as follows:

> ...the *Tritonia*, the *Stepping Stones*, the *Delaware*, eleven armed cutters from the various vessels, and 175 sailors, marines, and soldiers employed as skirmishes and pickets to drive back the small bodies of Confederates along the left bank so that the boats could safely pursue their search.[1]

In general, the Federal fleets involved were exceptionally good at sifting through the intricate channels, and few days went by without a "find." On one such excursion conducted by the USS *Philadelphia* up the Neuse River in North Carolina, Union officer Stephen C. Rowan reported:

> The obstructions in the river were very formidable, and had evidently been prepared with great care. The lower barrier was composed of a series of piling driven securely into the bottom and cut off below the water; Added to this was another row of iron-capped and pointed piles, inclined at an angle of about 45% down the stream. Near these was a row of thirty torpedoes, containing about 200 pounds of powder each, and fitted with metal fuzes connected with spring percussion locks, with trigger lines attached to the pointed piles....[2]

Throughout much of the South, the construction of low-slung attack vessels continued, with new innovations and ideas being presented by a variety of inventors. John B. Read, a citizen of Charleston, suggested that the Confederate Navy arm compact steamers with spar torpedoes, in order that they might conduct swift and unseen attacks on Federal monitors. General Beauregard, meanwhile, proposed a variation of Read's plan:

> It is stated that a proper-sized steamer, 400 or 500 tons, built like a blockade runner, but made shot-proof and armed with one of Lee's repeating submarine torpedo apparatus, could be built in about three months working time in England for the sum of about $250,000. I venture to say that with one of those vessels ... the blockade ... could be raised in less than a week.... Half a dozen of

these steamers would raise the blockade of our Atlantic and Gulf coasts, and enable us to recover the navigation of the Mississippi River. Indeed, a few years hence we will ask ourselves in astonishment how it was that with such a great discovery, offering such magnificent results, we never applied it to any useful purpose in this contest....[3]

In the capital city of Richmond, Virginia, a much different type of offensive craft was under construction during that same period. Known as the CSS *Squib*, she was a 42-foot steam launch, protected by a heavy coat of iron, and possessing a steersman cockpit at the stern and a torpedo windlass at the bow. Her commander was the innovative Hunter Davidson, whose earlier escapades with electrical torpedoes had earned him a heroic reputation.

In his secluded laboratory near Richmond, Davidson, while continuing to supervise his Submarine Battery Service, opted to pursue his own ideas concerning spar torpedo vessels. At the start of this particular phase of his illustrious career, he concentrated on the development of electrically-charged warheads. Yet the difficulty of arranging a contrivance which might close the circuit at the precise moment of contact with an enemy ship proved next to impossible. In an attempt to solve the dilemma, he turned his attention toward percussion fuses:

> To this end we made some sheet-lead tubes, the rounded end being of much thinner lead than the other part.
> These tubes were about three inches long and one inch in diameter. Into this tube was inserted a small glass tube, of similar shape, filled with sulphuric acid, and hermetically sealed. The vacant space about the glass tube was then tightly packed with a mixture of chlorate of potash and pulverized white sugar, and the mouth of the lead tube was closed by fastening a strip of muslin over it.
> Now, if the rounded end of the leaden tube is brought into contact with any hard substance, the thin lead will be mashed, the interior glass tube broken, and the sulphuric acid becoming mixed with the preparation of chlorate of potash and sugar, an immediate explosion is the result. We then prepared a copper cylinder capable of containing about fifty pounds of powder, and placed several of the leaden fuses in the head, so that at no matter what angle the butt struck the hull of a ship, one of the fuses would be smashed in, and flame from the potash and sugar [would] ignite the powder. At the bottom of the copper cylinder there was a socket made to fit on the end of a spar.[4]

The spar torpedo designed by Davidson would be, if not handled carefully, extremely dangerous. In their initial experiment, his crew rammed an empty encasement into an aging bulkhead located on the south side of Richmond. Next, they filled one with approximately 25 pounds of gunpowder and lowered a spar two feet beneath the water's surface. The effect of the resulting explosion "shattered the old wharf and threw up a column of water, completely drenching the occupants of the launch."[5]

Hunter Davidson instructed his men to prepare themselves for a full-scale assault on the enemy's fleet, which was anchored just off Newport News. Yet, before they could get underway, a serious flaw was discovered in their plan:

> The launch burned bituminous coal, the smoke from which could be discerned from a long distance, and the sparks from which at night would disclose its presence to an enemy. Some one suggested that we might obtain anthracite coal by dredging at the wharves and in the docks at Richmond. This was accordingly done, and we obtained a supply of the anthracite, for which an almost fabulous price was paid.[6]

Equipped with everything they needed for a surprise attack, Davidson boarded the CSS *Squib* with a crew of six, including the engineer and the fireman. They had selected as their prime target a 3,307-ton frigate known as the USS *Minnesota*.

Floating under the cover of darkness and hiding by day, the *Squib* was towed down a 100-mile stretch of the James River. Finally, during the first week of April 1864, she reached a point approximately 15 miles south of City Point. Then, on the night of April 7, the *Squib* steamed down toward the unsuspecting Union vessel. When dawn approached, Davidson decided to hide his craft within the confines of a secluded swamp until the following night.

Armed with a 53-pound torpedo, the CSS *Squib* zig-zagged her way through the imposing Federal fleet. In the past, she had been designated by the Confederate navy as a flag-of-truce vessel and, though she was subsequently spotted by several deck lookouts who questioned her intentions on this particular night, she did not stir up a great amount of anxiety within the enemy ranks.

The USS *Minnesota*'s exact position was known to Commander Davidson, who had gained a good deal of vital information from Confederate spies scattered throughout the region. At about 2:00 A.M., on the morning of April 9, Davidson decided to begin his advance. Yet, he understood that the *Squib* still had one more major obstacle to overcome: the USS *Poppy*, an armed tugboat, had been ordered to protect the *Minnesota* against all unidentified ships.

On most nights, the *Poppy* could be seen continually circumnavigating the mother ship, on the lookout for possible invaders. However, on this particular occasion, Davidson was delighted to discover her floating motionless in the water. He truly believed that Lady Luck was on his side.

At five minutes past two in the morning, beneath a bright star-lit sky, the USS *Minnesota*'s officer of the deck, Ensign James Bartwistle, spotted an unfamiliar ship steaming directly toward him. Quickly, he alerted the deck guard aboard the nearby USS *Poppy*, who proceeded to hail the unidentified vessel several times. Finally, he heard a faint voice shouting into the blackness, claiming that he was the commander of the ironclad USS *Roanoke*. As the tiny Confederate steamer continued on her collision course, the *Poppy*'s deck guard ordered her to stay clear or be fired upon.

"Aye, Aye," came the reply; yet Davidson had no intention of altering his course.

The *Poppy's* deck guard showered the CSS *Squib* with a spray of rifle shot, but the pellets seemed to glance off of some type of protective shield. In the meantime, Ensign Bartwistle had aroused his captain, and had then stationed himself at a nearby cannon. As he prepared the huge gun for firing, he shouted to the *Poppy's* deck guard once again, ordering him to use everything at his disposal to keep the intruder away from the *Minnesota*. But it was too late: before he could take aim, he was jarred by a violent explosion.

Below deck, Medical Officer John M. Batten, a new member of the *Minnesota's* crew, had just bedded down for the night. He was proud to be assigned to this, the largest war vessel in the Federal navy, under the command of Admiral S. P. Lee. Suddenly, without warning, he was rudely awakened by a deafening noise: "I could not for the life of me tell from where it came or whither it had gone ... it made the vessel tremble."[7]

Fear ran through his mind as Batten quickly dressed himself and hurried to topside, where he found the admiral and several other sailors assembled. It was only then that he discovered what had caused the loud explosion: an underwater torpedo had been detonated beneath the hull of the USS *Minnesota* while she was anchored at the very center of the Federal flotilla.

Medical Officer Batten looked on as officers and men scurried about the deck, panicking, and readying themselves for some measure of counter-attack. Led by Captain J. H. Upshur, who had been a classmate of Hunter Davidson's at the Academy, crew members lined the *Minnesota's* rail. As the drums pounded, Upshur gave his command, and guns opened fire on the tiny Confederate vessel below.

Aboard the CSS *Squib*, Hunter Davidson felt a good bit of satisfaction from the fact that his compact steamer had managed to sneak past the entire Federal squadron. Furthermore, he was proud that such a tiny vessel could inflict such damage to a seemingly oversized monster of a ship. The *Squib* had managed to ram the mighty *Minnesota* just below the water-line on her starboard side:

> The effect was terrific, the shock causing the *Minnesota* to tremble from stern to stern. Several of her guns were dismounted and a big hole was opened in her side by the explosion....[8]

Hunter Davidson was unable to make a clean and swift getaway, however, due to a problem with the *Squib's* engine. Reportedly, immediately after the collision, it somehow managed to "catch on center." The commander breathed a sigh of relief moments later, when the steamer's engine-works were quickly reactivated by the engineer, who would later be promoted two full ranks for his decisive and efficient actions:

Owing to the strong tide prevailing at the time, and the violence of the ramming, the launch [*Squib*] perceptibly rebounded, so that at the instant of the
explosion, which was not simultaneous with the blow, a cushion of water inter-
vened between the torpedo and the hull of the *Minnesota,* thus weakening the
effect and probably saving the ship. She was so thoroughly disabled, however, as
we afterward understood, that she had to be towed off, and underwent repairs
in the docks. Our men were greeted with showers of bullets from the deck of the
ship, but they struck harmlessly against the iron shield of the launch, which
quickly steamed away under cover of darkness, and escaped.[9]

In studying the aftermath of the CSS *Squib*'s attack upon the Federal
flagship, it should be understood that she came very close to being destroyed
by the retaliation of the Northern sailors. Every portion of her tiny hull was
hit by gunfire, with one shell even coming so near as to lift her compact keel
up out of the water. Minié balls tore through Hunter Davidson's hat and clothing: yet, miraculously, he was not injured.

In order that he might evade detection by any Union ships dispatched to
pursue them, Commander Davidson mapped a course in a direct route toward
Richmond, reversed his direction, and eventually escaped along exactly the
same pathway that he had come (up the James River). Finally, after passing
the mouth of the Nansemond River without spotting the enemy, he realized
that his ship and her crew were quite safe.

Two days later, Hunter Davidson dispatched a wire from his base camp
on Turkey Island to Secretary of the Navy Stephen R. Mallory:

> Passed through the Federal fleet off Newport News and exploded 53 pounds of
> powder against the side of the flagship *Minnesota....* She was not sunk, and I
> have no means of telling the injury.... My boat and party escaped without loss
> under the fire of her heavy guns and musketry....[10]

Later, when he arrived back in the capital city of Richmond, Davidson
was surprised to find a rather unenthusiastic President Jefferson Davis, who
coldly inquired as to the reason why the USS *Minnesota* was *not* totally
destroyed. Davis would soon alter his disappointed view concerning the attack,
however, and even went as far as to suggest a promotion for the "gallant and
meritorious conduct" of the *Squib*'s crew. The Confederate congress would
approve the promotion in June of that same year.

In reality, the *Minnesota* was not permanently damaged by the attack of
the *Squib*, although she was forced to undergo extensive repairs. Some of her
main support beams had been literally split down the middle, her hull plates
had been pushed inward from the force of the explosion, and a number of her
guns had been disabled. As for the USS *Poppy*, which had been ineffective in
warding off the attack, her captain was stripped of his command and demoted
in grade for his apparent inability to carry out his duties.

For several months following the attack, the Federal fleet took extraordinary precautions against similar incidents. In some cases, a thick webbing of nets were extended on booms around an entire vessel's hull, and *two* tugs were given the perilous task of protecting a single ship. Admiral John Dahlgren of the U.S. Navy hinted at his fears concerning the vulnerability of his ships: "The blockade is important, but the safety of the ironclads much more so...."[11]

At the same time, newspapers throughout the country seemed impressed by the Confederacy's persistence in designing a suitable torpedo attack ship. *Scientific America* put it in a nutshell when it commented: "A little more practice will make them perfect."[12]

Rear Admiral S. P. Lee, who had been the commanding officer aboard the USS *Minnesota* at the time of the assault, was angered by the entire affair. In a memo sent to Hunter Davidson, he heatedly complained about the use of the CSS *Squib* as an offensive vessel of war. Furthermore, he stated that if she were ever used as a flag-of-truce ship again, the Federal fleet would destroy her, for he was not of the opinion that such a "trusted" craft should be "engaged in civilized or legitimate warfare" under any circumstances.

Rear Admiral Dahlgren was also upset over the "misuse" of a recognized flag-of-truce vessel. Hunter Davidson could not have cared less for what the U.S. navy commanders thought. In fact, he expressed his feelings of Dahlgren's criticism by stating:

> ...[Admiral Dahlgren's words] glanced from my armor as many a worse shot did from my own side, for I felt that as he was the sufferer ... he saw the matter but from one point of view, but that time would set it even as I replied in substance ... respice finem.[13]

Eventually, as Hunter Davidson suspected, Admiral Dahlgren would change his opinion of incorporating torpedo boats as a viable and acceptable mode of attack. In fact, he even believed them to be the very best form of assault improvised by the Confederacy. Furthermore, he went one step further with his change of heart, urging Northern authorities to design and construct similar vessels, claiming that "we can make them faster than (the enemy) can."[14]

In the early morning hours of April 9, just after the attack on the USS *Minnesota*, the Union Navy began to formulate a plan to entrap and capture the elusive CSS *Squib*. They suspected correctly, that she must have hidden herself in one of the numerous shallow creeks that intersected the James River, and they believed that a small contingency of light-draft ships would be able to locate and take control of her.

Within a few days, Federal authorities were informed that the *Squib* had taken up temporary refuge in nearby Pagan Creek, a little-traveled waterway that led to the town of Smithfield from the James River's southern bank. On April 14, an expedition was formed, under the leadership of 35-year-old Acting

A secret Confederate torpedo station located along the James River, which was captured in 1864 (courtesy of National Archives).

Master Charles B. Wilder. The newly-installed search party's first mission was to verify the unsubstantiated information.

Wilder, who had previously been the acting executive officer aboard the *Minnesota*, boarded a small vessel equipped with a deadly howitzer, just in case the sketchy report proved to be true. He determined that if he did indeed locate the *Squib*, and if her crew attempted to escape, he would be able to threaten or shoot them into surrendering.

During the late morning hours of April 14, all seemed relatively quiet as Wilder's crewmen pushed their search vessel up the narrow Pagan Creek. Wilder himself stood in the bow section of the boat, giving orders and urging his men to keep a careful eye out for the Confederate *Squib*. Meticulously, they combed the banks and adjoining pools, but found little to indicate that the Southern torpedo boat had even been there.

Suddenly, as they were about to return to their home base, several rounds of rifle shot echoed through the still morning air, sending up rippling circles of water all around them. Wilder gave the command to prepare the howitzer, and to aim it in the general direction of a large clump of thickets on shore. Quickly, the Federal crew took aim and fired two explosive rounds, pausing only to reload. Just as the third round was being fired, Wilder was shot in the left temple by sniper fire, and he fell to the bottom of the boat, mortally wounded. A member of the Union search crew, H. H. Miller, was also wounded in the volley, as the Federals pulled hard on their oars to escape.

The Union Navy realized that a vessel such as the *Squib* could wreak havoc on the remainder of their blockading fleet anchored near the James River. Subsequently, a special Torpedo and Picket Division was established to pinpoint her location. The vessels which were part of this search team were instructed to "run down the torpedo craft," but they were unable to accomplish that objective.

Throughout the remainder of 1864, Union authorities persistently questioned prisoners and defectors from within the Confederate ranks. Yet, few talked of the Southern expertise concerning torpedo warfare, and even fewer could ascertain why Southern assaults had seemed to slow down. One Federal officer, who rarely believed that prisoners were telling the truth, reported that "they [the Confederates] say they haven't the sense to make a good torpedo; [but] they reckon on them more than all else besides."[15] Perhaps Confederate prisoners were only partially informed, however, concerning the apparent slow-down in the use of torpedo warfare. Much later, a member of Hunter Davidson's crew would offer a much more plausible explanation for the South's lack of offensive underwater maneuvers:

> During the last year of the war arrangements had been perfected to secure a large quantity [of supplies] ... from England, an officer having been sent there for that purpose. Every material requisite for the extension of our torpedo system throughout the entire South was obtained, and a small advance shipment did actually reach us through the blockade at Wilmington. The remainder was put on board a swift steamer, with the intention of running the blockade and returning with a full cargo of cotton; but from stress of weather, or other causes, the steamer put into the port of Fayal, and, as I understood, was wrecked in that port, either from the stupidity of the pilot or from treachery. The entire cargo was lost, and it was impossible to duplicate our material before the war ended.[16]

Despite the lull in offensive attacks by torpedo vessels, many Union officers felt that it was only a matter of time before the Confederates made their move. On June 1, 1864, Rear Admiral S. P. Lee sent a telegraph message to U.S. Secretary of the Navy Gideon Welles, stating that he had information that the Confederates were about to "mediate an immediate attack upon this fleet with fire rafts, torpedo vessels, gunboats, and ironclads, all of which carry torpedoes...." Furthermore, Lee stated that defensive measures against torpedoes might best be carried out by the implementation of the North's own underwater explosives. However, the Rear Admiral must have felt that he was not well enough equipped to conduct such defensive operations, for he also stated that "I have not [any underwater explosives] here, and am unable to fix torpedoes which are at all reliable."[17]

While the Union forces continued to wait for the "inevitable" attack, fear of the Confederate *Squib* remained in their minds. Many "threats" were far more exaggerated than truly necessary, however. At the end of February 1865, for example, a rather amusing incident occurred aboard Admiral Porter's flagship, the USS *Malvern*. On that particular occasion, Porter was informed by "reliable" sources that the CSS *Squib* was in his area, ready to attack the Union ship as she floated in the Cape Fear River.

As a defensive measure, Admiral Porter ordered that every ship in his fleet maintain a round-the-clock watch for the impending assault. Furthermore, two small tugs were assigned to each and every Federal monitor in the region, and they were to put out a blockade of nets in an attempt to foul the *Squib*'s propellers.

During the early morning hours, as Admiral Porter prepared himself for a restful night's sleep, he was suddenly aroused by panicked shouts coming from the deck of the USS *Malvern*. Moments later, he heard muffled pistol shots, and he hurried topside just in time to see a swarm of Federal search boats vaguely outlined beneath the dim light of lanterns. Reportedly, a mysterious vessel had been spotted moving steadily across the surface, though she had since been lost in the shroud of darkness.

Moments later, the *Malvern*'s lookout spotted the ominous shape coming in their direction once again. "Here he comes," he shouted excitedly, as a Coston signal flare lit up the surface of the water.

Anxious seconds passed before the lookout realized his mistake, sheepishly admitting that: "It was something worse than a [torpedo] ram; it was the biggest bull I ever saw. He was swimming across the channel...!"[18] Once again, the *Squib* had managed to evade capture, though no one truly knows if she was even in the area at all; and, once again, new fears within the Federal ranks had been provoked by the mere possibility of attack.

Chapter 14

Damn the Torpedoes

Alabama, one of the first states to sever its ties with the United States at the start of the Civil War, possessed a broad frontage on the Gulf of Mexico, as well as numerous inland waterways on which large vessels could travel. Following the closing of the Mississippi River in July 1863, the Federal navy, with Admiral David Farragut in command, decided to devote a good deal of effort toward the ultimate control of Mobile Bay.

Yet, as history has shown us, the Confederate forces were not willing to give up the control of Crimson Tide waterways without a struggle:

> Her [Alabama's] waters were destined to become the theatre of naval conflicts of varying magnitude, culminating in that death grapple of Titans at the battle of Mobile Bay; of scores of gallant exploits of seamanlike skill and daring; of marine raids by the adventurous hunters and fishermen of these semi-tropical sounds and bayous upon the enemy's transports and tenders, and of this side play of blockade-running which was a constant accompaniment to the main drama of the war.[1]

The Northern blockade was implemented against the city of Mobile on May 28, 1861, and the first Federal vessel to appear in the harbor was the frigate USS *Powhatan*. From that day forward, until Admiral Farragut's daring attack, this strategic port city underwent three grueling years of maritime closure, bypassed only by low, swift blockade-runners. The vessels that did make it through brought in cargoes of arms, ammunition, and gunpowder, and slipped away once again with shipments of cotton bound for Lancaster.

Three years was an ample amount of time for the Confederate forces in and around Mobile to strengthen their channel by laying out a variety of underwater explosives and to prepare themselves for the inevitable invasion. As early as January 1864, Admiral Farragut conducted a thorough reconnaissance of the harbor area. At that time, he determined that it was an ideal situation for a Union assault, for there was but a single Confederate transport vessel anchored in the lower bay. In a series of telegrams dispatched to the U.S. Department of the Navy he requested that at least one ironclad be sent to support his squadron of wooden ships then waiting to begin the attack. Even so, help did not come immediately.

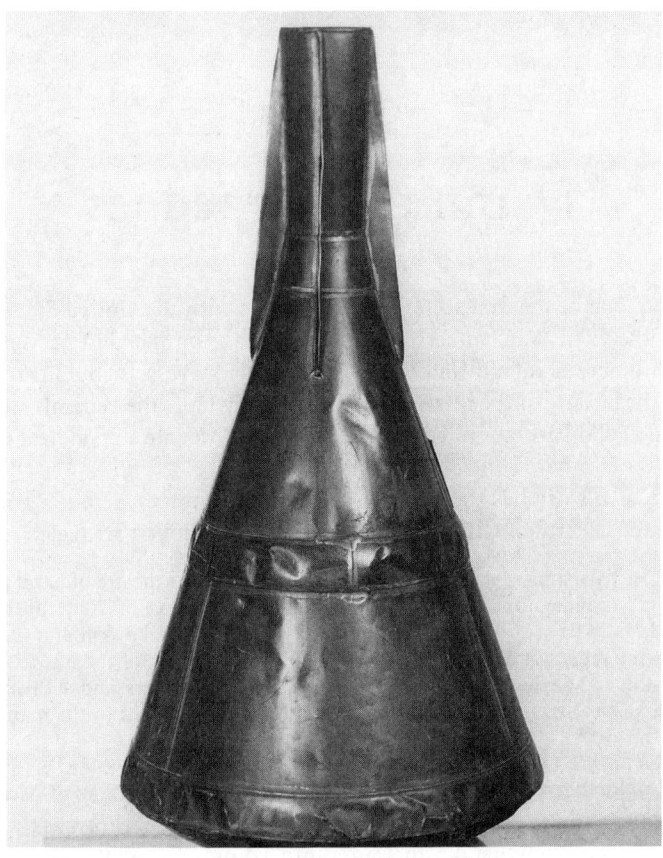

Copper-jacketed swaying torpedo, anchored with its broad air-chamber at the top. This type, most often with a tin rather than copper outer casing, was used as a line of defense at Mobile Bay (courtesy of West Point Museum Collection).

While the Union admiral waited impatiently, Confederate workmen were putting in overtime in order to complete the construction of at least three ironclad rams. With each passing day, Farragut looked on as his own situation grew more dismal; as torpedoes were planted in the harbor; and as Confederate troops steadily trained for action.

In the meantime, numerous Confederate navy men harbored a variety of ideas to help break up the Union blockade. One of the most daring exploits during this period was formulated by James C. Baker, who had earlier been assigned to the ironclad CSS *Louisiana* in New Orleans. Along with his brother, Page M. Baker, who was a master's mate aboard the CSS *Tuscaloosa*, he devised a unique plan to destroy one of Farragut's blockading vessels. To accomplish this end, they would incorporate an underwater explosive:

...Lieut. [James] Baker and his brother ... had in contemplation a project to destroy one vessel or more ... with torpedoes. They were to place a spar torpedo in a row-boat and pull out on a dark night to the ship selected for destruction. Lieut. [James] Baker was to keep the boat in position, while Master's Mate [Page Baker] was to dive overboard with the torpedo, swim under the side of the ship, and endeavor to explode it below her waterline. The merest statement of such a design is all that need be said to carry conviction of the devotion and heroism of these two young officers. They desired to attempt the task alone, being unwilling that anyone else should venture into the peril which it involved.[2]

When the detailed plan was initially submitted to Commodore Ebenezer Farrand of the Confederate navy, the superior officer condoned the idea, understanding that it meant certain death for those involved. However, after giving it further consideration, the commodore altered his point of view, instructing one of his lieutenants to

...inform Lieut. Jas. Baker, and ... also his brother, Master's Mate Page M. Baker, that, upon due deliberation, I am induced to withhold the verbal permission given them a few days since "to destroy by torpedo, in the manner proposed, any of the enemy's vessels in the bay," considering the whole scheme from beginning to end impracticable and attended with too great personal risk and danger....[3]

Hence, despite their willingness to sacrifice their own lives, the Baker plan was never carried out.

On February 23, 1864, the operations conducted by the Union navy for the destruction and capture of Mobile, Alabama, commenced. The central figure on the Federal side was Admiral David Farragut, who was described as being

...sixty-three years old, of medium height, stoutly built, with a finely proportioned head and smoothly shaven face, with an expression combining overflowing kindliness with iron will and invincible determination, and with eyes that in repose were full of sweetness and light, but, in emergency, could flash fire and fury.[4]

On the opposite side of the conflict was the Confederacy's Admiral Franklin Buchanan, who had been the commander of the CSS *Virginia* during her initial battle at Hampton Roads.

The city of Mobile was situated some 30 miles from the Gulf of Mexico, lying at the head of Mobile Bay. The inlet itself varied in width from 15 miles across at its lower end down to six at its northernmost reaches. The main entryway into the harbor arena was known as "Swash Channel," which flowed southwestward from the city and skirted an area called Mobile Point, a lengthy projection from the eastern mainland. On the western side of the bay was Dauphine Island, the easternmost island in a chain connecting Mobile to the Mississippi Sound.

The most prominent of land defenses to the above described waterway was Fort Morgan, built on the westernmost jetty of Mobile Point. It was this installation, constructed on the very same site where old Fort Bowyer had stood during the War of 1812, which controlled the channel. Designed in a pentagonal fashion, this brick-work fortification housed in both casemates and barbette a battery of guns which consisted of seven 10-inch, three 8-inch, and twenty-two 32-pound smooth bore cannons. Furthermore, she possessed two 8-inch, two 6.5-inch, and four 5.82-inch rifled cannons. And if these weren't enough to hold off an enemy invasion, Buchanan had armed her exterior batteries with an additional 29 assorted guns.

On the eastern shore of Dauphine Island, lying approximately three nautical miles from Fort Morgan, stood Fort Gaines. Also made of brick, it would be of secondary significance to the invading Federal fleet, which would move up the channel along the far side. Realizing that the Northern navy would remain well out of range from Fort Gaines, she housed only 27 total guns.

Much closer to Mobile, on a narrow stretch of land known as Tower Island, stood a half-finished Confederate battery known as Fort Powell. Although she had not yet reached completion, this fortification was already equipped with an arsenal that included an 8-inch Columbiad and a 10-inch Columbiad, as well as four reinforcing rifles.

Lying in wait for Farragut's flotilla was the most formidable Confederate ironclad ram then afloat:

> The *Tennessee* was 209 feet in length, with an extreme beam of 48 feet, and carried her battery in a casemate or shield amidships 79 feet long and 29 feet wide.... Her frame was composed of yellow pine beams, 13 inches thick, set close together vertically and planked with 5½ inches of yellow pine in horizontal courses, and 4 inches of oak in vertical courses. Within, the yellow pine frames were sheathed with 2½ inches of oak. The outer walls of the casemate were inclined at an angle of 45 degrees from the deck, and on this 25 inches of wood backing was laid the plate armor, which was 6 inches thick on the forward wall, and elsewhere 5 inches thick, and was fastened to the wood with bolts 1½ inches in diameter that went entirely through the wall.... The outside deck was plated with two inches of iron.[5]

In addition to the CSS *Tennessee*, the Confederate squadron consisted of three small gunboats, the CSS *Gaines*, the CSS *Morgan*, and the CSS *Selma*. Yet none of these possessed armor plating, except for a minute amount positioned around their boilers and machinery.

To reinforce the Confederate batteries, Mobile's defenses depended upon a line of piles positioned closely together, strung out southeasternly along a shallow sand reef in the general direction of Fort Morgan. Where the reef formed the western edge of the main channel, the piles ended. From that point on, a triple row of torpedoes was anchored beneath the water, ending at a distinct red buoy floating at a distance of less than 800 feet from Fort Morgan. Thus, the only safe navigable passageway left open to the Union admiral was less than 100 yards wide: he would be forced to take his flotilla past this prominently-reinforced installation.

Obviously, the Confederate Torpedo Division had been hard at work in the Mobile region, and their intricate system of defense had taken on elaborate proportions:

> About 180 torpedoes are said to have been planted in the bay in anticipation of Farragut's advance. One kind was made of tin in the form of a cone. The greater diameter was filled with an air chamber, which floated upward and carried a cap and trigger intended to be fired by a slight blow like that from a passing vessel. The lower compartment contained the charge, which so communicated with the cap that the explosion of the latter would reach it. The other class of torpedo was made of a barrel or beer keg, pitched to make it water tight and with wooden cones secured to the top and bottom to steady it. It was filled with powder and completed by the attachment of half a dozen sensitive primers, which would explode by concussion and transmit their flame to the charge. When prepared with care these torpedoes were much the more reliable as the caps of the can torpedoes got out of working order by long exposure to the action of the water.[6]

By sunset of August 4, 1864, Admiral Farragut had given his squadron their final instructions, and each of his commanding officers understood their individual assignments. The four Federal monitors present, recently arrived from various regions, included the USS *Tecumseh*, the USS *Manhattan*, the USS *Winnebago*, and the USS *Chickasaw*. They were ordered to travel in single file and a slight distance ahead of the seven pairs of wooden vessels. In addition to a warning concerning the powerful guns of Fort Morgan, Farragut offered his men the following:

> There are certain black buoys placed by the enemy from the piles on the west side of the channel across it towards Fort Morgan. It being understood that there are torpedoes and other obstructions between the buoys, the vessels will take care to pass eastward of the easternmost buoy, which is clear of all obstructions.[7]

August 5 dawned cloudless, with ideal wind conditions for Admiral Farragut's advance. During the night a light breeze had managed to push a dense fog away from the harbor. At a quarter before six, the commander's fleet was in motion, moving slowly up the channel. Admiral Buchanan, aboard the CSS *Tennessee*, had positioned his four ships across the channel, just behind the line of torpedoes. The Confederate leader fully expected that his own vessel would engage the USS *Tecumseh*, whose 15-inch guns had been loaded with 60 pounds of powder and cylindrical, flat-headed steel bolts. These, it was believed, would have no problem penetrating the steel plating of the *Tennessee*.

Even before this fateful day had arrived, Admiral Farragut had made known his feelings concerning Confederate underwater explosives: he believed them to be totally unethical for use in warfare. Yet, in anticipation of a rebel attack upon his own fleet prior to his invasion of Mobile, he had "bent" his morals somewhat and set explosives around his own anchored squadron:

> Torpedoes are not so agreeable when used on both sides; therefore, I have reluctantly brought myself to it. I have always deemed it unworthy a chivalrous nation, but it does not do to give your enemy such a decided superiority over you.[8]

The shooting began at precisely 7:07 A.M., and by a quarter past the hour the fighting had grown to intense proportions. A thick black cloud of smoke settled over the calm bay, above which hovered the tall masts and spars of Admiral Farragut's steadily advancing fleet.

Still Admiral Buchanan, situated with a bird's-eye view in the pilot house of the CSS *Tennessee*, held his fire, waiting for the USS *Tecumseh* to come within close range. Momentarily, there was a strange lull in the heated exchange, as all eyes turned toward these floating gladiators about to commence dueling.

Buchanan remained determined that the confrontation would begin at the closest of quarters, and he gave the order "not to fire until the vessels are in actual contact."[9]

It was then that Captain Tunis A. M. Craven, commander aboard the USS *Tecumseh*, made his fatal mistake: either influenced by the narrowness of the channel, or determined to attack the CSS *Tennessee* on a direct route, he turned his ship to the west, disregarding the orders given earlier by Admiral Farragut:

> In a moment, and when the ships were less than a hundred yards apart, a muffled explosion was heard, a column of water like a fountain springing from the sea shot up beside the Federal monitor; she lurched violently, her head settled, her stern went up into the air so that her revolving screw could be plainly seen, and then the waves closed over her....[10]

Of the total number of officers and crewmen aboard the USS *Tecumseh*, 93 of 114 went down with the ship, including Captain Craven. And, of the 21 men who survived, two officers and five seamen found refuge in one of the *Tecumseh*'s lifeboats, while four others swam to shore near Fort Morgan, where they were captured.

Meanwhile, John Collins, the *Tecumseh*'s pilot, and nine others who had been in the turret section of the ship, leaped into the water just seconds before she went down. Seeing the men floundering helplessly amid the intense battle, Federal officer Acting Ensign Henry C. Nields rowed his ship, the USS

Metacomet, up under the guns of Fort Morgan and through a deadly onslaught of shot and shell in a valiant attempt to save them. During this gallant effort, Nields found it necessary to pass around the stern section of the *Tecumseh's* wreck, under the broadside of the USS *Hartford,* and across the USS *Brooklyn's* bow section. Hence, he placed his vessel directly in the line of fire from Admiral Farragut's fleet, as well as that of the fort. The nine seamen, along with pilot Collins, were rescued, however, in what might very well have been one of the most daring adventures of the war.

Later, John Collins related his own version of exactly what had taken place aboard the USS *Tecumseh* as she was sinking. The following is quoted from a secondary source:

> Craven and Mr. John Collins, the pilot of the *Tecumseh,* met, as their vessel was sinking beneath them, at the foot of the ladder leading to the top of the turret.... It may be, then, that Craven, in the nobility of his soul — for all know that he was one of the nature's noble men, — it may be, I say, that, in the nobility of his soul, the thought flashed across him that it was through no fault of his pilot that the *Tecumseh* was in this peril; he drew back. "There was nothing after me," relates Mr. Collins, "when I reached the upmost round of the ladder, the vessel seemed to drop from under me."[11]

Meanwhile, the heated fighting continued. A lookout standing on the deck of the USS *Brooklyn* spotted some suspicious-looking objects floating in the water just in front of the ship. The vessel's captain immediately backed her engines, in an apparent maneuver to avoid them. Admiral Farragut, who had earlier climbed into the USS *Hartford's* rigging in order to locate a better vantage point, looked on in disgust as the *Brooklyn* reversed directions. Lashed to the after-shroud by a piece of lead line fastened around his waist, the confident admiral ordered his flagship to bypass the retreating vessel. As the *Hartford* went by on the port side of the *Brooklyn,* the captain informed Farragut that there was a "heavy line of torpedoes ahead."[12]

"Damn the torpedoes!" shouted Farragut from his perch, as the USS *Hartford,* followed by the rest of the column, steamed forward. One by one, the Union vessels crossed the minefield into the bay.

Inside the hulls of the attacking fleet, crewmen held their breath and said a silent prayer as they heard the steel rods of the torpedoes smashing against the fuses. Luckily, there were no further explosions, as the Federals pressed forward to confront and, eventually, defeat Admiral Buchanan's forces. Later, it was surmised that the underwater explosives had failed due to wet gunpowder.

Within a week following the destruction of the USS *Tecumseh,* Federal divers were given the grim detail of inspecting the sunken ship. While they were examining the wreck, they discovered, surprisingly, that nearly all of her crew remained at their respective posts:

The chief engineer, who had been married in New York only two weeks before, and who had received from the flag-ship's mail his letters while the line was forming, stood with one hand upon the revolving bar of the turret engine, and in the other an open letter from his bride, which his dead eyes still seemed to be reading.[13]

During the second week of August, Lieutenant F. S. Barrett, who was in charge of the torpedo defenses in Mobile Bay, sent a telegraph message to Brigadier General Gabriel J. Rains. From his office in Richmond, Virginia, Rains then proceeded to contact the Secretary of War concerning the USS *Tecumseh*'s destruction:

> I have the honor to enclose the within telegram with the remark that previous to leaving Mobile I had 67 torpedoes planted where this one acted, and had nine submarine mortar batteries underway (three completed) to close the main channel, such as the enemy report kept them out of Charleston, they being unable to move them. But my instructions and wishes were frustrated after I left; the place [was] left open and the enemy made use of it.[14]

Neither Barrett nor Rains, however, made the final comment concerning the destruction of the USS *Tecumseh*. A few days later, Major General Dabney H. Maury asserted that the Federal ironclad had not been sunk by a torpedo at all, but rather by gunfire from nearby Fort Morgan.

Upon hearing this determination, Gabriel Rains angrily rose to the defense of his bureau, arguing that the truth could be found in a report published by the enemy in the August 9 issue of the New Orleans *Picayune*:

> The enemy's report ... states ... that "so rapidly [was the vessel sunk] that two acting masters who escaped from the top of the turret stepped off directly in the water." The time of submersion determines whether shot or torpedo sunk the vessel. We have no evidence that her magazine was penetrated. How otherwise could a shot have occasioned her sinking in half a minute![15]

Perhaps the best evidence concerning what really caused the sinking of the *Tecumseh* comes not from any "official" source, but rather from an observant civilian. Greatly disturbed by a statement quoted in the Mobile *Register*, claiming that the Federal monitor had been devastated by guns from the fort, a Miss Emily Lee McCleskey sent a letter to Brigadier General Rains. In it she stated that such an idea was "a thing which had never been thought of before." Furthermore, she said,

> It really seems that the prejudice which the army and navy have against torpedoes cannot be eradicated. They hate to think anything so little credited yet shall invariably do the fleet of the foe more damage than their fine fighting, but the people now have faith in torpedoes and little else.[16]

Admiral Farragut's invasion and conquest of Mobile did not diminish Confederate determination to continue planting torpedoes throughout the region. Just a single day after the battle, a wagon-load of 12 underwater explosives left the Mobile area bound for the mouth of the Dog River, located just outside the city.

Once again, Lieutenant F. S. Barrett was in charge of the operation, and, with the assistance of two escaped slaves, he made his way over the rough roads with four mules pulling the wagon. Suddenly, as one of his helpers drove the team, Barrett, who was riding his horse a few strides ahead, heard a series of violent explosions. The lieutenant was blown from his horse into a nearby briar patch sprouting along the road's edge. Picking himself up and looking around, he discovered that the torpedoes had literally disintegrated the wagon. Evidently, he surmised, the man riding in the rear of the wagon had been absent-mindedly unscrewing the safety guards of the charges as they traveled. Barrett described the scene:

> ...three mules dead in the road ... [my] horse running wildly about, the ... driver dead ... and the author of the mischief a dozen steps off on the beach, mortally wounded.[17]

In spite of the accident, Barrett continued to prepare and plant torpedoes, placing them in the Dog River, as well as the Blakely and the Apalachee. More explosives were positioned near the batteries opposite the city of Mobile, in an effort to counteract any further Federal attacks.

Just after 10:00 P.M. on December 7, 1864, Ensign William G. Jones took his 101-ton gunboat, the USS *Narcissus*, toward the Confederate obstructions near Fort Morgan. Intending to perform picket duty, he weighed anchor in approximately eight feet of water. At precisely 10:30, a sudden gale blew in from the northeast, pushing his ship violently toward the shore. Fearing that the strong winds would cause the *Narcissus* to run aground, Jones moved south about one mile, letting his anchor drop in deeper waters:

> While paying out chain, the vessel struck a torpedo which exploded, lifting her [the USS *Narcissus*] nearly out of the water and breaking out a large hole in the starboard side, amidships, besides doing other damage.[18]

As the Federal ship filled with hot steam from broken pipes, men scurried from below deck to topside. Afraid that her boilers might explode, Ensign Jones ordered his Second Class Fireman, James Kelly, to "haul the fires." In carrying out this order, Kelly was severely scalded, along with an officer and two other crewmen. Despite their brave efforts, however, the *Narcissus* sank to the bottom of Mobile Bay.

Chapter 15

The Trout Boat
St. Patrick

As we have stated before, a number of builders laid claim to the invention of the first totally submersible craft which might be used against the Federal blockading forces. Still, despite the disagreement, only the *H. L. Hunley* submarine was successful in sinking an enemy vessel.

Abraham Lincoln narrowly missed becoming the father of modern underwater warfare nearly two and one-half years prior to the sinking of the USS *Housatonic*. The inventor behind the plan to attack Confederate vessels of war was a French citizen named Brutus de Villeroi, who traveled from his place of birth to offer the Northern government a down-scaled version of his original design. This, his second model, measured 35 feet in length, and was powered by a screw propeller. The Federal navy's commander-in-chief was so taken with the concept that he ordered an even larger craft, which would be meticulously constructed by Martin Thomas, a skilled ship-builder from Philadelphia. De Villeroi, of course, insisted on overseeing the entire project from start to finish.

Evidently the Frenchman was extremely well-versed in the design and construction of underwater vessels. As early as 1835, in his hometown of Nantes, he had successfully submerged himself in a ten-foot-long model for a period of two hours. This unique experiment very possibly proved quite fascinating to a seven-year-old neighbor boy of de Villeroi's, whom history would come to know as Jules Verne.

The present underwater craft, initially proposed by de Villeroi in early September 1861, possessed an innovative chemical device which had the unique ability to purify the inner air supply of his submarine. Furthermore, with this device installed, he claimed that the vessel's occupants could remain submerged for up to three hours without difficulty.

Following extensive testing of de Villeroi's initial scale model by the Union Navy, a much larger, 47-foot version went under construction in early 1862. A few weeks before her completion, de Villeroi became embroiled in a heated argument with the submarine's contractor concerning the specifications of the

Illustration of the incident which took place on the USS *Octorara* on February 26, 1865, involving a crewman who grasped the smokestack of the attacking CSS *St. Patrick* in an attempt to defend his vessel. His action was successful (courtesy of Valecia Bryner).

breathing apparatus. Furthermore, he held some grave reservations concerning the ship's updated non-mechanical means of propulsion. Disgusted, the hot-tempered Frenchman opted to sever his relationship with the Union government, returning home without seeing the project through to the end.

The *Alligator*, as she was now known, was later dispatched from Philadelphia to the Hampton Roads area on June 19, 1862, under the command of

Samuel Eakin. Meanwhile, the Assistant Secretary of the U.S. Navy, Gustavus V. Fox, notified Rear Admiral Samuel F. DuPont, "We have sent you down the semi-submarine boat '*Alligator*' that may be useful in making reconnaissances...."[1] Driven by a set of folding oars rather than a screw-propeller as was originally intended, the four and one-half-foot-wide *Alligator* poked around the bottom of the James River housing an ample crew of 17 within her roomy confines. However, as destiny would have it, she would never see action, for she was lost at sea in the perilous waters off Cape Hatteras, North Carolina.

Despite the apparent setback, President Lincoln continued his search for a well-designed, workable underwater attack vessel. During the same week of the now famous *Monitor–Merrimac* sea battle, in fact, the Northern commander-in-chief presented an idea to the Federal navy for a "rocket-powered" submarine. The ingenious craft had been designed by a Washington, D.C., inventor named Pascal Plant. However, navy officials brushed the concept aside, believing it to be impractical, if not impossible.

Not one to give in easily, Plant soon developed an idea that did catch the attention of U.S. navy officials: the world's first rocket-driven torpedo. In a subsequent test, conducted at the Washington Navy Yard, which was witnessed by Secretary of the Navy Gideon Welles, the innovative explosive proved its worth inconclusively. The first torpedo struck a mudbank along the shoreline, harmlessly blowing muck in all directions. A second explosive veered slightly off course, sinking a nearby schooner named the USS *Dianna*.

A few months later, in January 1863, another test was conducted before a small contingent of Union officials. With all eyes watching intently, Plant fired his underwater torpedo. Zig-zagging uncontrollably beneath the calm waters of the Anacostia River, the explosive broke the surface at a high rate of speed approximately 20 feet from its launch site. Flying dangerously through the air, it splashed down once again nearly one hundred yards farther down river. Sadly, the airborne missile overshadowed the significance of the near-successful launching, and disgusted Union officials cancelled all future testing of the device.

On the Confederate side, experiments with submerged vessels of war seemed to be more readily accepted by top-ranking naval officials. During the final months of 1861, an underwater craft was completed at the Tredegar Iron Works of Richmond, Virginia. In a demonstration conducted on the James River, the craft managed to destroy a large scow anchored near midstream.

The operation was carried out by three volunteers wearing rubber diving suits. After attaching the tiny submersible to the underside of the barge with a large suction cup device, the divers screwed the torpedo into the target vessel's wooden hull. When they had moved a safe distance away from the ship, one of the submarine's crewmen yanked hard on a lengthy lanyard, and the scow was "lifted bodily out of the water."

Evidently, the attachable torpedo was not thought feasible for large-scale construction, however, for nothing more is heard of it throughout the remainder of the war.

On the other hand, one invention was taken seriously by Confederate officials during the latter half of the conflict. The designer was one John P. Halligan, of Selma, Alabama, who intended for his semi-submersible craft, known as the *St. Patrick*, to be employed to break up the Northern blockading forces at nearby Mobile.

During the early weeks of 1863 Halligan had come to realize that the ideal attack submarine would be able to approach an enemy vessel on the surface of the water. Then when it came near enough to run the risk of detection, the craft would be able to submerge quietly and quickly beneath the surface. Finally, as the submarine passed beneath the hull of her intended victim, she would be able to detonate her explosive charge on contact. With these general concepts in mind, Halligan went to work on his underwater boat.

While the earliest stages of development and construction were underway, Halligan began promoting his idea to a variety of influential Confederate officials. One of those contacted was Dabney H. Maury, the Southern general in charge of the defense of Mobile. In a hand-written letter, Maury was informed that the *St. Patrick* would be completed in July 1864.

With the practice of espionage in full swing throughout the region, it is not surprising that the Federals were fully aware of the tiny submersible long before she was ready for action. Writing U.S. Secretary of the Navy Gideon Welles on April 12, 1864, Major General Stephen Augustus Hurlbut spoke about the preparations being carried out in the construction of the *St. Patrick*:

> The craft, as described to me, is a propeller about 30 feet long, with engine of great power for her size, and boiler so constructed as to raise steam with great rapidity. She shows above the surface only a small smoke outlet and pilot house, both of which can be lowered and covered. The plan is to drop down within a short distance of the ship, put out the fires, cover the smoke pipe and pilot house, and sink the craft to a proper depth; then work the propeller by hand, drop beneath the ship, ascertaining her position by a magnet suspended in the propeller, rise against her bottom, fasten the torpedo by screws, drop their boat away, pass off a sufficient distance, rise to the surface, light their fires, and work off....[2]

Just two months later, in June 1864, Commander Catesby R. Jones, head of the Confederate Naval Gun Foundry and Ordnance Works based in Selma, contacted General Maury in Mobile, informing him that the *St. Patrick* would be launched "in a few days." Furthermore, he stated,

> It [the *St. Patrick*] combines a number of ingenious contrivances, which, if experiments show that they will answer the purposes expected, will render the boat very formidable. It is to be propelled by steam (the engine is very compact), though under water by hand. There are also arrangements for raising and descending at will, for attaching the torpedo to the bottom of vessels, etc. Its first

field of operation will be off Mobile Bay, and I hope you may soon have evidence of its success.[3]

However, "evidence of its success" would be somewhat slow in coming for the Confederate forces, for General Maury soon thereafter became quite distressed to learn that Halligan's submarine was behind construction schedule. Hoping to employ the 30-foot-long, six-foot-high *St. Patrick* against Admiral Farragut's blockading fleet, Maury anxiously pressed the builder to complete the vessel.

Weeks passed before Maury's desires were met. Finally, in September, Halligan hired a contractor to tow the craft down the Tensaw River to Mobile. On the journey down, it was reported that the submarine proved "to be a good sailor on the river."[4] Upon arrival, however, Confederate officials were once again troubled by the fact that Halligan seemed to be stalling for more time. The inventor, evidently in no hurry to partake in an assault against enemy blockaders, offered a number of "excuses" as to why the *St. Patrick* was not yet ready for battle.

The vessel itself, which had been dubbed the "Trout Boat" by Mobile area seamen, would transport five volunteers packed like sardines in her belly. After two brief test runs in shallow waters, one Confederate official reported that Halligan had recently installed "some arrangement of machinery that times the explosion of torpedoes, to enable the operators to retire to a safe distance."[5]

With John P. Halligan at the helm, the versatile *St. Patrick* conducted several more practice dives in the choppy waters of Mobile Bay. Despite the apparent successes, however, numerous problems continued to plague Maury's plans for actual combat duty. Eventually, these delays proved to be quite costly to Southern forces. Furthermore, they began to stretch the patience of those who had hoped, by this time, to destroy a Federal ironclad.

By the first week of December, while the *St. Patrick* continued to be "preparing" for her maiden underwater attack, Confederate officials began to realize that they had missed their prime opportunity to attack Admiral Farragut's fleet. Many Southerners involved in the plan began to lose faith in Halligan's intentions, as seen in a letter from General Maury to the Confederate secretary of war, James A. Seddon:

> Farragut has moved North. The *Hartford* and other heavy vessels have disappeared from down bay.... Halligan, recently appointed lieutenant, has not yet used his torpedo boat. I do not believe he ever will. His boat is reported a most valuable invention.[6]

Within a 24-hour period, General Maury had lost all patience with John P. Halligan. In fact, he decided to take action by suggesting to his superiors that the inventor be relieved from his command of the *St. Patrick*. In a memo to Commodore Ebenezer Farrand, the commanding naval officer in Mobile, he stated:

> Every opportunity and facility having been afforded Mr. Halligan to enable him to use his boat against the enemy, and he evidently not being a *proper* man to conduct such an enterprise, please order a suitable officer of your command to take charge of the *St. Patrick* at once and attack without unnecessary delay.[7]

Within a few weeks, the submarine was indeed transferred to the control of the Confederate States Army, under the direction of General Dabney Maury himself. In turn, Maury appointed an energetic young naval officer, Lieutenant John T. Walker, to command the vessel.

During the second week of January 1865, when Lieutenant Walker boarded the *St. Patrick* for inspection, he discovered that Halligan had absconded with numerous parts of her valuable machinery. He immediately ordered that the unscrupulous inventor be located.

Tracing Halligan's movements carefully, Walker's informants discovered that he was "comfortably established" in a room at the Battle House Hotel, located in midtown Mobile. Within hours, the valuable missing equipment had been recovered "by energetic and good management."[8]

Lieutenant Walker wasted no time in reassembling the *St. Patrick* to working order. However, over the course of the next ten days, he also implemented a number of alterations in an apparent attempt to improve upon her capabilities. Perhaps the most notable change concerned the Trout Boat's mode of attack. She was outfitted with a 40-pound copper torpedo extending from a 12-foot long wooden spar. Finally, after one last test run, General Maury declared her fully prepared for an assault.

On the evening of January 26, 1865, the *St. Patrick* was boarded by Lieutenant Walker, accompanied by four Confederate navy volunteers stationed in Mobile. Slowly she built up steam and departed from the dock, moving through the unsettled waters of the bay toward the Federal blockaders. Earlier, Walker had selected as his primary target the USS *Octorara*, one of Admiral Farragut's vessels which had taken part in the invasion of Mobile.

At approximately two hours past midnight, Lieutenant Walker spotted his prey. Quickly, he ordered his fireman to increase steam, veering the *St. Patrick* so that she was on a direct collision route with the *Octorara*. The Confederate sailors braced themselves for the inevitable explosion. Striking the enemy ship abaft the wheelhouse, however, they were disappointed when nothing happened. Obviously, their spar torpedo had misfired, and any hopes to try again on this particular night were hampered by the heroics of the Federal lookout aboard the *Octorara*. The exact details of the incident were later reported in the February 25 issue of *Harper's Weekly*:

> On the night of the 26th a torpedo-boat came out from Mobile Bay.... At about 2 A.M., though the night was very dark, an object was discovered not many yards

astern, and making direct for the vessel. The look-out hailed lustily, "Boat ahoy!" The response came, "Ay, ay!" as though from one of our own boats. The officer of the deck immediately sang out to them to "lie on their oars;" to which they answered, "Ay, ay!"

A moment after they rasped along the vessel's side from aft forward to the guards. The knowledge that it was the torpedo-boat of the rebels now flashed upon all. The intrepidity of the captain of the after-guard is worthy of the highest praise. Though all expected momentarily to be blown up, this man, seeing how readily they [Federal guards] could gain an advantage over the enemy by prompt action, grasped her smoke-pipe as it came by the guards of the ship, at the same time crying out lustily for a rope to make the devil fast with.

The remaining sailors, acting under different impulses, recoiled to the opposite side of the deck. Several shots were fired at this brave man, and as his exertions were hardly sufficient to retain his hold upon the hot pipe, he preferred to let go rather than be dragged overboard.[9]

The CSS *St. Patrick* quickly disappeared into the night amid a hailstorm of gunfire from the *Octorara*, yet returned to the docks of Mobile. Though for the most part she was undamaged by her adventure, Confederate officials would not call her into further service. And though she had contributed to the South's expertise in designing and constructing underwater attack vessels, the brief exploits of the little-recognized Trout Boat were now a part of history.

Chapter 16

Justice in
North Carolina Waters

During the spring of 1864, Confederates were hard at work completing the construction process of the CSS *Albemarle* at Edwards Ferry, located on the Roanoke River some 30 miles below Weldon, North Carolina. Designed by John L. Porter and built under the watchful eye of contractor Gilbert Elliott, she was

> ...of solid pine frame timbers, each 8×10 inches thick, dovetailed together, and sheathed with 4-inch plank. The *Albemarle* was 152 feet long, 45 feet beam, and drew 8 feet [of water]. The *Albemarle*'s shield, octagonal in form, was 60 feet long, and was protected by two layers of 2-inch iron plating. The prow, or "ram," was of solid oak, plated with 2-inch iron, tapering to an edge. She had two engines of 200 horse-power each.[1]

In April of that same year, the CSS *Albemarle* was dispatched to patrol the shallow waters of Albemarle Sound surrounding Plymouth, North Carolina. During her initial mission, she successfully attacked and destroyed the USS *Southfield*, then blockading the city.

The Union navy was completely perplexed when it came to developing a strategy for mounting an offensive against this, the newest of Confederate ironclad rams. Certainly Federal experts believed its wooden ships were no match for the mighty *Albemarle*. Furthermore, the North's heavy iron monitors drew far too much water to pass over the shallow sandbars leading into the sound.

Despite this knowledge, however, two attempts to sink the seemingly indestructible Confederate vessel were made during early May 1864. The first was carried out on water, and involved a concentrated attack by a fleet of double-ended gunboats. One of these Union vessels, the USS *Sassacus*, was even able to get close enough to the *Albemarle* to ram her. Still, the assault failed miserably, with the *Sassacus* being destroyed in the process.

A second assault on the *Albemarle* was conducted by land, as five Union volunteers carried a pair of 100-pound torpedoes, disguised as patients on

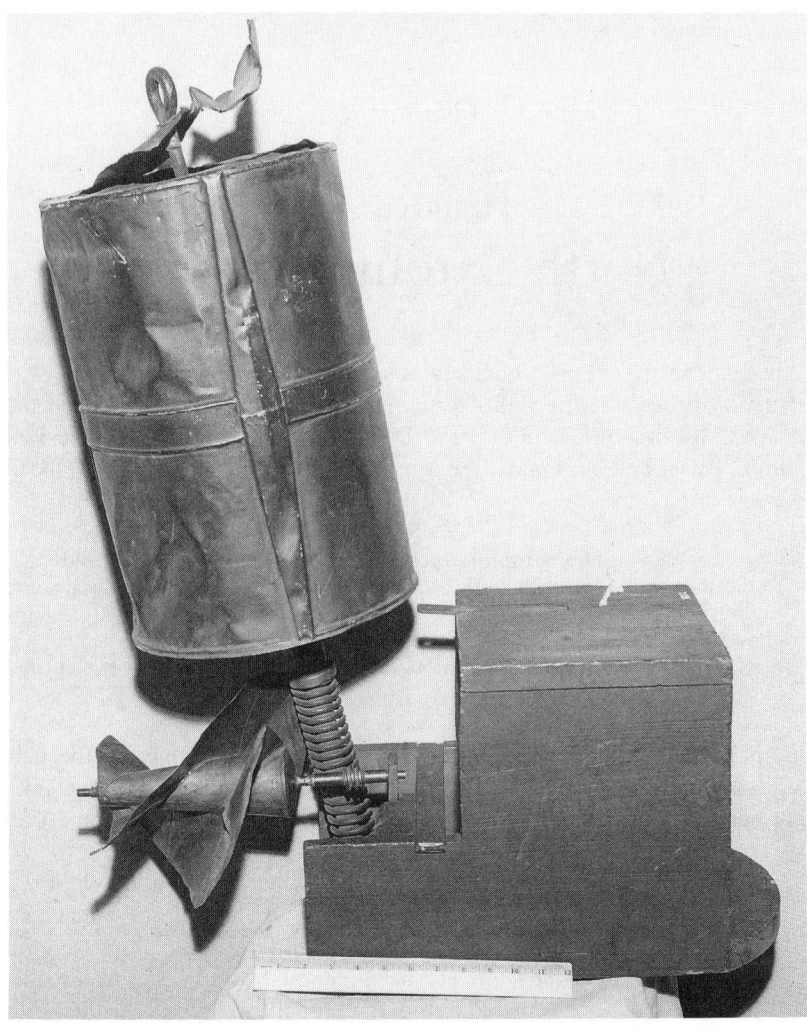

A current torpedo designed to float just below the surface against the hull of enemy vessels. The propeller, activated by the current from a ship's wake, would release the spring-driven plunger and detonate the explosive (courtesy of West Point Museum Collection).

hospital stretchers, across a swamp. When they reached the Albemarle Sound, the Federals floated the explosives toward their target, guiding them by two able-bodied swimmers. But, as they neared the *Albemarle*, the two Northerners were discovered and captured. Thus, the second attempt at destroying the Confederate ram had also failed, and she was destined to remain a major threat to Union blockaders for the rest of that summer.

Finally, on the night of October 27, 1864, Lieutenant William B. Cushing, of the Union navy, carried out a well-conceived assault upon the Confederate ironclad. Employing a small picket boat outfitted with a spar torpedo, he proceeded with his plan:

> We passed within thirty feet of the pickets without discovery, and neared the vessel ... just as I was sheering in close to the wharf, a hail [of gunfire] came, sharp and quick, from the iron-clad, and in an instant was repeated. I at once directed the cutter to cast off, and go down to capture the guard left in our rear, and, ordering all steam, went at the dark mountain of iron in front of us. A heavy fire was at once opened upon us, not only from the ship, but from men stationed on the shore. This did not disable us, and we neared them rapidly. A large fire now blazed upon the bank, and by its light I discovered the unfortunate fact that there was a circle of logs around the Albemarle, boomed well out from her side, with the very intention of preventing the action of torpedoes. To examine them more closely, I ran alongside until amidships, received the enemy's fire, and sheered off for the purpose of turning, a hundred yards away, and going at the booms squarely, at right angles, trusting to their having been long enough in the water to have become slimy — in which case my boat, under full headway, would bump up against them and slip over into the pen with the ram.... As I turned, the whole back of my coat was torn out by buckshot, and the sole of my shoe was carried away....
> ...in another instant we had struck the logs and were over, with headway nearly gone, slowly forging up under the enemy's quarterport. Ten feet from us the muzzle of a rifle gun looked into our faces, and every word of command was distinctly heard on board.
> My clothing was perforated with bullets as I stood in the bow, the heel-jigger in my right hand and the exploding-line in the left. We were near enough then, and I ordered the boom lowered until the forward motion of the launch carried the torpedo under the ram's overhang. A strong pull of the detaching-line, a moment's waiting for the torpedo to rise under the hull, and I hauled in the left hand, just cut by a bullet.
> The explosion took place at the same instant that 100 pounds of grape, at 10 feet range, crashed among us, and the dense mass of water thrown out by the torpedo came down with a choking weight upon us....[2]

Aboard the CSS *Albemarle*, it was reported to the captain that a "hole in her bottom big enough to drive a wagon in" had been inflicted upon the once-untouchable ram. Soon, her crewmen "found her resting on the bottom in eight feet of water, her upper works above water."[3]

The attack carried out by Lieutenant Cushing was the only successful torpedo assault conducted by the Union navy during the entire Civil War. Twenty years later, J. R. Soley would write:

> When it is reflected that Cushing had attached to his person four separate lines: the detaching lanyard, the triggerline, and two lines to direct the movements of the boat, one of which was fastened to the wrist and the other to the ankle of the engineer; that he was also directing the adjustment of the spar by the halliard; that the management of all these lines, requiring as much exactness and delicacy

of touch as a surgical operation, where a single error in their employment, even a pull too much or too little, would render the whole expedition abortive, was carried out directly in front of the muzzle of a 100-pound rifle, under a fire of musketry so hot that several bullets passed through his clothing, and carried out with perfect success, it is safe to say that the naval history of the world affords no other example of such marvelous coolness and professional skill as were shown by Cushing in the destruction of the *Albemarle*.[4]

What Soley had failed to point out in his description of Lieutenant William B. Cushing's "unmatched" exploit was that the Federal officer had, in fact, borrowed a Confederate weapon and tactic incorporated months earlier by volunteer navy men from the South. Furthermore, similar attacks on Union vessels during the same time period throughout North Carolina have been downplayed and all but forgotten.

Confederate experts continued to agree that underwater explosives might help them to be victorious in a war that seemed to be slipping away from them day by day. They planted their deadly devices throughout North Carolina, including the Cape Fear, Roanoke, and Rappahannock rivers. And, as the weeks passed, they came to realize that their actions grew out of pure patriotism, despite an earlier threat by Union government officials that they would be severely punished for such "murderous" activities:

> It is only the breaking or crushing of the hull of a vessel by the upheaving force of a column of water which makes torpedoes so destructive. It is not the flames of powder, or its suffocating or burning gases, which produce the awful death, in many instances, of all on board, but the instantaneous disruption of the hull, driven inward by the weight of the water, crushing everybody between decks, and instantaneously sinking the craft, and drowning those who are carried down by the rapid sinking of the wreck. An ironclad is more quickly and easily destroyed than any other class of vessel, for the reason that such an immense weight of metal armor carries down to the bottom everybody between decks the instant the hull is shattered by a torpedo.... I believe [that] several instances occurred in Southern rivers, during the war, where wooden vessels, coming in contact with mechanical torpedoes containing only a small quantity of powder, were simply lifted out of the water at the bows, without serious injury to the hull.[5]

Before the "fearlessness" of Lieutenant Cushing had managed to destroy the CSS *Albemarle*, Confederate troops had recaptured the city of Plymouth. Their well-organized land and sea attack had pushed the Federals into taking refuge at nearby Batchelor's Bay, where the Roanoke River intersects Albemarle Sound. There they began to formulate their next assault.

Late in the summer of 1864, General Ulysses S. Grant had opted to order a joint army-navy attack on Fort Branch, which was situated some 20 miles north of Plymouth. It was his opinion that the very best plan of action would be to land a large army detail under the protective guns of the Federal navy on the nearby beach. Then, slowly and meticulously, they would work their way inland, followed by a formidable flotilla of Union vessels strengthening their rear along the Roanoke River. At the same time, other Federal battalions would conduct similar operations throughout the state of North Carolina. Eventually, Grant surmised, these assault units would be successful in isolating the Confederates throughout the region:

> The operation is an important one, as closing the last port of the rebels, and destroying their credit abroad, by preventing the exportation of cotton, as well as preventing the reception of munitions and supplies from abroad.[6]

Union Rear Admiral David D. Porter was commanding the North Atlantic Squadron, and every Northern fleet was depleted in order to strengthen his invading force. The massive assault was set to begin on October 15. In the meantime, more than 150 vessels were gathering together for the impending attack.

On December 1, Commander W. H. Macomb, who was in charge of the Division of the Sounds of North Carolina, was informed that he should cooperate with the invading army in the attempt to capture Fort Branch. Anticipating such an order, however, he had already begun organizing his forces a few days earlier:

> Lieutenant Cushing reached the Valley City about midnight on the night of October 28th–29th. On the next day, the 29th, at 11:15 A.M., Commander Macomb got under way, and his fleet proceeded up the Roanoke River. Upon the arrival of the fleet at the wreck of the Southfield, after exchanging shots with the lower batteries, it was found that the enemy had effectually obstructed the channel by sinking schooners alongside the wreck, and the expedition was therefore compelled to return....[7]

Having learned from an advanced reconnaissance party, dispatched from the USS *Valley City*, that the nearby Middle River was clear of all obstructions, Commander Macomb decided to approach Plymouth from that direction. His flotilla zig-zagged up the waterway, shelling Plymouth from behind a stand of trees, until they reached the mouth of the Middle River, where it intersected the Roanoke:

> At 9:30 on the morning of the 31st of October the line was formed, the *Commodore Hull* being placed in advance, as her ferry-boat construction enabled her to fire ahead. The *Whitehead*, which had arrived with stores [of ammunition] just before the attack, was lashed to the *Tacony*, and the tugs *Bazely* and *Belle* to the *Shamrock* and *Otsego*, to afford motive power in case of accident to the machinery. Signal was made to "Go ahead fast," and soon after 11 the fleet was hotly engaged with the batteries on shore, which were supported by musketry from rifle-pits and houses. After a spirited action of an hour at short range, receiving and returning a sharp fire of shell, grape, and canister, the *Shamrock* planted a shell in the enemy's magazine, which blew up, whereupon the Confederates hastily

abandoned their works. In a short time Plymouth was entirely in possession of the Union forces....[8]

Within a week, Commander Macomb was prepared to move his forces up the Roanoke River toward Fort Branch. His fleet included the USS *Wyalusing*, under the command of Lieutenant Earl English; the USS *Valley City*, under the guidance of Acting Master J. A. J. Brooks; the USS *Otsego*, with Lieutenant H. N. T. Arnold at the helm; the tugboat *Belle*, under the direction of Acting Master James G. Green; the tugboat *Bazely*, controlled by Acting Master Mark D. Ames; and a rather small picket boat, not unlike the one used by Lieutenant Cushing a few weeks earlier in the attack on the CSS *Albemarle*.

The formidable flotilla departed from Plymouth at precisely 5:00 A.M. on December 9, threading its way up the river in single file. As they closed in on their intended destination, the crewmen noticed that the waterway was becoming increasingly narrow, with huge red clay bluffs overhanging their decks and thick vegetation crowding the banks. Earlier, Commander Macomb had been absolutely assured that all obstructions, including underwater torpedoes, had been located and removed. Furthermore, he had been promised that his battalion would have no trouble reaching Jamesville, located approximately a dozen miles upriver. Even so, before departing he had taken extra precautionary measures, throwing nets across the bows of his vessels in order to "scoop up any stray mines."

During the first few miles of the voyage, the USS *Wyalusing* led the pack, followed close behind by the USS *Valley City* and the USS *Otsego*. Then, having suffered a few engine problems, the *Wyalusing* dropped back to the third position, allowing the *Otsego* to assume the second place in line. Little did he realize it at the time, but Lieutenant Arnold, of the *Otsego*, had made his first fatal mistake of the journey.

Reaching the township of Jamesville at approximately 9:00 P.M., the Union vessels were ordered to drop anchor for the night. Just as crewmen prepared to do so aboard the *Otsego*, a deadly Singer torpedo exploded off their port deck, sending up a huge geyser of water and muck. Though the 974-ton gunboat was rocked violently by the explosion, she was not seriously damaged, and her crewmen prepared to move a bit further away from the bank. Seconds later, however, another explosion was heard, this time directly under the forward pivot gun. The 100-pound Parrott rifle teetered and fell, as the force of the torpedo blasted a hole up through the ship's vulnerable wooden decking.

The second charge had inflicted considerable damage to the unsuspecting *Otsego*, and she quickly settled to the bottom of the shallow river. Crewmen aboard the accompanying vessels looked on in horror as steam and smoke spurted from her opening. Within minutes she hit bottom, with her spar deck resting beneath three feet of water. Fortunately, because of the immediate reaction on the part of other crewmen, no one was killed in the explosion. Furthermore, a later report claimed but a single minor injury.

Early the following morning, Commander Macomb ordered his remaining vessels to dispatch search parties, in order to sweep the area around the fallen ship. Soon they managed to locate "a perfect nest of torpedoes," which they quickly destroyed.

Acting Master Mark D. Ames, in command of the USS *Bazely*, was instructed to make a return trip to Plymouth, transporting the *Otsego*'s men with him. As his ship moved up alongside the wreck for the transferral of men, she struck another torpedo and was "blown literally to pieces." Though her captain, pilot, and paymaster escaped without so much as a scratch, two sailors were killed in the mishap.

Shaken by the extremely close encounter, Acting Master Ames informed Commander Macomb that "the *Bazely* is gone up." A member of Macomb's staff, however, saw the destruction of this, the second craft in the fleet, in a totally different light: "By that time she had gone down!"[9]

Only a short time later, still another explosion rippled the waters surrounding Macomb's flotilla. This time, Picket Boat Number 5 was severely damaged and, eventually, sunk. The commander was in an angry uproar, and he ordered his men to search every single inch of waterway in the region.

Employing the sunken *Otsego* as a gun battery post to protect this portion of the river from enemy fire on shore, Macomb dispatched smaller boats to conduct the tedious task of locating underwater explosives. In short order, another half dozen torpedoes were found nestled very near the three wrecks. Furthermore, to Macomb's surprise, two others were discovered entangled in the *Otsego*'s "protective" netting. Though absolute care was taken while moving them toward shore, two of them accidentally exploded. No one was injured, however, and the remaining three were later destroyed.

Just two days passed before a number of underwater mines were located approximately eight miles beyond Jamesville. Then, on December 14, crewmen aboard the USS *Valley City* uncovered a total of 29 torpedoes near Shad Island Bend, describing them to be "in the richest and choicest clusters, in some places eight or nine ... across the river in a line...."[10] This deadly obstruction was later determined to be the masterful work of Lieutenant Francis L. Hoge, a member of the Confederate navy, who was quite well-known for his numerous exploits in battles against the Federal fleet.

Meanwhile, as mines continued to be discovered throughout the region, Union forces were preparing to attack Fort Fisher, which protected the city of Wilmington on the Cape Fear River:

> The channels of Cape Fear River ... were carefully planted by the Confederates with electric and barrel torpedoes; and the operators for the electric torpedoes were stationed with their firing apparatus in bomb-proofs of the forts.[11]

Despite the careful measures employed by the Rebels, Union navy personnel managed to carry out what was to be perhaps the most bizarre explosives attack of the entire war. The plan called for the intentional detonation of an aging steamer, the USS *Louisiana*, which would be filled to capacity with 180 tons of gunpowder. Though Admiral Porter was "an unwilling party to the scheme" at the outset, he eventually changed his way of thinking. Subsequently, the floating bomb was towed in along the beach, approximately 400 yards from Fort Fisher. Then, the fuse, which was designed to burn for about 90 minutes, was lit:

> The more sanguine believed that Fort Fisher, with its garrison, guns, and equipment, would be leveled to the ground, while others were equally certain it would prove a fizzle. Commander A. C. Rhind, with a crew of volunteers, successfully performed the perilous duty, and, applying the match at midnight, the crew rowed safely away to the Wilderness, a swift gun-boat, in waiting. The whole fleet having moved off shore, under low steam, awaited the result in anxiety. A glare on the horizon and a dull report were the indications that the floating mine had been sprung. In the morning, when the fleet steamed in, all eyes were toward the fort. There it was, as grim as ever, apparently uninjured, with its flag floating as defiantly as before....[12]

At the time of the explosion Midshipman Clarence Cary of the Confederate navy occupied a deserted hut located a short distance up the beach, between the *Louisiana* and the fort. Though he was much closer to the immense blast, he managed to sleep peacefully throughout the night:

> Possibly the first ton or so of powder ignited blew the remainder harmlessly into the sea, or it may be the ship got adrift in the hour and a half the time fuse allowed her after she was abandoned, and thus wreaked her expected havoc at some remote point, where only the fish and sea-gulls, instead of sleeping men, were within range.[13]

Despite the disappointing failure of the well-conceived plan to demolish Fort Fisher, Federal forces continued their efforts. Following two immense assaults, the second of which included no less than 6,000 Union soldiers, navy men, and marines, the fort fell on January 22, 1865.

Almost immediately, Federal gunboats began sweeping the Cape Fear River and its small channels, hoping to find any torpedoes left behind by the enemy. While digging trenches in the soft sand near Fort Caswell, located across the estuary from Fort Fisher, they discovered a strange grouping of wires. Following them into the water, crew members found four huge electric mines, three of which were raised and destroyed. The fourth was left in its place after being disarmed.

Near Fort Anderson, located halfway up the Cape Fear River near the township of Brunswick, more odd-looking wires were uncovered. Tracing the wires to their respective ends, the searchers found what would prove to be the most advanced torpedo system yet devised. On land was located a magneto battery, then known as the "Wheatstone Magnetic Exploder." Devised by Matthew Fontaine Maury in Great Britain, it was made up of three magnetos enclosed in a single mahogany box. To the side of the enclosure was an ingenious crank that, when turned, could detonate a series of up to two dozen explosions in rapid succession.

Late in the afternoon, on February 20, 1865, a flotilla of Union vessels was ordered by Admiral Porter to search the waters of the Cape Fear River. Earlier in the day, he had received an urgent message warning him that the Confederates had dispatched nearly 100 torpedoes all along the waterway, establishing a minefield which was floating toward his squadron.

At approximately 8:00 P.M., a barrel-type torpedo was spotted by Porter himself as it bobbed up and down on the surface. A launch from the USS *Shawmut* was sent out for a closer inspection. After examining it thoroughly, the launch's commanding officer, Ensign W. B. Trufant, decided that it was, indeed, an explosive device. He drew his loaded pistol and fired a shot into its side at close range. Suddenly, as might have been expected, the floating torpedo exploded, severely wounding Trufant, killing two of his men, and totally destroying his vessel.

On the following evening, the search parties were dispatched once again. This time, however, when a torpedo was found, it was destroyed from a safe distance. Though the men had taken extra precautions, one of the floating charges managed to slip through their nets. The hidden explosive was then drawn into the paddle wheels of the USS *Osceola*. When the blast occurred, the 974-ton gunboat suffered only minor damage, and was able to remain afloat.

Further orders to continue the tedious search and destroy mission just two weeks later proved to be quite perilous. On that occasion, an Army transport, the USS *Thorne*, was struck by a torpedo near Fort Anderson. Within moments, she had sunk to the bottom of the river. Later, Admiral Porter had this to say about the situation:

> ...the Confederates sent down 200 floating torpedoes from Wilmington upon the fleet. One damaged the gunboat *Osceola*, and the second blew to pieces a cutter from the *Shawmut*, killing and wounding four men.[14]

Though the war was now drawing to a close, torpedo warfare on the part of the Confederates would greatly intensify during the upcoming weeks of action.

Chapter 17

A Valiant Effort
in South Carolina

After January 1, 1865, it soon became crystal clear to both sides that the Confederate land forces could not hold out much longer. In the weeks ahead, they would suffer quick and successive problems within the government, beginning near the top and trickling down to the lower ranks:

> The *Examiner* this morning says very positively that Mr. Secretary Seddon has resigned. Not a word about Messrs. Benjamin and Mallory—yet....[1]

During the first week of the new year, Confederate Secretary of the Navy Stephen R. Mallory submitted a detailed report to President Jefferson Davis concerning the current conditions of the Southern munitions of war. In it, he described the efforts of the Naval Powder Works, based at Columbia, South Carolina:

> This establishment is worked to its full capacity and makes 20,000 pounds of powder per month with ten experts. In the course of a few weeks the capacity will be doubled by the addition of new machinery and five more experts....[2]

Further to the southeast, in Charleston, members of the Confederate Torpedo Division worked diligently around the clock to produce newer and more innovative weaponry. Two and a half years of experimentation and planning had managed to create full-fledged experts out of one-time "tinkerers" in the field of explosives. Furthermore, their established department had grown immensely. In fact, nearly 60 men were now involved on a full-time basis, and their efforts to keep Federal blockaders and invaders at bay continued to pay off.

Rains-style keg and barrel torpedoes were continually floated in the waters throughout South Carolina during the early months of 1865. Still under the close direction of Captain M. Martin Gray, operators braved bone-chilling night winds as well as detection by the enemy in order to carry out their instructions.

168

On the night of January 15, for example, a pair of Confederate volunteers were dispatched into the Charleston Harbor to reinforce the rope obstructions with a fresh batch of underwater explosives. One of these brave men, Francis Wood, was born and raised in the Charleston area, and he knew every nook and cranny of the channel like the back of his hand. The second volunteer, Robert Thompson, was from Norfolk, Virginia, and had been a trusted member of the Charleston operations for several months. Together, they managed to deposit 16 new torpedoes near the barrier, and then proceeded to plant numerous others near the entrance of Hog Island Channel, situated just north of the city limits.

By the time that Wood and Thompson had completed their mission, Federal monitors had begun brisk operations throughout the bay area. The Union's Admiral Dahlgren had, in fact, instructed the commanders of his ironclad squadron to search the waterway with meticulous care and precaution. The reason for his extraordinary concern for a clear harbor was simple; he was preparing to embark on a coordinated attack with General Sherman's army, which was then marching northward from Georgia. In orders issued on January 15, he required that each vessel be outfitted with a pair of 50-foot pine logs, attached in an "X" shape across the bow. From these were hung heavy nets which would, it was hoped, snare and entrap any underwater explosive prior to contact with a ship's hull.

Despite the extra precautionary measures taken by the admiral, however, one of his vessels would suffer a grave fate during the upcoming invasion. On the night of January 15, just hours after Dahlgren's orders had been carried out, the USS *Patapsco* and the USS *Lehigh*, two picket monitors, made their way toward Charleston through the harbor. As they steamed carefully between forts Moultrie and Sumter, protecting the search operations of several scout boats that were hunting for torpedoes with grapnel hooks, they unknowingly became surrounded by deadly explosives.

With the *Patapsco* leading the way for a pair of smaller tugs, the captain of the USS *Lehigh* remained a good distance to the port side. Lieutenant Commander S. P. Quackenbush, aboard the lead vessel, decided to call it a night at approximately ten minutes before 8:00 P.M. Subsequently, he ordered his men to stop the engines and to drop anchor. However, noticing that his ship seemed to be drifting slightly toward the shallows, he instructed his fireman to restore power once again:

> ...suddenly, there was a shock, a sound of explosion, a cloud of smoke on the port side, and in less than half a minute her deck was under the surface of the water. The torpedo had struck the vessel under the overhang and had lifted the deck. The first impression of Lieutenant Sampson, the executive officer, was that she had been hit by a shot, but the column of water and smoke which immediately shot up convinced him of the real nature of the explosion. So quickly did the *Patapsco* go down that, although a dozen boats were within a few hundred yards, only forty-seven of her 109 officers and men escaped drowning.[3]

As daylight approached, it was very apparent to the men aboard the remaining Union search vessels that the 844-ton ironclad was a total loss. All that was visible of the USS *Patapsco*'s once-formidable hulk was, in fact, the uppermost portion of her curved smoke stack. One member of the Charleston-based Torpedo Division summed up his own feelings concerning the incident in only a few words, saying that it had been his ambition to "teach them a lesson."[4]

Following the loss of the USS *Patapsco*, which had gone down approximately 800 yards off the banks leading to Fort Sumter, Admiral Dahlgren called his captains together for a major top-secret conference. He advised them at that time that they would be called upon to put forth an added effort to capture the city of Charleston. Furthermore, he discussed the possibility that they might simultaneously attack Sullivan's Island and Fort Johnson, while still another flotilla would make a run past Fort Sumter all the way through the harbor for a direct assault on the city. A good number of Dahlgren's commanding officers were somewhat skeptical of the plan: although they did approve of an attack on Sullivan's Island, they felt that the other portions of the admiral's plan were far too risky.[5]

Meanwhile, the Confederate Torpedo Division at Charleston was attempting to piece together the most powerful torpedo boat squadron then in existence. A total of nine vessels had either been completed or were very close to completion. Unlike those employed previously in other locations, however, they were designated by number rather than by name. Lieutenant General W. J. Hardee, who had recently been placed in charge of them, hoped to formulate a single, devastating force:

> In organizing the [torpedo boat] force, I propose to select one officer to control the whole service, who should make his headquarters in this city; one to command a flotilla on the coast ... and one to command the Georgia fleet. A number of officers are anxious to serve if the organization is perfected....[6]

By the end of January 1865 it was clear that the city of Charleston would soon fall. In an eloquent appeal by the women of the region, who had earlier sold their valuable jewelry to help finance the gunboat CSS *Palmetto State*, the Southern army was urged to continue its valiant efforts:

> We implore, as the greatest boon, fight for Charleston! At every point, fight for every inch, and if our men must die, let them die amid the blazing ruins of our homes.[7]

On the night of February 17 the order was given to abandon Charleston. Before departing, however, select members of the Confederate army took the time to set fire to the area surrounding an enormous Blakely gun, situated at the corner of East Battery and South Battery. The resulting explosion was of such magnitude that a 500-pound chunk of the weapon landed on the roof of a residence located more than 100 yards distant.

In the nearby public square, a huge pile of raw cotton was also burned, along with thousands of bushels of rice. A few young children, who had innocently discovered that black gunpowder would create a smokey "pop" when tossed on the fire, amused themselves by carrying handfuls of it to the blaze from a nearby storage depot. Inadvertently, they left a scattered trail of powder from the storage area to the burning cotton. This in turn was ignited by a stray spark, and when the depot exploded nearly 150 people were killed. Hundreds of others were severely wounded.

A second explosion was heard when the gunboat CSS *Palmetto State* was purposely set ablaze at her wharf. A short time later there was yet a third massive explosion: it was the CSS *Chicora*. Lastly, there was a final, ear-deafening blast that shook the entire city of Charleston. More than 20 tons of black gunpowder had been loaded aboard the gunboat CSS *Charleston*, which was then deliberately ignited. Huge pieces of her once-proud hull came out of the sky along nearby wharves, setting them ablaze as well.

The Federal invaders did manage to take possession of the ironclad CSS *Columbia*, along with the steam tugs CSS *Mab*, CSS *Transport*, and CSS *Lady Davis*. During their search along the expansive docks spreading all along the coast they also discovered a pair of torpedo boats, lying at the base of the railway wharf. Boat Number 3 was found partially submerged near Chilolm's Mills. The seawater had ruined her decking, boilers, and engine parts. Nearby, also underwater, were two other torpedo vessels, in much the same condition. In all, no fewer than eight assault vessels, hoisting spars for torpedoes, were found.

After the evacuation of Charleston was complete, the job of clearing the harbor and nearby rivers of underwater explosives fell on the shoulders of Admiral Dahlgren. On February 19, the hazardous undertaking was begun by Captain M. Martin Gray, the one-time head of the Charleston Torpedo Division. Two other members of his elite team, Francis Wood and Robert Thompson, also offered their assistance in the project.

Gray, who had spent the past six months in a Federal prison camp, was extremely willing to assist the enemy in this matter. Having been detained and, eventually, arrested for "irregularities in purchasing rope" for the booms on his torpedo-boat spars, he was later released and placed under the watchful eyes of the authorities. In a statement made to Admiral Dahlgren, Gray claimed that since the previous August he had attempted, on numerous occasions, to desert the Confederate ranks. Furthermore, he said that he had knowingly and purposely sabotaged numerous hidden underwater mines. Evidently, he had felt that their deployment was against all rules of war, and he was now ready to make reparations by pinpointing their locations for Union officials.

With Gray leading the way, Federal search parties found a pair of contact mines just below the surface in the shipping channel near Fort Sumter. Most likely, these were two of the 16 placed there just a single month earlier (one of which had destroyed the USS *Patapsco*). In addition, Gray pointed out three large electrically-controlled underwater explosives located between Middle Ground and Battery Bee. He explained that the copper wires leading onto the shoreline had been severed since August, and that he was not only the only one who knew this, but totally responsible for their disarming.

Captain Gray also generalized about the probable locations of contact mines which had been floated in many areas. For example, a great number were found in the Wando River region, near Cat Island. Others were discovered a bit farther downstream, near the mouth of the waterway where it intersected the Cooper River.

Even without the assistance of Captain Gray, Federal searchers were able to locate a number of explosives. A series of frame torpedoes, for example, was discovered beneath the waters of the Ashley River by the tugs USS *Jonquil* and USS *Gladiolus*. As work was initiated to remove them, along with several 50-foot-long wooden obstacles which surrounded them, Admiral Dahlgren left on a journey to nearby Georgetown, South Carolina. Early in the morning on March 1, 1865, he prepared to make the return trip to Charleston aboard a 645-ton side-wheeler gunboat known as the USS *Harvest Moon*. Anxious to get back, he paced the floor of his cabin, occasionally spying the shoreline through his binoculars:

> Suddenly, without warning came a crashing sound, a heavy shock, the partition between the cabin and wardrobe was shattered and driven towards me, while all loose articles in the cabin flew in different directions. Then came the hurried tramp of men's feet, and a voice of someone in the water ... shrieking .... My first notion was that the boilers had burst; then the smell of burnt gunpowder suggested that the magazine had exploded.
>
> ...Frightened men were struggling to lower the boats.... Passing from the gangway to the upper deck ladder, the open space was strewed with fragments of partitions. My foot went into some glass. The Fleet Captain was rushing down, and storming about. I ascended the ladder to get out on the upper deck to have a full view of things. A torpedo had been struck by the poor old "Harvest Moon," and she was sinking. The water was coming in rapidly through a great gap in the bottom. The main deck had also been blown through....[8]

The torpedo had exploded just a few feet beneath the hull of the USS *Harvest Moon* as she steamed along her journey just a few miles from Battery White. In the belief that the Georgetown Bay area had been cleared of all remaining underwater mines, no precautions had been taken to protect the ship from such an incident. Though Admiral Dahlgren was rescued by a nearby gunboat, he lost everything he had brought with him except the clothes on his back. Furthermore, as proof of his close encounter with injury and death, one crewman was killed and the ailing vessel sank in less than five minutes.

On March 6 the USS *Jonquil* left port on a mission to drag the Ashley River in search of more frame torpedoes. Later that morning, her 50-foot-long grapnel hook snagged a set of obstructions attached to four cast-iron encasements. Slowly, the entire bundle was hoisted to the surface, and searchers noticed that one of the four torpedoes was missing. Continuing on their perilous mission, the remaining three were moved toward shore, where they were to be destroyed.

Suddenly, the missing torpedo struck the *Jonquil*'s hull and exploded violently. The force was so great that three of the ship's crewmen were seriously injured, while nine others were thrown completely overboard. All nine were eventually rescued from their plight, but damage to the vessel was extensive; every glass window on board had been shattered, three cross-beams were sprung, and the forward howitzer was damaged by the blast. In spite of the incident, however, the *Jonquil*'s captain ordered his crew back out the following morning.

At precisely 5:25 in the afternoon on St. Patrick's Day, March 17, the Coastal Survey steamer USS *Bibb* was returning to Charleston when she was struck by an underwater explosive. The force damaged her engines, as it threw up a column of water high into the air alongside the ship's port bow. Although she rolled violently to one side, losing 60 feet of mooring chain in the process, the *Bibb* was able to retain her upright position.

Just two days after the USS *Bibb*'s close encounter with disaster, the 1,155-ton navy transport USS *Massachusetts* reportedly "grazed one" torpedo, though it failed to detonate. Before her crew members could scoop it up out of the water, however, the failed mine sank out of sight.

Aside from the numerous electrically-detonated explosives which had been located during the month-long search, a total of 61 contact mines had been discovered floating throughout South Carolina's waterways. All were constructed out of small encasements, fitted with nose cones, and covered with pitch to prevent leakage. Furthermore, most contained approximately 70 pounds of gunpowder, with a small number housing even more. According to Gray, they were not "new" mine fields, but rather replacements for those which had been washed out to sea by the strong currents.

Eventually, Federal officials came to the belief that they were now truly in control of Charleston, and they continued their efforts to render all underwater explosives harmless. Of all the sites throughout the South, it was here that the entire concept of underwater warfare had remained a mystery to the North until the final evacuation of the city. However, mine warfare was certainly no mystery to the citizens of Charleston, who had witnessed its birth in early March 1839. It was at that time that public experiments had been conducted in the harbor by two men known only as "Taylor and Goodyear." These two enterprising inventors had shown their expertise by diving into the harbor and affixing a wooden keg containing 75 pounds of gunpowder to the wooden hull of a small schooner. Just two minutes and 40 seconds after the lighting of a lengthy fuse, the schooner had been "torn into fragments, nay, almost atoms, by the explosive force."[9] And now, 26 years later, the city of Charleston had gained the reputation of being one of the last Confederate strongholds defended by underwater explosives.

Chapter 18

Closing Operations in Mobile

Following the invasion and subsequent takeover of Mobile Bay by the Union navy's Admiral Farragut in August 1864, the Confederates prepared for a direct assault on the city of Mobile itself. After Farragut's retirement from the service in September that same year, the West Gulf Squadron came, for a brief period of time, under the direction of Commodore James S. Palmer. He in turn was relieved of duty in February 1865 by Acting Rear Admiral Henry K. Thatcher. In conjunction with General Edward R. S. Canby, Thatcher personally organized the final assault on Mobile:

> His force included among other vessels the iron-clads *Cincinnati, Winnebago, Chickasaw, Milwaukee, Osage,* and *Kickapoo.* Among the wooden vessels were the double-enders *Genesee, Sebago, Octura,* and *Metacomet,* the gun-boats *Itasca* and *Sciota,* the tin-clads *Rodolph, Elk, Meteor, Tallahatchie, Nyanza,* and *Stockdale* [flagship]....[1]

In the waters surrounding Mobile, the Confederate Torpedo Division was indeed hard at work to protect the city from final invasion. Under the leadership of General Dabney H. Maury, the nephew of Matthew Fontaine Maury, the "upper waters of the bay were thickly sown with stationary torpedoes, and great numbers of floating mines were sent down from above, so that the [North's] naval operations were full of danger."[2]

General Maury, a die-hard commander known to his men as "Old Puss in Boots," employed the most educated operators available to carry out the huge order of underwater mine displacement. His chief engineer was a German-born mercenary by the name of Victor von Sheliha, and it was he who eventually took charge of the crewmen involved in this intricate undertaking.

As a student of science, von Sheliha had graduated from the Prussian Military School, and had gone on to gain valuable experience as an officer in the Prussian army's Sixth Infantry Regiment. Later, during the 1850s, he had chosen to migrate to the New Orleans region.

After joining the Confederate Army in the spring of 1861, von Sheliha was captured by Federal soldiers and became a prisoner of war at Fort Warren, Massachusetts, where he remained for nearly 15 months. Two months after his release, in October 1863, he was assigned to the elite Mobile torpedo unit. There, he took an active role in underwater explosives research, and after the war he wrote a valuable, little-known book on the subject.

Von Sheliha, like so many other researchers who worked with underwater mines, experienced a great deal of anxiety-provoking delay when it came to locating and securing supplies for his weaponry. However, unlike the others, he took such delays as a personal affront to his command, and was quickly drained of patience by the seemingly never-ending string of red tape. In fact, even after he complained several times to both the governor of Alabama and General Dabney Maury about the lack of adequate workmen, no results were forthcoming. Hence, von Sheliha resigned his commission in the Confederate service in October 1864. His resignation, however, was promptly refused by government officials.

Later, as 1864 came to an end, von Sheliha complained that he was continually in pain from a "chronic disease of the liver." Because of this, he requested a leave of absence for "health reasons." His plea was granted on this occasion, and his supervision of the underwater mining detail in and around Mobile was delegated to Lieutenant J. T. E. Andrews. By the time the German had departed, to spend six months of rest and recuperation soaking in the springs of Bohemia, his entire explosives network was in place:

> Every avenue of approach to the outworks or to the city of Mobile was guarded by submarine torpedoes, so that it was impossible for any vessel drawing three feet of water to get within effective cannon range of any part of our defenses. Two ironclads attempted to get near enough to Spanish Fort to take part in the bombardment. They both suddenly struck the bottom on Apalachee Bar, and thence-forward the fleet made no further attempt to encounter the almost certain destruction which they saw awaited any vessel which might attempt to enter our torpedo-guarded waters.[3]

Before beginning their well-devised plan of assault on the city of Mobile, Federal search vessels were dispatched on a daily basis, in an attempt to locate and destroy hidden underwater explosives. In all, "150 large submerged torpedoes were removed from Blakely River and the adjacent waters by the *Metacomet*, [with] Commander Pierce Crosby" in charge of the operation.[4]

On March 12, 1865, Ensign F. A G. Bacon maneuvered his 72-ton screw-propeller gunboat, USS *Althea*, along the Blakely River near Battery Ruger. Mounting but a single cannon for defense purposes, the *Althea*'s major job was to sweep the river's murky bottom in an attempt to pinpoint the location of explosives. Her long chain, which had been suspended from a strong spar extending from her stern section, dragged along as the ship steamed slowly over the surface. It dredged up mud, tree branches, and other debris as it went.

The chain became accidentally entangled in an old sunken craft which crewmen had failed to spot in time. After several minutes of trying to work it free, the frustrated captain ordered that the chain be loosened and dumped. They would be forced to return the following day with a new length of iron links.

Soon after beginning the slow journey back to port, the USS *Althea* was struck by a torpedo which exploded beneath her port side just behind the pilot house. The ensuing shock tore a huge hole in her hull, and she sank to the bottom almost immediately. Two of her crewmen were killed in the incident, while three others, including Ensign Bacon, were seriously injured.

Just nine days later, on March 21, Federal warships moved against Mobile, as support soldiers invaded the city by land. Spanish Fort, situated directly across the bay east of Mobile, had 2,100 men at her disposal, and it was designated as the initial Confederate installation to be attacked:

> The defense of Spanish Fort was the last death-grapple of the veterans of the Confederate and Federal armies. They brought to it the experience of four years of incessant conflict, and in the attack and defense of that place demonstrated every offensive and defensive art then known to war. It is not too much to say that no position was ever held by Confederate troops with greater hardiness and tenacity....[5]

Confederate gunboats, anchored just east of Mobile, were unable to assist in the defense of the fort. However, hundreds of Singer torpedoes were submerged in the harbor, and another 205 Rains-style explosives were buried beneath the soft sands surrounding the Confederate installation's outer walls. Despite the dangerous mine-laden waters and battlegrounds, however, Union forces commenced their invasion on March 28.

Later that same day, the USS *Winnebago* and USS *Milwaukee* were dispatched with orders to travel up the Blakely River. Their mission was to shell a Southern army transport which was believed to be heavily loaded with supplies for the Spanish Fort garrison. Afterward, the two Union vessels were further instructed to return to the "safer waters" of the harbor. However, after completing the first half of their orders, they ran into a major problem:

> ...as they were returning to the fleet the *Milwaukee* struck a torpedo, and in three minutes was on the bottom in ten feet depth of water. All her people escaped to the other vessels. She was one of the largest and strongest Federal iron-clads, having two turrets and two fifteen-inch and two eleven-inch guns.[6]

The underwater explosive had detonated beneath the USS *Milwaukee*'s port side just 40 feet from the stern, breaking the ship into two pieces. Though the tail section of the huge 970-ton vessel sank almost immediately, the bow was slow to fill with water, giving her crewmen ample time to escape. During the nearly 60 minutes it required for the second portion to be completely submerged, Lieutenant Commander James H. Gillis looked on as his men scurried from their posts:

There was naturally some confusion at first, the hatches being closed ... and those who were not on deck being dependent on those who were, for other means of egress; but a single command served to restore order, and all came on deck in a quiet, orderly manner.[7]

The following day, March 29, at approximately 1:00 P.M., the USS *Winnebago* found itself being pushed toward the shoreline by a brisk east wind in a direct course toward the USS *Osage*. Lieutenant Commander William M. Gamble, aboard the *Osage*, decided to take evasive action in order to avoid the collision. He ordered his men to weigh anchor and to move ahead a short distance. Suddenly, he felt a tremendous vibration as his vessel struck a torpedo, rocking the 523-ton, turtle-backed ironclad violently to one side. Soon, she began to settle slowly in the 12-foot-deep waterway, eventually sinking out of sight:

> Four of her crew were instantly killed, and six wounded, of whom two subsequently died. The destruction of these heavy ships [USS *Milwaukee* and USS *Osage*] caused much exultation among the Confederates, which found expression in salutes from Spanish Fort and the guns of the Nashville. To the Federals the two disasters, one following the other so closely, were depressing. As they had swept the channel for torpedoes regularly, and had taken up 120 within a few days previously, they concluded that those which had wrecked the *Milwaukee* and *Osage* were floating instruments of destruction let loose from the rear of the Confederate obstructions to sweep down with the tide, and with this fresh peril confronting them they doubled their vigilance, a detail of boats being constantly on duty as torpedo searchers.[8]

Despite these additional precautions, however, encounters with torpedoes continued to occur. On the same day that the USS *Osage* was devastated, Admiral Thatcher himself narrowly escaped death. A floating mine, which had been scooped up and supposedly "cleaned of its deadly contents," was then transferred to the Admiral's flagship, the USS *Stockdale*, for close scrutiny. Following his strict directions, two of his crewmen began to extract the percussion caps from the encasement. Without warning, one of the torpedo's nipples was inadvertently detonated, and the ensuing explosion severely wounded both seamen. Amazingly, Admiral Thatcher, who was seated less than five yards away at the time, was unharmed.

At exactly 1:00 in the afternoon, on April 1, the 217-ton tinclad USS *Rodolph*, a stern-wheeled gunboat, was dispatched with orders to move a barge filled with salvage gear toward the wreck of the USS *Milwaukee*. Slowly, she pulled the equipment through the perilous waters toward the hulk, with lookouts maintaining a constant vigilance for any strange-looking floating objects. Suddenly, at approximately 2:40 P.M., as the *Rodolph* steamed midway between the USS *Winnebago* and USS *Chickasaw*, she rammed a mine. The resulting explosion left a ten-foot long gash in her belly, and she immediately began to take on an immense amount of water. Four of her crewmen were lost and 11 others were wounded in the incident.

Federal work crews continued to clear the harbor and its adjoining waterways of torpedoes, under the close supervision of Commander Crosby, whose base was aboard the USS *Metacomet*. The step-by-step procedure had been, by this time, memorized by every member of his search team. First, large hemp nets controlled on each end by 10 to 12 rowboats were stretched out across the channel. Then, taking it slowly and cautiously, the team would move the netting up and down the waterway between six and ten times. A normal haul, after each section of the river or harbor had been searched thoroughly, was two dozen or more torpedoes.

Early in the morning on April 13, the tugboat USS *Ida*, weighing just over 104 tons, was ordered to report to the captain of the USS *Genesee*. Before reaching her destination vessel, which was then anchored in the mouth of the Blakely River, the *Ida* chanced to graze a floating mine. The torpedo was detonated on contact, and in turn, set off a chain reaction of explosions. After watching the *Ida*'s boilers burst wide open, a crew member aboard the nearby USS *Albatross* described the scene:

> I think, her smoke stack must have gone fifty feet into the air. There seemed to be a thick mist about her, hiding her completely from sight. When ... cleared ... she had sunk....[9]

On April 14, two days after the Confederate army had evacuated the city of Mobile, the 507-ton wooden gunboat USS *Sciota* met with disaster. Earlier in the day, she had spent a good deal of time loading up her bins with coal. Afterward, she was assigned the duty of transferring Federal crewmen to different vessels anchored in the bay. These ships, in turn, were then dispatched one-by-one to continue the search for underwater explosives. While steaming out toward the USS *Elk*, with a troop of men, the *Sciota* struck a torpedo, which exploded beneath her starboard side: "The explosion was terrible, breaking the beams of the spar deck, tearing open the waterways, ripping off starboard fore-channels, and breaking the fore-topmast...."[10] The *Sciota* was a total loss, with five of her crewmen killed in the incident, and six others wounded.

Though the war was officially over just a few days earlier, other Union vessels would continue to feel the wrath of the Confederate Torpedo Division:

> On the 14th [of April] the cutter of the iron-clad *Cincinnati* hit a torpedo in the bay with the usual result, and on the same day the gunboat *Itasca* was blown up; five men were killed and six injured by these two disasters. Late the same afternoon the steamer *Rose* was destroyed, and two men were killed and three wounded. A few days later the transport *St. Mary's* was blown up by a torpedo in the Alabama River, and the steamer [*R. B.*] *Hamilton* from New Orleans, with the Third Mich. Cavalry on board, was struck by a torpedo in the Lower

Gap channel entrance to Mobile, making a wreck of the boat, and killing and wounding thirteen persons....[11]

Thus ended the barrage of attacks by submerged explosives employed throughout the war by the Confederate army and navy. Today, underwater warfare is recognized as a legitimate means of both offensive and defensive fighting. Though numerous people who fought and lived during the Civil War era believed the use of such weaponry to be "fiendish acts, unknown among civilized nations," modern observers all over the world must credit the fact that the Confederacy was the first to develop underwater warfare into a formidable strategy. Perhaps Dabney H. Maury put it best when he wrote:

Had we understood their [torpedoes'] power in the beginning of the war as we came to do before its end, we could have effectually defended every harbor, channel or river throughout the Confederate States against all sorts of naval attacks. It is noteworthy that the Confederate ironclad *Virginia*, by her fearful destruction of the Federal warships in Hampton Roads early in the war, caused all the maritime powers of the world to remodel their navies and build ironclads at enormous expense, only to learn by the Confederate lessons of Mobile that ironclads cannot avail against torpedoes; for, as the Federal naval captain who had been engaged in clearing Mobile bay of the torpedoes and of the wrecks they had made, after the close of the war remarked to the writer: "It makes no difference whether a ship is of wood, or is tin-clad, or is iron-clad, if she gets over a torpedo it blows the same size hole in the bottom of all alike...."[12]

Notes

Introduction: Beginnings of Underwater Explosives

1. David Bushnell, in a letter written to Thomas Jefferson, dated October 1787, Manuscripts Division, Library of Congress.

Chapter 1: Maury, at Your Service

1. Diana Fontaine Maury Corbin, *A Life of Matthew Fontaine Maury* (London: London Press, 1888), p. 192.

2. *Ibid.* This statement was made by Matthew Fontaine Maury on October 29, 1861, to Grand Admiral Constantine of Russia.

3. Richard L. Maury, "The First Submarine Torpedoes," *Southern Historical Society Papers* vol. 31 (1903), p. 329.

4. *Ibid.*, pp. 326–328.

5. The National Archives, *The Maury Family Papers*, vol. 15, LC; quoted in a letter written by Matthew Fontaine Maury to B. Franklin Minor, dated October 8, 1861.

6. Orders dispatched from Franklin Buchanan, Captain in charge of C.S.N. Office of Orders and Details, to Lieutenant Robert D. Minor, dated October 5, 1861, *Official Records of the Union and Confederate Navies in the War of the Rebellion*, ser. I, vol. 6, Manuscripts Division, Library of Congress (1894–1928), p. 304.

7. *Ibid.*, ser. 1, vol. 4, pp. 566–567.

8. LaFayette C. Baker, *History of the United States Secret Service* (Philadelphia, 1867), p. 77.

9. National Archives, *The War of the Rebellion: A Compilation of the Official Records of the Union and Confederate Armies*, Ser. 1, vol. II, part 3 (1860–1901), p. 487.

10. *Official Records of the Union and Confederate Navies*, Ser. I, vol. 7, p. 780.

11. *Ibid.*, pp. 543–544.

12. *The Maury Family Papers*, vol. 25, LC, National Archives, Washington, D.C.; Matthew Fontaine Maury, in a lecture on the topic of torpedo warfare, held in Paris, France, May 21, 1866.

Chapter 2: The Anaconda and the Rabbit

1. Victor Ernest Rudolph von Sheliha, *A Treatise on Coast-Defence: Based on the Experiences Gained by Officers of the Corps of Engineers of the Army of the Confederate States* (London, 1868), p. 220.

2. Scharf, *History of the Confederate States Navy* (New York: Rogers & Sherwood, 1887), p. 430.

3. *Official Records of the Union and Confederate Navies in the War of the Rebellion*, ser. 1, vol. 6, Manuscripts Division, Library of Congress (1894–1928), pp. 288–289.

4. *New York Herald*, issued dated March 7, 1861.

5. Winfield Scott to George B. McClellan, *Official Records of the Union and Confederate Armies*, ser. 1, vol. 51, pp. 338–339.

6. Robert Henry Newell, *Orpheus C. Kerr Papers* (New York: AMS Press, 1862), vol. 1, p. 205.

7. James Russell Soley, *The Navy in the Civil War* (New York: Charles Scribner's Sons, 1903), p. 19.

8. *Ibid.*

9. Gideon Welles, *The Diary of Gideon Welles* (New York: W. W. Norton & Company, 1960), vol. 1, p. 42.

10. *New York Herald*, issue dated December 24, 1861.

11. Brigadier General J. D. Hittle, *Jomini's Art of War* (Harrisburg, Pa.: Stackpole Books, 1947), p. 88.

12. *Official Records of the Union and Confederate Navies*, vol. 7, p. 543.

13. R. O. Crowley, "The Confederate Torpedo Service," *Century Magazine,* vol. 46 (1898), p. 206.

14. *Ibid.*, p. 201.

15. *Ibid.*, p. 200.

16. *Ibid.*, p. 203.

Chapter 3: With Patience Comes Success

1. *Harper's Weekly*, article dated August 2, 1862; *Official Records of the Union and Confederate Navies in the War of the Rebellion*, vol. 7, 1894–1928, p. 543.

2. J. B. Jones, *A Rebel War Clerk's Diary* (Philadelphia, 1866), vol. 1, p. 6

3. J. S. Barnes, *Submarine Warfare* (New York, 1869), pp. 96–100.

4. Burke Davis, *The Civil War: Strange and Fascinating Facts* (New York: 1982), p. 144.

5. Scharf, *History of the Confederate States Navy*, p. 764.

6. Crowley, "The Confederate Torpedo Service," p. 210.

Chapter 4: Supply and Demand

1. Brigadier General Josiah Gorgas, *Personal Journal*, the Manuscripts Division, Library of Congress, Washington, D.C., entry dated October 29, 1863.

2. Governor Francis Wilkinson Pickens, in a letter written to the Confederate States Congress, dated September 1, 1861.

3. *Official Records of the Union and Confederate Navies in the War of the Rebellion*, ser. 4, vol. 2, pp. 26–30; vol. 3, pp. 695–702.

4. Gorgas, *Personal Journal*, entry dated October 29, 1863.

5. John Bigelow, *France and the Confederate Navy* (New York: Harper & Brothers, 1888).

6. George Washington Rains, *History of the Confederate Powder Works* (Augusta, Ga.: Chronicle and Constitutionalist, 1882).

Chapter 5: Torpedoes on the Yazoo

1. Scharf, *History of the Confederate States Navy*, p. 751.
2. Thomas Yoseloff, *Battles and Leaders of the Civil War* (New York: Thomas Yoseloff, Inc., 1956), vol. 3, p. 580.
3. Thomas O. Selfridge, *Memoirs of Thomas O. Selfridge, Jr., Rear Admiral, U.S.N.* (New York, 1924), p. 75.
4. H. D. Brown, "The First Successful Torpedo and What It Did," *Confederate Veteran*, vol. 18 (1910), p. 169.
5. *Official Records of the Union and Confederate Navies in the War of the Rebellion*, ser. 1, vol. 23, p. 567.
6. *Ibid.*, p. 568.
7. *Ibid.*, p. 602.
8. Isaac N. Brown, "Confederate Torpedoes in the Yazoo," from *Battles and Leaders of the Civil War*, vol. 3 (New York: Thomas Yoseloff, Inc., 1956), p. 580.
9. J. S. Barnes, *Submarine Warfare* (New York: D. Van Nostrand, 1869), pp. 71–73.
10. *The Daily Courier*, Charleston, South Carolina, issue dated June 20, 1863.
11. *Official Records of the Union and Confederate Navies*, ser. 1, vol. 3, p. 281.
12. Isaac N. Brown, "Confederate Torpedoes," p. 580.

Chapter 6: Birth of the Spar Torpedo

1. Scharf, *History of the Confederate States Navy*, pp. 553–54.
2. General George A. Mercer, *Mercer Diary*, Manuscripts Division, Library of Congress, October 1862.
3. Scharf, p. 639.
4. Stephen R. Mallory, *Stephen R. Mallory Diary*, typescript in the Southern Historical Collection, University of North Carolina Library, Chapel Hill, North Carolina, pp. 13–14.
5. A letter from Nelson Tift to J. Thomas Scharf, dated June 9, 1890, the Atlanta folder, Confederate Subject and Area File, Group 45, National Archives, Washington, D.C.
6. Scharf, p. 641.
7. *Official Records of the Union and Confederate Navies in the War of the Rebellion*, ser. I, vol. 13, pp. 819–820.
8. Letter from Josiah Tattnall to Secretary of the Navy Stephen R. Mallory, dated April 23, 1863, quoted in Charles C. Jones, Jr., *The Life and Services of Commodore Josiah Tattnall* (Savannah: Morning News Steam Printing House, 1878), p. 224.
9. William N. Still, Jr., *Iron Afloat: The Story of the Confederate Ironclads* (Nashville: Vanderbilt University Press, 1971), p. 132.
10. Scharf, p. 644.
11. Frank Moore, *The Rebellion Record: A Diary of American Events with Documents, Narratives, Illustrative Incidents, Poetry, etc.*, 11 vols. (New York: Harper and Brothers, 1864–68), vol. 7, p. 73.
12. *Ibid.*

Chapter 7: The Rains Torpedo

1. James H. Tomb, "The Last Obstruction in Charleston Harbor, 1863," *Confederate Veteran* vol. 23 (1924), pp. 98–99.

2. *Official Records of the Union and Confederate Armies*, ser. 11, pt. 3, p. 510.

3. Gabriel J. Rains, "Torpedoes," *Southern Historical Society Papers*, vol. 3 (1877), p. 260.

4. *Ibid.*

5. J. Thomas Scharf, *History of the Confederate States Navy*, p. 757.

6. Gabriel J. Rains, *ibid.*, p. 256.

7. Scharf, p. 751.

8. *Ibid.*, p. 638.

9. J. B. Jones, *A Rebel War Clerk's Diary* (Philadelphia: 1866), vol. 1, p. 245.

10. *Official Records of the Union and Confederate Navies in the War of the Rebellion*, Washington, D.C., 1880–1901, ser. 18, p. 1,082.

11. Jefferson Davis, *The Rise and Fall of the Confederate Government* (New York, 1881), vol. 2, pp. 424–25.

12. *Official Records of the Union and Confederate Armies in the War of the Rebellion*, Washington, D.C., 1880–1901, ser. 35, pt. 1, p. 517.

13. *Ibid.*, pp. 517, 538–39.

14. George H. Gordon, *A War Diary of Events in the War of the Great Rebellion 1863–1865* (Boston: 1882), pp. 268–69.

Chapter 8: Captain Lee's Torpedo Ram

1. Milton F. Perry, *Infernal Machines* (Baton Rouge: Louisiana State University Press, 1965), p. 63.

2. General P. G. T. Beauregard, "The Defense of Charleston," in *Battles and Leaders of the Civil War* (New York: Thomas Yoseloff, Inc., 1956), vol. 4, p. 6.

3. Stephen R. Mallory to the Hon. Porcher Miles, in a letter dated December 19, 1863, and enclosed in a letter from Porcher Miles, to General Beauregard, December 30, 1863, National Archives, p. 597.

4. A letter sent from P. G. T. Beauregard to Porcher Miles, dated January 5, 1864, National Archives, Washington, D.C.

5. *Official Records of the Union and Confederate Navies in the War of the Rebellion*, ser. 1, vol. 13, p. 814.

6. A letter sent from Francis D. Lee to Brig. General Jordan, 1862, National Archives.

7. *The War of the Rebellion*, vol. 14, ser. 1, p. 648.

8. E. Milby Burton, *The Siege of Charleston, 1861–1865* (Columbia, S.C.: University of South Carolina Press, 1970), p. 212.

9. W. T. Glassel, "Torpedo Service in Charleston Harbor," *Southern Historical Society Papers* (1877), p. 226.

10. *The War of the Rebellion*, vol. 14, ser. 1, p. 820.

11. Glassel, "Torpedo Service in Charleston Harbor," *Southern Historical Society Papers* (1877), pp. 227–28.

12. *Ibid.*, p. 228.

13. *The War of the Rebellion*, vol. 14, ser. 1, p. 837.

14. *Ibid.*, p. 843.

15. William H. Parker, *Recollections of a Naval Officer, 1841–1865* (New York: 1883), p. 306.

16. Scharf, *History of the Confederate States Navy*, p. 688.

17. *Official Records of the Union and Confederate Navies*, ser. 1, vol. 14, p. 688.

18. Beauregard, "The Defense of Charleston," p. 5.
19. *The War of the Rebellion*, vol. 14, ser. 1, p. 965.
20. *Official Records of the Union and Confederate Navies*, ser. 1, vol. 14, p. 498.
21. *Ibid.*, p. 497.
22. *Ibid.*, vol. 28, pt. 2, p. 322.

Chapter 9: The Little David

1. C. C. Fulton comments on torpedoes in the Confederate States, in *Official Records of the Union and Confederate Navies in the War of the Rebellion*, ser. 1, vol. 14, p. 58.
2. *The War of the Rebellion*, ser. 1, vol. 14, p. 288.
3. Francis D. Lee, letter dated July 25, 1863, Division of Naval History, Smithsonian Institution.
4. Scharf, *History of the Confederate States Navy*, p. 756.
5. Glassel, "Torpedo Service in Charleston Harbor," *Southern Historical Society Papers* (1877), p. 230.
6. *Ibid.*, pp. 231–232.
7. *Ibid.*, p. 232.
8. *Ibid.*
9. *The War of the Rebellion*, ser. 1, vol. 14, pp. 648–649.
10. Madeleine Vinton Dahlgren, *The Memoir of John A. Dahlgren* (Boston, 1882), p. 19.
11. *The War of the Rebellion*, ser. 1, vol. 35, p. 546.
12. *Ibid.*, p. 548.
13. Dahlgren, *The Memoir of John A. Dahlgren*, p. 147.
14. *Official Records of the Union and Confederate Navies*, ser. 1, vol. 19, p. 631.
15. *Ibid.*, ser. 1, vol. 15, p. 733.
16. *The War of the Rebellion*, vol. 35, pt. 2, p. 396.
17. *Ibid.*, vol. 47, pt. 2, p. 1,201.
18. *Official Records of the Union and Confederate Navies*, ser. 1, vol. 16, p. 338.

Chapter 10: A Pioneer in Southern Waters

1. *New Orleans Daily Crescent*, dated April 12, 1861.
2. James R. McClintock, to Matthew Fontaine Maury, the *Maury Family Papers*, National Archives, undated.
3. Scharf, *History of the Confederate States Navy*, p. 750.
4. *Official Records of the Confederate and Union Navies in the War of the Rebellion*, vol. 14, pp. 399–400.
5. *Ibid.*, p. 400.
6. Yoseloff, *Battles and Leaders of the Civil War*, vol. 2, p. 91.
7. *Ibid.*, pp. 91–92.
8. Simon Lake, *The Submarine in War and Peace* (Philadelphia: J. B. Lippincott, 1918).
9. James R. McClintock, to Matthew Fontaine Maury, the *Maury Family Papers*, National Archives, undated.
10. W. A. Alexander, "Thrilling Chapter in the History of the Confederate States Navy. Work of Submarine Boats," *Southern Historical Society Papers*, vol. 30 (1902), p. 165.

Chapter 11: The H. L. Hunley *Submarine*

1. A letter from Lieutenant R. H. Lamson to Rear Admiral S. P. Lee, dated May 25, 1864, in *War of the Rebellion*, ser. 1, vol. 10, pp. 92–93.

2. A letter from J. A. Quintero to J. P. Benjamin, dated April 9, 1863, Library of Congress, Washington, D.C.

3. W. A. Alexander, "Thrilling Chapter in the History of the Confederate States Navy. Work of Submarine Boats," *Southern Historical Society Papers* (1902), p. 165.

4. *Ibid.*, pp. 165–66.

5. *Ibid.*, p. 167.

6. *Ibid.*

7. *Ibid.*

8. *War of the Rebellion*, pt. 2, vol. 28, p. 285.

9. *Ibid.*, pt. 1, vol. 28, p. 670.

10. Letter from Theodore A. Honour, dated August 30, 1863, South Carolina Library.

11. The Charleston *Daily Courier*, issue dated August 31, 1863.

12. W. R. Fort, "First Submarine in the Confederate Navy," *Confederate Veteran* (October 1918), p. 459.

13. Alexander, "Thrilling Chapter," p. 168.

14. *Journal of Operations in Charleston Harbor* (October 1863).

15. Alexander, "Thrilling Chapter," pp. 169–70.

16. *Ibid.*, pp. 170–71.

17. *Ibid.*, pp. 171–72.

18. *Ibid.*, p. 174.

19. *Ibid.*

20. *Official Records of the Union and Confederate Navies in the War of the Rebellion*, ser. 1, vol. 26, p. 187.

21. James R. McClintock, to Matthew Fontaine Maury, the *Maury Family Papers*, National Archives, Washington, D.C., undated.

Chapter 12: A Flurry in Northern Florida

1. General P. G. T. Beauregard, "Narrative by General Beauregard," *Southern Historical Society Papers* (January-June, 1878).

2. Scharf, *History of the Confederate States Navy*, p. 763.

3. *Ibid.*, p. 721.

4. *War of the Rebellion*, pt. 1, vol. 35, p. 115.

5. *Ibid.*, p. 388.

6. *Ibid.*

7. Abraham Lincoln to Major General Gilmore, "The Battle of Olustee, or Ocean Pond, Florida," in *Battles and Leaders of the Civil War*, Thomas Yoseloff, ed. (New York: Thomas Yoseloff, Inc., 1956), p. 76.

8. *Norfolk New Regime*, issue dated April 25, 1864.

9. *Official Records of the Union and Confederate States Navies in the War of teh Rebellion*, vol. 16, p. 425.

10. Gabriel J. Rains, "Torpedoes," *Southern Historical Society Papers* (1877), p. 256.

11. *Ibid.*, p. 257.

Chapter 13: Attack of the Squib

1. *War of the Rebellion*, ser. 1, vol. 10, pp. 92–93.

2. *Message of the President of the United States to the Two Houses of Congress at the Commencement of the Third Session*, vol. 3 (Washington, D.C.: Government Printing Office, 1862), p. 110.

3. P. G. T. Beauregard, "Remarks ... Relative to Ironclad Boats," in *War of the Rebellion*, ser. 1, vol. 15, p. 695.

4. Crowley, "The Confederate Torpedo Service," *Century Magazine* vol. 46 (1898), p. 298.

5. *Ibid.*

6. *Ibid.*

7. John M. Batten, *Reminiscences of Two Years in the United States Navy* (Lancaster, Penn., 1881), p. 14.

8. Crowley, "The Confederate Torpedo Service," pp. 298–299.

9. *Ibid.*, p. 299.

10. Hunter Davidson, "The Electrical Submarine Mine, 1861–1865," *Confederate Veteran* vol. 16 (1908), p. 458.

11. *War of the Rebellion*, ser. 1, vol. 15, p. 273.

12. *Scientific American*, issue dated April 30, 1864.

13. Dunbar Rowland, *Jefferson Davis, Constitutionalist, His Letters, Papers and Speeches* (Jackson, Miss., 1923), vol. 7, p. 387.

14. Report of Admiral Dahlgren, dated October 7, 1863, in *War of the Rebellion*, ser. 1, vol. 15, pp. 13–14.

15. *Official Records of the Union and Confederate Navies in the War of the Rebellion*, vol. 10, pp. 112–113.

16. Crowley, "The Confederate Torpedo Service," p. 299.

17. *Official Records of the Union and Confederate Navies*, vol. 10, pp. 112–113.

18. David D. Porter, *Incidents and Anecdotes of the Civil War* (New York, 1886), pp. 267–277.

Chapter 14: Damn the Torpedoes

1. Scharf, *History of the Confederate States Navy*, pp. 533–534.

2. *Ibid.*, p. 545.

3. *Ibid.*

4. John Coddington Kinney, "Farragut at Mobile Bay," in *Battles and Leaders of the Civil War*, Thomas Yoseloff, ed. (New York: Thomas Yoseloff, Inc., 1956), p. 383.

5. Scharf, *History of the Confederate States Navy*, pp. 553–554.

6. *Ibid.*, p. 556.

7. Kinney, "Farragut at Mobile Bay," p. 388.

8. *Ibid.*, p. 380.

9. Scharf, *History of the Confederate States Navy*, p. 560.

10. *Ibid.*, p. 561.

11. Kinney, "Farragut at Mobile Bay," p. 388.

12. William N. Still, Jr., *Iron Afloat: The Story of the Confederate Armorclads* (Nashville: Vanderbilt University Press, 1971), p. 208.

13. Scharf, *History of the Confederate States Navy*, p. 562.

14. *Ibid.*

15. *War of the Rebellion*, ser. 1, vol. 39, pt. 2, pp. 431–432.

16. *Ibid.*, p. 435.

17. Royal B. Bradford, *History of Torpedo Warfare* (Newport, R.I., 1882), pp. 57–58.

18. W. G. Jones to J. S. Palmer, dated December 10, 1864, in *Letters Received by Secretary of the (U.S.) Navy from West Gulf Blockading Squadron*, National Archives, Record Group 45.

Chapter 15: The Trout Boat St. Patrick

1. Gustavus V. Fox to Samuel F. DuPont, letter dated March 26, 1863, National Archives, Washington, D.C.

2. *War of the Rebellion*, ser. 1, vol. 4, p. 42.

3. *Ibid.*, p. 74.

4. *Ibid.*, p. 134.

5. *Ibid.*, p. 135.

6. Dabney Maury to James A. Seddon, letter dated December 4, 1864, National Archives.

7. Dabney Maury to Commodore Ebenezer Farrand, letter dated December 5, 1864, National Archives.

8. *Official Records of the Union and Confederate Navies in the War of the Rebellion*, ser. 1, vol. 22, p. 267.

Chapter 16: Justice in North Carolina Waters

1. Gilbert Elliott, "The First Battle of the Confederate Ram 'Albemarle,'" from *Battles and Leaders of the Civil War*, Thomas Yoseloff, ed. (New York: Thomas Yoseloff, Inc., 1956), vol. 4, p. 626.

2. W. B. Cushing, "The Destruction of the *Albemarle*," in *Battles and Leaders of the Civil War*, vol. 4, pp. 635–637.

3. A. F. Warley, "Note on the Destruction of the 'Albemarle,'" from *Battles and Leaders of the Civil War*, vol. 4, p. 642.

4. Phillip Van Doren Stern, *Secret Missions of the Civil War* (New York: Rand McNally & Company, 1959), p. 248.

5. Crowley, "The Confederate Torpedo Service," p. 296.

6. Scharf, *History of the Confederate States Navy*, p. 418.

7. Soley, "The Destruction of the *Albemarle*," from *Battles and Leaders of the Civil War*, vol. 4, p. 641.

8. *Ibid.*

9. John M. Batten, *Reminiscences of Two Years in the United States Navy* (Lancaster, Penn., 1881), p. 65.

10. *Official Records of the Union and Confederate Navies in the War of the Rebellion*, ser. 1, vol. 11, p. 164.

11. Scharf, *History of the Confederate States Navy*, p. 766.

12. Selfridge, "The Navy at Fort Fisher," from *Battles and Leaders of the Civil War*, vol. 4, p. 655.

13. Scharf, *History of the Confederate States Navy*, p. 766.

14. *Ibid.*, pp. 766–767.

Chapter 17: A Valiant Effort in South Carolina

1. J. B. Jones, *A Rebel War Clerk's Diary*, entry dated January 21, 1865.
2. Mallory, in a letter to President Jefferson Davis, *Davis Papers*, Rare Books Division, Library of Congress.
3. Scharf, *History of the Confederate States Navy*, p. 705.
4. *Official Records of the Union and Confederate Navies in the War of the Rebellion*, vol. 16, p. 178.
5. Madeleine Vinton Dahlgren, *Memoir of John A. Dahlgren*, p. 492.
6. *The War of the Rebellion*, pt. 2, vol. 35, p. 648.
7. *Charleston Mercury*, issue dated January 24, 1865.
8. Dahlgren, *Memoir*, p. 504.
9. E. Milby Burton, *The Siege of Charleston, 1861–1865* (Columbia S.C.: University of South Carolina Press, 1970), p. 266.

Chapter 18: Closing Operations in Mobile

1. Soley, "Closing Operations in the Gulf and Western Waters," in *Battles and Leaders of the Civil War*, Thomas Yoseloff, ed. (New York: Thomas Yoseloff, Inc., 1956), vol. 4, p. 412.
2. *Ibid.*
3. Dabney H. Maury, "Defence of Mobile," *Southern Historical Society Papers* (1877), p. 11.
4. Soley, "Closing Operations in the Gulf and Western Waters," in *Battles and Leaders of the Civil War*, p. 412.
5. Scharf, *History of the Confederate States Navy*, p. 593.
6. *Ibid.*, p. 594.
7. *Official Records of the Union and Confederate Navies in the War of the Rebellion*, vol. 22, p. 71.
8. Scharf, *History of the Confederate States Navy*, p. 594.
9. Frank E. Alward, "A Sailor's Service," *The Maine Bugle*, vol. 2 (1895).
10. *Official Records of the Union and Confederate Navies*, vol. 22, p. 130.
11. Scharf, *History of the Confederate States Navy*, p. 767.
12. Dabney H. Maury, "Defence of Mobile," p. 11.

Bibliography

Alexander, W. A. "Thrilling Chapter in the History of the Confederate States Navy. Work of Submarine Boats." *Southern Historical Society Papers*, vol. 30 (1902).

Alward, Frank E. "A Sailor's Service." *The Maine Bugle*, vol. 2 (1895).

Baker, LaFayette C. *History of the United States Secret Service*. Philadelphia, 1867.

Barnes, J. S. *Submarine Warfare*. New York, 1869.

Batten, John M. *Reminiscences of Two Years in the United States Navy*. Lancaster, Penn., 1881.

Beauregard, Pierre G. T. Letter written to Porcher Miles, National Archives, Washington, D.C., January 5, 1864.

____. "Narrative by General Beauregard." *Southern Historical Society Papers* (January–June 1878).

____. "Torpedo Service at Charleston." *Annals of the War Written by Leading Participants North and South, vol. 1*. Philadelphia, 1879, pp. 514–525.

Bigelow, John. *France and the Confederate Navy*. New York: Harper & Brothers, 1888.

Bradford, Royal B. *History of Torpedo Warfare*. Newport, R.I., 1882.

Brown, H. D. "The First Successful Torpedo and What It Did." *Confederate Veteran*, vol. 18 (1910).

Burton, E. Milby. *The Siege of Charleston, 1861–1865*. Columbia: University of South Carolina Press, 1970.

Bushnell, David. Letter written to Thomas Jefferson, October 1787. Library of Congress.

Calhoun, John C. "The South Carolina Exposition." South Carolina, 1828. Washington, D.C.: National Archives.

Charleston Mercury, January 24, 1865.

Corbin, Diana Fontaine Maury. *A Life of Matthew Fontaine Maury*. London: London Press, 1888.

Crowley, R. O. "The Confederate Torpedo Service." *Century Magazine,* vol. 46 (1898).

Dahlgren, Madeleine Vinton. *The Memoir of John A. Dahlgren*, Boston, 1882.

Daily Courier, Charleston, South Carolina, issues dated June 20, 1863, and August 31, 1863.

Daily Crescent, New Orleans, Louisiana, April 22, 1861.

Daily Delta, New Orleans, Louisiana, August 17, 1861.

Davidson, Hunter. "The Electrical Submarine Mine, 1861–1865." *Confederate Veteran* vol. 16 (1908).

Davis, Burke. *The Civil War: Strange and Fascinating Facts*. New York: Fairfax Press, 1982.

Davis, Jefferson. *The Rise and Fall of the Confederate Government*. vol. 2. New York, 1881.

"Declaration of Paris." Article 1. Paris, France, 1856. Washington, D.C.: National Archives.

Fort, W. R. "First Submarine in the Confederate Navy." *Confederate Veteran* (October 1918).

Fox, Gustavus V. Letter dated March 26, 1863, National Archives.

Glassel, W. T. "Torpedo Service in Charleston Harbor." *Southern Historical Society Papers* (1877).

Gordon, George H. *A War Diary of Events in the War of the Great Rebellion, 1863–1865.* Boston, 1882.

Gorgas, Josiah. *Personal Journal.* Manuscripts Division, Library of Congress.

Grant, U. S. 3rd. *Military Strategy of the Civil War.* Paper read at the meeting of the Civil War Round Table, January 8, 1957, in Washington, D.C.

Harper's Weekly, articles dated August 2, 1862, and February 25, 1865.

Hittle, J. D. *Jomini's Art of War.* Harrisburg, Penn.: Stackpole Books, 1947.

Honour, Theodore A. Letter written August 30, 1863. South Caroliniana Library.

Jeff Davis Piracy Case. Full Report of Trial of William Smith for Piracy as One of Crew of Confederate Privateer Jeff Davis. Philadelphia: King & Baird, 1861.

Jomini, Baron Henri. *A Summary of the Art of War.* London, 1838.

Jones, Charles C. *The Life and Services of Commodore Josiah Tattnall.* Savannah: Morning News Steam Printing House, 1878.

Jones, J. B. *A Rebel War Clerk's Diary.* vol. 1, Philadelphia, 1866.

Jones, W. G. Letter written to the Secretary of the U.S. Navy, December 10, 1864. Record Group 45, National Archives.

Journal of Convention of Georgia. Milledgeville, Georgia. January 29, 1860.

Journal of Convention of South Carolina. Charleston, South Carolina. December 31, 1860.

Journal of Operations in Charleston Harbor. (October 1863).

Journal of the Congress of the Confederate States of America, 1861–1865. vol. 1. Washington, D.C.: Government Printing Office, 1904.

Lake, Simon. *The Submarine in War and Peace.* Philadelphia: J. B. Lippincott, 1918.

Lee, Francis D. Letter written to Brig. General Thomas Jordon. National Archives.

_____. Letter written July 25, 1863. Division of Naval History, Smithsonian Institution.

Levey, Gordon. "Torpedo Boats at Louisiana Soldier's Home." *Confederate Veteran.* vol. 17 (1909).

Mallory, Stephen R. Letter written to the Honorable Porcher Miles, December 19, 1863. National Archives.

_____. *Davis Papers*, Rare Books Division, Library of Congress.

_____. *Stephen R. Mallory Diary.* Typescript in the Southern Historical Collection, University of North Carolina Library.

Maury, Betty Herdon. *Maury Papers.* Manuscripts Division, Library of Congress.

Maury, Dabney H. "Defence of Mobile," *Southern Historical Society Papers* (1877).

Maury Family Papers. Manuscripts Division, Library of Congress.

Maury, Richard L. "The First Submarine Torpedoes," *Southern Historical Society Papers* vol. 31 (1903).

Mercer, General George A. *Mercer Diary.* Manuscripts Division, Library of Congress.

Message of the President of the United States to the Two Houses of Congress at the Commencement of the Third Session. Washington, D.C.: Government Printing Office, 1862.

Miles, Porcher. Letter written to P. G. T. Beauregard, December 30, 1863. National Archives.

Moore, Frank. *The Rebellion Record: A Diary of American Events with Documents, Narratives, Illustrative Incidents, Poetry, etc.*, vol. 7. New York: Harper and Brothers, 1864–68.

Newell, Robert Henry. *Orpheus C. Kerr Papers*, vol. 1. New York: AMS Press, 1862.

New Regime. Norfolk, Virginia (April 25, 1864).

New York Herald. Issues dated March 7, 1861, and December 24, 1861.

Nicolay, John G. *A Short Life of Abraham Lincoln.* New York: The Century Company, 1903.

Official Records of the Union and Confederate Navies in the War of the Rebellion. 1894–1928. Manuscripts Division, Library of Congress.

Ordinance of Nullification. Charleston, South Carolina, November 1832.

Parker, William H. *Recollections of a Naval Officer, 1841–1865.* New York, 1883.

Perry, Milton F. *Infernal Machines.* Baton Rouge: Louisiana State University Press, 1965.

Pickens, Governor F. W. Letter written to the Confederate States Congress, September 1, 1861. Manuscripts Division, Library of Congress.

Porter, David D. *Incidents and Anecdotes of the Civil War.* New York, 1886.

Porter, Horace. *Campaigning with Grant.* New York, 1879.

Rains, Gabriel J. "Torpedoes." *Southern Historical Society Papers*, vol. 3 (1877).

Rains, George W. "History of the Confederate Powder Works." *Chronicle and Constitutionalist* (1882).

Richardson, James D. *Compilation of the Messages and Papers of the Confederacy.* Nashville, Tenn.: United States Publishing Company, 1906.

Robinson, William Morrison. *The Confederate Privateers.* New Haven: Yale University Press, 1928.

Ross, Fitzgerald. *Cities and Camps of the Confederate States.* Urbana: University of Illinois Press, 1958.

Rowland, Dunbar. *Jefferson Davis, Constitutionalist, His Letters, Papers and Speeches.* vol. 7. Jackson, Miss., 1923.

Schaff, Morris. "The Explosion at City Point." *Civil War Papers Read Before the Commandery of the State of Massachusetts, Military Order of the Loyal Legion of the United States.* vol. 2. Boston, 1900.

Scharf, J. Thomas. *History of the Confederate States Navy.* New York: Rogers & Sherwood, 1887.

Schwab, John Christopher. *The Confederate States of America.* New York: Charles Scribner's Sons, 1901.

Scientific America (April 30, 1864).

Selfridge, Thomas O. *Memoirs of Thomas O. Selfridge, Jr., Rear Admiral, U.S.N.* New York, 1924.

Soley, James Russell. *The Navy in the Civil War.* New York: Charles Scribner's Sons, 1903.

South Carolina Historical Magazine (January 1953).

Stern, Phillip Van Doren. *Secret Missions of the Civil War.* New York: Rand McNally & Company, 1959.

Still, William N., Jr. *Iron Afloat: The Story of the Confederate Armorclads.* Indianapolis: Vanderbilt University Press, 1971.

Tift, Nelson. Letter written to J. Thomas Scharf dated June 9, 1890. The Atlanta folder, Confederate Subject and Area File, Group 45, National Archives.

Toombs, James H. "The Last Obstruction in Charleston Harbor, 1863." *Confederate Veteran*, vol. 32 (1924).

von Sheliha, Victor Ernest Rudolph. *A Treatise on Coast-Defence: Based on the Experiences Gained by Officers of the Corps of Engineers of the Army of the Confederate States.* London, 1868.

War of the Rebellion: A Compilation of the Official Records of the Union and Confederate Armies. National Archives, 1860–1901.

Welles, Gideon. *The Diary of Gideon Welles.* Vol. 1. New York: W. W. Norton, 1960.

Wesley, Charles H. *The Collapse of the Confederacy.* New York: Russell & Russell, 1937.

Yoseloff, Thomas, ed. *Battles and Leaders of the Civil War.* 4 volumes. New York: Thomas Yoseloff, Inc., 1956.

Index

*Numbers in **boldface** refer to pages with illustrations or photographs.*